LAW, POWER,
AND THE
SOVEREIGN STATE

The Pennsylvania State University Press
University Park, Pennsylvania

LAW, POWER, AND THE SOVEREIGN STATE

The Evolution and Application of the Concept of Sovereignty

Michael Ross Fowler
Julie Marie Bunck

Foreword by
Inis L. Claude, Jr.

Library of Congress Cataloging-in-Publication Data

Fowler, Michael, 1960–
    Law, power, and the sovereign state : the evolution and
    application of the concept of sovereignty / Michael Ross Fowler,
    Julie Marie Bunck ; foreword by Inis L. Claude, Jr.
        p.   cm.
    Includes bibliographical references and index.
    ISBN 0-271-01470-9 (cloth)
    ISBN 0-271-01471-7 (paper)
    1. Sovereignty. I. Bunck, Julie Marie, 1960– . II. Title.
  JX4041.F69 ~~1996~~ 1 9 9 5
  320.1′5—dc20   94-45483
                                                                          CIP

It is the policy of The Pennsylvania State University Press to use acid-free paper
for the first printing of all clothbound books. Publications on uncoated stock
satisfy the minimum requirements of American National Standard for Information
Sciences—Permanence of Paper for Printed Library Materials, ANSI Z39.48–1992.

AFJ - 2346

To Inis L. Claude, Jr.

Inis L. Claude, Jr., is Professor Emeritus of Government and Foreign Affairs at the University of Virginia. With unceasing lucidity, sparkling wit, and penetrating insight Mr. Claude deftly introduced many decades of students to numerous concepts in international relations, including sovereignty. This work draws in part on a framework of theory that he originally elucidated.

Contents

Foreword

The importance of the notion of sovereignty in the conduct of international relations and in discourse and argumentation about that subject certainly warrants the development of more and better analytical treatment of that concept than the literature of international relations contains. This study, a thoughtful and well-balanced appraisal of sovereignty by two able young scholars, is a fine contribution to that development.

Sovereignty arouses ambivalence in the community of academic specialists in international relations. For many of us, the term seems unfortunate because it suggests separateness and independence in an era increasingly marked by togetherness and interdependence; it stands for freedom of action by states when the need is for central coordination and control; and it evokes the fear of unpredictable and irresponsible state behavior instead of progress toward the international rule of law. On the other hand, we value sovereignty as a protective mantle and deplore such disrespect for it as is entailed by acts of aggression against states and arbitrary interventions into their affairs. Moreover, we tend to react favorably to invocations of the principle of national self-determination by peoples previously swallowed up by colonial or other empires—usually without reflecting on the fact that we are actually endorsing sovereignty, for the typical objective and result of the drive for self-determination is the acquisition of sovereign status.

Sovereignty, however, is not merely something to be embraced or deplored, supported or opposed, in accordance with the disposition either to associate it with such values as national freedom and immunity from improper interference or to emphasize the danger of its being abused to impede useful international cooperation and to justify domestic tyranny or violations of international order. Rather, the claim to and acknowledgment of sovereignty are significant facts of life in the multistate system, elements of reality that students of the system need to understand and take into account. Indeed, I find it impossible to conceive of a multistate system without either a concept of sovereignty or a functional equivalent masquerading in other semantic guise. The notion of sovereignty identifies the units that give the system its multistate character and is the essential indicator of the currently asserted and currently accepted implications of the status enjoyed by those units: the rights, immunities, responsibilities, and limitations attributed to states. Sovereignty, in short, has much to tell us about statehood and stateliness.

The key to the main gate controlling access to the understanding of international relations is the realization that the multistate system undergoes endless change. Among the most basic changes that occur are alterations in convictions about what follows from the possession of sovereign status. Hence, the definition of sovereignty—if that is taken to include the delineation of the implications of being a sovereign state—is a perpetually tentative undertaking; one can only cite the latest edition and anticipate the next revision. What Professors Bunck and Fowler have to tell us in this volume is, therefore, not definitive. It is, however, appropriately alert to recent and probable future developments in the meanings associated with the venerable concept of sovereignty.

Inis L. Claude, Jr.
University of Virginia

Acknowledgments

In the course of writing a relatively short book on an exceedingly large topic, we have amassed considerable debts to various colleagues and friends. We must first single out Inis Claude not only for stimulating our interests in the discipline of political science, the subject of international relations theory, and the topic of sovereignty, but for encouraging and guiding us through various versions of this and other works over many years and, often, over very formidable distances. We realize full well how valuable it has been to have such a master architect prepared to consult on each successive draft.

We would also like to extend special thanks to the other scholars who read the manuscript and advised on how it might be improved. The critiques offered by Richard Falk of the Center of International Studies at Princeton University and Donald Seekins of Meio University in Nago, Okinawa, Japan, proved especially profitable. We are also thankful for the observations of our dear friend, Adam Watson, of Richard Little of the University of Bristol, Paul Taylor of the London School of Economics, and the anonymous reviewers commissioned by the *Review of International Studies*. We took to heart many of their suggestions.

The writing of this work owes a great deal as well to the generosity of various institutions, including the Institute for the Study of World Politics in Washington, D.C., the Japan–United States Educational Commission, and the Council for the International Exchange of Scholars, which sponsored Fulbright Scholarships for each of us. We thank the University Press of America for granting permission to use our essay from *Community, Diversity, and a New World Order: Essays in Honor of Inis L. Claude Jr.* in preparing Chapters 3 and 4.

We are also most indebted to Sandy Thatcher, director of the Pennsylvania State University Press, for believing in this project and seizing the opportunity to bring it to fruition with publication. And we are immensely grateful for our editor, Cathy Thatcher, who skillfully, patiently, and cheerfully helped us to polish and hone the final product.

Finally, we acknowledge the many friends and family members who cheerfully tolerated our absorption in the manuscript and attended to matters that otherwise would have taken time away from our scholarship. In this regard we are especially thankful for the assistance of Russell Riley of the University of Pennsylvania. Not only did he lend substantive assistance with the manuscript but during our years abroad he also acted as our chief liaison to American academia and as our trusty cargo superintendent—roles that proved so useful that we have been exceedingly reluctant to allow him to forfeit them since our return to the States.

To the many others who lent a hand, one way or another, we offer sincere thanks. Naturally, those who participated by critiquing the blueprints, pounding in a nail here, or pointing out a crooked beam there, should in no way be taken to endorse the soundness of the finished product.

Abbreviations

UNSCOR   *United Nations Security Council Official Records*

UNTS   *Treaties and International Agreements Registered or Filed and Reported with the Secretariat of the United Nations* ("United Nations Treaty Series")

UST   *United States Treaties and Other International Agreements* (United States Department of State—"United States Treaties")

Other

BDF   Belize Defence Force

DEA   United States Drug Enforcement Administration

ICJ   International Court of Justice

OECS   Organization of Eastern Caribbean States

PCIJ   Permanent Court of International Justice

PLO   Palestine Liberation Organization

PRC   People's Republic of China

SADR   Saharan Arab Democratic Republic

SAR   Special Administrative Region

TRNC   Turkish Republic of Northern Cyprus

Introduction:
Why Is Sovereignty
Ambiguous?

> Nothing is today more greatly needed than clarity upon
> ancient notions. Sovereignty, liberty, authority, personality—
> these are the words of which we want alike the history and
> the definition; or, rather, we want the history because its
> substance is in fact the definition.
>
> —Harold Laski[1]

Some time ago, sounding sovereignty's death knell came into academic vogue. In discussions of future international relations, functionalism, supranational integration, and international organization
occupied center stage. Sovereign states, long the focal point of
attention, no longer automatically commanded the lead roles. In
keeping with the notion that the concept was lapsing in relevance,
one prominent scholar wrote of "the ghosts of the theories of
sovereignty."[2] Another predicted, "the sovereign nation-state is in
the process of becoming obsolete."[3] Yet another went so far as to

---

1. Harold J. Laski, *The Foundations of Sovereignty and Other Essays* (New York:
Harcourt Brace & Co., 1921), p. 314, quoted in F. H. Hinsley, *Sovereignty* (New York:
Basic Books, 1966), p. viii.

2. Joseph Frankel, *The Making of Foreign Policy: An Analysis of Decisionmaking*
(London: Oxford University Press, 1963), p. 66.

3. Hans J. Morgenthau, "The Intellectual and Political Functions of a Theory of
International Relations," in *The Role of Theory in International Relations*, ed. H. V.

write, "Nowadays the problem of sovereignty is, for social scientists, a dead duck."[4] Still another claimed the term to have "lost meaning and analytic relevance."[5] Two academics chose to title their book *The End of Sovereignty?*[6] Others pictured sovereignty as perforated,[7] defiled,[8] cornered,[9] eroded,[10] extinct,[11] anachronistic,[12] bothersome,[13] even interrogated.[14]

Harrison (Princeton: D. Van Nostrand Co., 1964), p. 116, quoted in Alan James, *Sovereign Statehood: The Basis of International Society* (London: Allen & Unwin, 1986), p. 3.

4. J. P. Nettl, "The State as a Conceptual Variable," *World Politics* 20 (1968): 560. Nettl introduced this thought as follows: "More than thirty years ago, Frederick Watkins pushed sovereignty to the margin of political science concerns by insisting that it be regarded as a 'limiting concept'—an ideal-typical situation that had to be qualified in all sorts of ways."

5. Stephen D. Krasner, "Sovereignty: An Institutional Perspective," in *The Elusive State: International and Comparative Perspectives*, ed. James A. Caporaso (Newbury Park, Calif.: Sage Publications, 1989), p. 88. Krasner claimed: "*Sovereignty* is a term that makes the eyes of most American political scientists glaze over."

6. Joseph A. Camilleri and Jim Falk, *The End of Sovereignty? The Politics of a Shrinking and Fragmented World* (Brookfield, Vt.: Elgar, 1992).

7. Ivo D. Duchacek, Daniel Latouche, and Garth Stevenson, eds., *Perforated Sovereignties and International Relations: Trans-Sovereign Contacts of Subnational Governments* (New York: Greenwood Press, 1988).

8. Jarat Chopra and Thomas G. Weiss, "Sovereignty Is No Longer Sacrosanct: Codifying Humanitarian Intervention," *Ethics and International Affairs* 6 (1992): 95–117.

9. See Raymond Vernon, *Sovereignty at Bay: The Multinational Spread of U.S. Enterprises* (New York: Basic Books, 1971), and Raymond Vernon, "Sovereignty at Bay: Ten Years After," *International Organization* 35 (1981): 517–29.

10. Geoffrey L. Goodwin, "The Erosion of External Sovereignty?" in *Between Sovereignty and Integration*, ed. Ghita Ionescu (New York: John Wiley and Sons, 1974), pp. 100–117.

11. Ali Khan, "The Extinction of Nation-States," *American University Journal of International Law and Policy* 7 (1992): 197–234.

12. Between 1985 and 1993 at least five scholars titled works "Beyond Sovereignty." See Mary Catherine Bateson, "Beyond Sovereignty: An Emerging Global Civilization," in *Contending Sovereignties: Redefining Political Community*, ed. R.B.J. Walker and Saul H. Mendlovitz (Boulder, Colo.: Lynne Reinner Publishers, 1990), pp. 145–58; Martin S. Soroos, *Beyond Sovereignty: The Challenge of Global Policy* (Columbia: University of South Carolina Press, 1986); Max Mark, *Beyond Sovereignty* (Washington, D.C.: Public Affairs Press, 1985); Neil MacCormick, "Beyond the Sovereign State," *The Modern Law Review* 56 (1993): 1–18; and Kaarle Nordenstreng and Herbert Schiller, eds., *Beyond National Sovereignty: International Communication in the 1990s* (Norwood, N.J.: Ablex Publishing Co., 1992).

13. Kenneth N. Waltz, "Political Structures," in *Neorealism and Its Critics*, ed. Robert O. Keohane (New York: Columbia University Press, 1986), p. 90.

14. R.B.J. Walker and Saul H. Mendlovitz, "Interrogating State Sovereignty," in *Contending Sovereignties: Redefining Political Community*, ed. R.B.J. Walker and Saul H. Mendlovitz (Boulder, Colo.: Lynne Reinner Publishers, 1990), pp. 1–12.

The thoughtful skeptic may find this rush to pen sovereignty's obituary unsettling. One objective of this book is to question whether news of the concept's imminent demise may have been exaggerated. As a scholar once questioned, "Is it the word we wish to throw out, or the concept, or the implications of the concept or the word?"[15] Perhaps the implications of sovereignty for international affairs differ sharply from past eras. Yet even as the most salient issues confronting the international community have changed dramatically over the centuries, those involved in the study or practice of international relations have continued to rely on the venerable concept of sovereignty. Though the frequency of its use has waxed and waned, sovereignty has never strayed far from the center of discourse about international relations. Today, one might say, sovereignty is the Banquo's ghost of the academic feast—rattling the soothsayers by reappearing at inconvenient intervals just when many assumed its final departure was at hand.

To date, those tolling sovereignty's death knell have been unable to convince the world that the concept is now obsolete.[16] These days Third World leaders regularly invoke sovereignty to underscore their independence. Representatives to the United Nations and other multilateral and regional institutions constantly appeal to sovereignty, or the like phrase "domestic jurisdiction." Those debating political unification in Europe, economic groupings in Asia or the Americas, or the future of the newly born states delivered from the former Soviet Union and Yugoslavia constantly refer to the term. So too do those discussing separatist movements in Quebec,[17] Puerto Rico, and elsewhere. Indeed, the number of sovereign states that have come into being since World War I now eclipses the number created since the dawn of the state system. Although the face of international relations has changed dramatically with the end of the Cold War, references to sovereignty continue to abound. It is thus perhaps appropriate to reexamine the

15. Charles E. Merriam, Jr., *Systematic Politics* (Chicago: University of Chicago Press, 1945), cited in Georg Schwarzenberger, "The Forms of Sovereignty," in *In Defense of Sovereignty*, ed. W. J. Stankiewicz (New York: Oxford University Press, 1969), p. 160.

16. See Quncy Wright, *Mandates Under the League of Nations* (New York: Greenwood Press, 1968), p. 281.

17. See Sharon Anne Williams, *International Legal Effects of Secession by Quebec* (North York, Ontario: York University, Centre for Public Law and Public Policy, 1992).

relevance and application of sovereignty to modern international affairs.

The Multiple Meanings of Sovereignty

In international relations discourse, scholars, diplomats, politicians, and government officials often casually refer to sovereignty without identifying the sense in which they are using the term. Many apparently assume that the meaning of sovereignty is universally recognized. Yet as one authority observed years ago: "The word sovereignty holds various conflicting connotations and by no means arouses identical patterns in the minds of different students."[18] Audiences must regularly attempt to derive the precise meaning of sovereignty solely from the context of the remarks. As was once stated of the similarly elusive term "the balance of power," the concept of sovereignty has been used not only in different senses by different people, or in different senses at different times by the same people, but in different senses by the same person in rapid succession.[19]

The English word sovereignty originally derived from the French term *souverain*: a supreme ruler not accountable to anyone, except perhaps to God.[20] On the heels of the dynastic and imperial struggles of the Middle Ages, monarchs in early modern Europe advanced the notion of sovereignty to strengthen their grip on the reins of the state[21] and to counter feudal claims by the nobility and

18. Vernon A. O'Rourke, *The Juristic Status of Egypt and the Sudan* (Baltimore: Johns Hopkins University Press, 1935), p. 10.

19. A. F. Pollard made this point about the balance of power. See A. F. Pollard, "The Balance of Power," *Journal of the British Institute of International Affairs* 2 (1923): 51–64, cited in Inis L. Claude, Jr., *Power and International Relations* (New York: Random House, 1962), p. 12.

20. Ivo D. Duchacek, *Nations and Men: International Politics Today* (New York: Holt, Rinehart and Winston, 1966), p. 47. In some states rulers may also have been expected to defer to customary law. See James, *Sovereign Statehood*, p. 4; see also Hinsley, *Sovereignty*, p. 122.

21. In tracing the history of this effort Joseph Strayer wrote: "[W]hen feudal theory had been elaborated to the point where it allowed the thing to regulate all justice and to tax all men, suzerainty was coming very close to sovereignty." See Joseph R. Strayer, *On the Medieval Origins of the Modern State* (Princeton: Princeton University Press, 1970), p. 43.

religious claims by the papacy.[22] In this period of religious schism and the dismembering of empire, rulers who trumpeted their sovereignty often intended other neighboring peoples to hear their claim to supremacy. A declaration of sovereignty stood as a ringing assertion of absolute political authority at home, one that could imply designs on territory abroad.[23]

Over the centuries, as international communities expanded in reach and ranks, diversity and complexity, and eventually merged into a single international society,[24] the implications of sovereignty did not remain fixed.[25] As various systems of states developed, people used sovereignty to focus not just on domestic authority within a state but on the relative independence of individual states. At home, sovereignty meant supremacy over all other potential authorities within that state's boundaries. In foreign affairs, the concept connoted concentrated power sufficient to secure independence from other states.[26] Thus, sovereignty came to denote the independence of a state interacting in a system of states rather than the potential supremacy of one state over other rivals. Paired with the emphasis on independence came the idea of reciprocity. In

22. See Quincy Wright, *The Existing Legal Situation as it Relates to the Conflict in the Far East* (New York: Institute of Pacific Relations, 1939), p. 18. More generally, see Evan Luard, *Types of International Society* (New York: The Free Press, 1976), pp. 312–29. See also Janice E. Thomson, *Mercenaries, Pirates, and Sovereigns: State-Building and Extraterritorial Violence in Early Modern Europe* (Princeton: Princeton University Press, 1994), and Michael Wilks, *The Problem of Sovereignty in the Later Middle Ages: The Papal Monarchy with Augustinus Triumphus and the Publicists* (Cambridge: Cambridge University Press, 1964).

23. George Kennan observed: "[T]his concept of sovereignty, the supremacy of a single ruler, was often conceived to have universal significance—to be applicable, that is, to all of the known civilized world. The particular ruler in question laid claim to be superior to any other ruler in authority. His supremacy was expected to be acknowledged by anyone else who had any authority over people anywhere." George F. Kennan, *Around the Cragged Hill: A Personal and Political Philosophy* (New York: W.W. Norton, 1993), p. 87.

24. The best historical account of this process is Adam Watson, *The Evolution of International Society* (London: Routledge, 1992).

25. See Jean Bodin, *On Sovereignty: Four Chapters from the Six Books on the Commonwealth*, ed. and trans. Julian H. Franklin (New York: Cambridge University Press, 1992). For a general analysis of Bodin's contribution to thought on sovereignty see Hinsley, *Sovereignty*, pp. 122–25. For an interesting, yet dated, discussion of the development of different meanings of sovereignty see Robert Lansing, *Notes on Sovereignty: From the Standpoint of the State and of the World* (Washington, D.C.: Carnegie Endowment for International Peace, 1921).

26. See generally Hinsley, *Sovereignty*, pp. 107, 122–32.

the international interactions of the day—whether arranging royal marriages, resolving disputes, or negotiating military or commercial agreements—a sovereign was to respect the sovereignty of its peers.

Over time, as political institutions developed further, people tailored the term to suit changed surroundings. Sovereignty thus brought to mind somewhat different notions for people in different centuries. The test of the locus of internal sovereignty developed from the right to give final judicial decisions to the possession of executive power to the right to make law.[27] And as states moved from absolutist to representative rule, democratically elected governments co-opted a term that had originally been linked with the supreme powers of a state's ruler and used it to assert their own sovereign powers delegated to them by their citizens.[28] Moreover, as the form of the modern society of states crystallized for its participants, the concept of sovereignty moved beyond declarations of the rights of a sovereign to encompass novel ideas of legitimacy, responsibility, and international recognition. Thus, during the gradual evolution of the international system, the content of the concept of sovereignty also changed.

Today the flavor of sovereignty depends upon the context in which the word is used. Since different usages are applied in different circumstances, the meaning of sovereignty varies according to the issue that is being addressed or the question that is being asked. For instance, if one states that "a critical difference between Gibraltar and Malta in the Mediterranean, or between Puerto Rico and Haiti in the Caribbean, is sovereignty," the reference likely denotes a particular status in international relations. The international community considers Malta and Haiti to be sovereign states but takes Gibraltar and Puerto Rico to be dependent parts of the British and American commonwealths.

At other times, however, sovereignty is used to refer not so much to status as to a particular degree of political freedom that might be termed de facto independence. If one states: "During the Cold War the Soviet Union's strict control over the government of Outer Mongolia brought into question that country's sovereignty," one

27. Strayer, *On the Medieval Origins of the Modern State*, p. 102.

28. For a discussion of this process see George L. Mosse, *The Struggle for Sovereignty in England: From the Reign of Queen Elizabeth to the Petition of Right* (New York: Octagon Books, 1968).

may well be using sovereignty in the sense of a particular degree of political independence. Someone questioning Outer Mongolian sovereignty[29] during the Cold War may not be doubting that the Outer Mongolian government enjoyed sovereign status in the international community. Rather, that person may be expressing the opinion that Outer Mongolia failed to demonstrate that measure of political independence that is normally associated with sovereign states.

In still other contexts sovereignty denotes a particular degree of legal freedom for a state, or what might be termed de jure independence. If one states: "During the Cold War a critical difference between the Baltic states and Outer Mongolia was that Outer Mongolia retained its sovereignty," the reference might be to this third popular usage of the term. Since the Baltic states were constitutionally bound to the Soviet Union during the Cold War, their situation differed from that of the nominally independent state of Outer Mongolia.

This assortment of meanings gathered under the broad rubric "sovereignty," as well as others that might readily be added, sometimes coexist comfortably, sometimes overlap uneasily, and sometimes contradict one another sharply.[30] They attest to the fact that the content of the concept of sovereignty varies dramatically with the subject under discussion. Though this trend toward using sovereignty with varying definitions in mind may be irreversible, we regard it as regrettable: "[A] word that means almost everything means virtually nothing, a conceptual tool used indiscriminately has its analytical edge irreparably dulled."[31] Thus, the principal focus of this book is upon sovereignty as a particular status and will take de facto and de jure independence to be its constituent parts. In our view political entities aspiring to sovereign status must customarily show both de

29. For the early history of Outer Mongolian political ties to China and the Soviet Union see Wright, *The Existing Legal Situation*, pp. 59–60.

30. Philosopher Jacques Maritain observed: "Of course we are free to say 'Sovereignty' while we are thinking full autonomy or right to decide without appeal—as we are free to say 'omnipotence' while . . . thinking limited power, or 'drum' while . . . thinking flute. Yet the result for our own way of thinking and for intelligible intercommunication would appear questionable." See Jacques Maritain, "The Concept of Sovereignty," in *In Defense of Sovereignty*, ed. W. J. Stankiewicz (New York: Oxford University Press, 1969), p. 61.

31. Inis L. Claude, Jr., "The Peace-Keeping Role of the United Nations," in *The United Nations in Perspective*, ed. E. Berkeley Tompkins (Stanford, Calif.: Hoover Institution Press, 1972), p. 49.

facto and de jure independence in order to be accepted as sovereign members of the international community.

Issues Addressed in this Book

In this study of sovereignty we analyze the concept through several different lenses. First, we identify and assess the importance of the term. In what capacities do scholars, leaders, and policymakers employ the concept? We examine the links between the status of sovereignty and power and rhetoric in the international arena.

The second chapter considers what precisely constitutes a sovereign state. We theorize that attaining sovereignty depends upon showings of de facto and de jure independence. We explore the ambiguities inherent in each requirement and sketch out the complex political process by which the international community confers sovereign status on aspirant states.

In the third and fourth chapters we ask how is the concept of sovereignty applied to international relations in theory and practice? We focus specifically on two approaches. The first views sovereignty as monolithic, indivisible, and applied in a uniform manner to all juridically equal sovereigns. The contrasting approach envisions sovereignty as a variable, divisible, and relative phenomenon. How have these views conflicted in scholarship and statescraft? Under what circumstances has one view or the other prevailed? Which view best reflects the reality of how states interact in contemporary international politics?

The fifth chapter considers the usefulness of sovereignty in the study and conduct of international affairs. To some, sovereignty is a pejorative term: an unpleasant reminder of all the flaws and deficiencies in our current system of states. It smacks of arrogance, irresponsibility, and abuse of power. The term exposes the weaknesses in the current international order and reflects the need for the system to evolve. To others, sovereignty is a laudable concept: one that should be hailed as a sturdy pillar that stabilizes the international system and offers hope to nations[32] intent on exercis-

---

32. Rather than taking a "nation" to be synonymous with a "state," we use "nation"

ing their right to self-determination. We critically assess the various perspectives of prominent defenders and critics, from the Marxist and the world federalist to the supranationalist, from the views of Third World leaders to those of human rights advocates. And, we ask: Is the concept of sovereignty more respected today, more encroached upon, or both?[33]

We conclude this work by asking, What does the future hold for the constantly evolving concept of sovereignty? That political communities around the world are now celebrating the end of the Cold War by claiming, or reclaiming, sovereign statehood raises questions as to whether many scholars are hurrying in the wrong directions. Did critics of the term act erroneously or simply prematurely? Is sovereignty approaching the end of a long and useful life, or is the concept likely to survive, even as particular uses fall from favor?

These are the theoretical issues that frame our inquiry into the concept of sovereignty. While scholars have long rued the retarded development of international relations theory,[34] they have never wholly agreed on just what theory is.[35] A few seem to have equated theory with jargon, or a long-winded, convoluted writing style. A more formidable group has focused on what it considers to be the appropriate process of arriving at a scholarly conclusion concerning international affairs. In recent years this methodological approach

---

to mean a group of people that claims a distinct identity and usually shares a language, customs, history, and common racial origins, and that frequently desires self-government. Thus the boundaries of a nation do not necessarily coincide with the boundaries of any particular state.

33. Israeli diplomat Abba Eban argued that sovereignty is now simultaneously more respected and more encroached upon. See Abba Eban, *The New Diplomacy: International Affairs in the Modern Age* (New York: Random House, 1983), p. 10. Eban apparently had in mind the European states in which fears of invasion have subsided, yet the necessity for compromise and concession in the European Union have increased. See also Stanley Hoffmann, *Primacy or World Order: American Foreign Policy Since the Cold War* (New York: McGraw-Hill, 1978), p. 132.

34. See, for instance, Martin Wight, "Why There is No International Theory?" in *Diplomatic Investigations*, ed. Herbert Butterfield and Martin Wight (Cambridge, Mass.: Harvard University Press, 1968), pp. 17–34. More generally, see Kenneth W. Thompson, *Fathers of International Thought: The Legacy of Political Theory* (Baton Rouge: Louisiana State University Press, 1994).

35. The following points draw on Inis L. Claude, Jr., "Introduction—The Place of Theory in the Conduct and Study of International Relations," *Journal of Conflict Resolution* 4 (1960): 264.

to theory has been dominated by those who would ground international relations scholarship in scientific methods, and particularly in the discipline of mathematics. Still other scholars have focused not so much on the proper tools as on the proper objectives: in particular, they have sought to advance our ideas concerning what is actually happening in international relations. Those who adopt this substantive perspective attempt to distinguish theoretical thinking about international affairs from empirical, or historical, or normative, or other conceivable angles on the subject.

Our work on sovereignty is theoretical in the sense that it attempts to interpret how states actually interact in international relations. And, as the titles to each chapter suggest, it focuses especially on answering a set of important questions about state behavior. From our perspective, then, theorizing about international relations is a matter of posing significant, unresolved issues about the subject and advancing hypotheses that purport to explain behavior in the international realm, grounded in what can actually be observed of the behavior of states. If this work does not offer definitive answers to all students of sovereignty, we hope that it will at least identify pertinent questions to stimulate further study of this elusive yet extraordinarily long-lived and steadily evolving concept.

1

Why Is Sovereignty Important?

> Of all the rights that can belong to a nation, sovereignty is
> doubtless the most precious.
>
> —Emerich de Vattel[1]

For centuries now the sovereignty of states has been a matter of
cardinal importance for those conducting international relations.
While originally the term referred to the absolute supremacy of
the ruling monarch, over time sovereignty came to denote the
independence of states: their supremacy at home and their freedom
from interference in external affairs. As the international community of states evolved, these notions of domestic supremacy and
external independence took on weighty implications.

Sovereignty as a Status in International Politics

Sovereignty is first, and perhaps foremost, a noteworthy legal and
political expression. Within the modern society of states the pres-

1. Emerich de Vattel, *The Law of Nations*, ed. Joseph Chitty (Philadelphia: T. and
J. W. Johnson & Co., 1883), p. 154, cited in Michael Scaperlanda, "Polishing the
Tarnished Golden Door," *Wisconsin Law Review* 1993 (1993): 1002 n. 181.

ence or absence of sovereignty determines the status of particular political entities. One might conceive of it as a ticket of general admission to the international arena.[2] A political entity that has attained the status of sovereign statehood is presumed by its peers to be capable of receiving fundamental international rights. Under international law sovereign states may take advantage of various substantial rights, including those of expropriation,[3] of diplomatic and sovereign immunity,[4] and of jurisdiction over legal matters at home and, increasingly, abroad.[5] Among many other notable entitlements sovereign states may recognize new states, negotiate treaties and sign agreements, declare war and conclude peace, protect national citizens traveling abroad, cast votes in international organizations, even register ships to sail on the high seas.[6] In this way sovereign status identifies a special set of members in the international community: the exclusive club of sovereign states.

What may be less frequently recognized is that to claim sovereignty is also to incur international obligations. Sovereignty is a declaration of political responsibility for governing, defending, and promoting the welfare of a human community. When Argentina attempted to assert its sovereignty over the Falkland, or Malvinas, Islands, the Argentine generals seem to have expected political support from the Third World against Great Britain, the archetypical colonial power. One reason that much of the international community reacted negatively was the perception that the Argentine junta

2. Oliver J. Lissitzyn called sovereignty "the essential qualification for full membership in international society." See Alan James, Sovereign Statehood: The Basis of International Society (London: Allen & Unwin, 1986), p. 7.

3. See Kamal Hossain and Subrata Roy Chowdhury, Permanent Sovereignty over Natural Resources in International Law: Principle and Practice (New York: St. Martin's Press, 1984), and Mannaraswamighala Sreeranga Rajan, Sovereignty over Natural Resources (Atlantic Highlands, N.J.: Humanities Press, 1978).

4. See Ian Brownlie, Principles of Public International Law (Oxford: Clarendon Press, 1979), p. 126. See also Elmer Plischke, Conduct of American Diplomacy (Princeton: D. Van Nostrand Co., 1961), pp. 57–58.

5. For a useful distinction among the legislative, executive, and judicial jurisdictions of a state and the development of judicial jurisdiction from the territorial principle to the nationality, protective, universality, and passive personality principles, see Malcolm N. Shaw, International Law, 3d ed. rev. (New York: Cambridge University Press, 1991), pp. 393–429.

6. See Plischke, Conduct, pp. 57–58. For a historical work on registering ships see Rodney Carlisle, Sovereignty for Sale: The Origins and Evolution of the Panamanian and Liberian Flags of Convenience (Annapolis, Md.: Naval Institute Press, 1981).

was more concerned with extending its rights over adjacent territory than with carrying out the responsibilities of governing the
inhabitants of the Falklands, who seemed thoroughly dismayed at
the prospect of Argentine rule.[7] This incident nicely reflects how
members of the international society have increasingly viewed
sovereignty as a grave assertion of responsibility.[8]

And since the international community expects sovereigns to
control actions within their territories, sovereignty stands for the
acceptance by states of a significant measure of accountability. As
the distinguished Swiss jurist Max Huber pointed out in the *Island
of Palmas* case, "Territorial sovereignty . . . involves the exclusive
right to display the activities of a State. This right has as corollary a
duty: the obligation to protect within the territory the rights of other
States, in particular their right to integrity and inviolability in peace
and war, together with the rights which each State may claim for its
nationals in foreign territory."[9] When an international delinquency
occurs, as when Iranian students seized and held hostage American
diplomats,[10] the international community expects the sovereign
state at fault to accept responsibility.

International law has long required sovereigns to protect diplomatic representatives received from other states and to refrain from
mistreating them.[11] Sovereign states are also legally obligated to act

7. Leslie Blake suggested: "It may be that the right word to describe the wants of
Argentina is 'dominion' rather than 'sovereignty.' She would have the islands with or
without the present inhabitants (preferably without). Sovereignty connotes a degree of
care over people, in their spiritual, cultural, and physical lives." See Leslie L. Blake,
Sovereignty: Power Beyond Politics (London: Shepheard-Walwyn, 1988), p. 6.

8. See Inis L. Claude, Jr., "The Common Defense and Great-Power Responsibilities,"
Political Science Quarterly 101 (1986): 719–32. See also Claude's chapter "Myths About
the State," in his *States and the Global System: Politics, Law, and Organization* (New
York: St. Martin's Press, 1988), especially pp. 25–26.

9. *Island of Palmas* [US/Neth.], 2 *Reports of International Arbitral Awards* (hereafter
R. Int'l. Arb. Awards) 839 (1928). Huber concluded: "Territorial sovereignty cannot limit
itself to its negative side, i.e., to excluding the activities of other States; for it serves to
divide between nations the space upon which human activities are employed, in order
to assure them at all points the minimum of protection of which international law is
the guardian."

10. See *United States Diplomatic and Consular Staff in Tehran* [US v Iran], 1980
International Court of Justice Reports of Judgments, Advisory Opinions, and Orders
(hereafter *ICJ*) 1 (Judgment).

11. See Grant McClanahan, *Diplomatic Immunity: Principles, Practices, Problems*
(New York: St. Martin's Press, 1989).

to prevent their territory from being used by terrorists intent on attacking other states or peoples.[12] Indeed, in 1830 France invaded and occupied Algiers, and thus threatened the sovereignty of the Barbary States, to punish Tunis and Tripoli for failing to suppress piracy.[13] More recently the human rights movement has attempted to require sovereign states to protect the human rights of their own citizens.[14] In each of these particulars the notion of sovereignty has helped the international community to express the duties of states as well as their rights.

Sovereignty also serves to remind states that when an issue arises touching upon another sovereign's territory or people the international community expects the sovereigns to deal with one another rather than to attempt to resolve the matter unilaterally.[15]

12. The implications of this legal obligation are subject to debate. Using the examples of the military campaigns against Palestine Liberation Organization (PLO) bases in Jordan (1970) and Lebanon (1982), Israel's former United Nations ambassador, Benjamin Netanyahu, argued: "Sovereignty imposes not only the right but the obligation to control one's territory." See Benjamin Netanyahu, "Terrorism: How the West Can Win," in *Terrorism: How the West Can Win*, ed. Benjamin Netanyahu (New York: Farrar, Straus & Giroux, 1986), p. 222. Eugene Rostow similarly concluded: "Israel . . . had an altogether legal right to enter Lebanon to eliminate the source, not only of attacks against Israel itself, but of attacks against Israeli interests throughout the world. Lebanon had a categorical legal obligation to prevent its territory from being used for such purposes. . . . Since Lebanon was incapable of putting down the PLO, Israel had a right to enter Lebanese territory to do what the Lebanese should have done themselves." See Eugene Rostow, "Overcoming Denial," in *Terrorism: How the West Can Win*, ed. Benjamin Netanyahu (New York: Farrar, Straus & Giroux, 1986), p. 148.

13. Janice E. Thomson, "Sovereignty in Historical Perspective: The Evolution of State Control over Extraterritorial Violence," in *The Elusive State: International and Comparative Perspectives*, ed. James A. Caporaso (Newbury Park, Calif.: Sage Publications, 1989), p. 240.

14. See, for instance, Jack Donnelly, "Human Rights and International Organizations: States, Sovereignty, and the International Community," in *International Organization: A Reader*, ed. Friedrich V. Kratochwil and Edward D. Mansfield (New York: HarperCollins College Publishers, 1994), pp. 202–18. See also Scaperlanda, "Polishing the Tarnished Golden Door," pp. 965–1032; Jarat Chopra and Thomas G. Weiss, "Sovereignty Is No Longer Sacrosanct: Codifying Humanitarian Intervention," *Ethics and International Affairs* 6 (1992): 95–117; and Jennifer Noe Pahre, "The Fine Line Between the Enforcement of Human Rights Agreements and the Violation of National Sovereignty: The Case of the Soviet Dissidents," *Loyola of Los Angeles International and Comparative Law Journal* 7 (1984): 323–50.

15. For an interesting essay on a related topic see Quincy Wright, "Espionage and the Doctrine of Non-Intervention in Internal Affairs," in *Essays on Espionage and International Law*, ed. Roland J. Stanger (Columbus: Ohio State University Press, 1962), pp. 3–28.

In 1960 Israeli citizens abducted from Argentina the fugitive Nazi war criminal Adolf Eichmann and brought him to Israel to stand trial for crimes against the Jewish people.[16] Despite diplomatic correspondence in which Israel expressed its regret if it had "interfered with matters within the sovereignty of Argentina," and despite a letter of apology sent from Prime Minister David Ben-Gurion to Argentine President Arturo Frondizi, Argentina protested to the United Nations Security Council the violation of its sovereignty by foreigners exercising law enforcement authorities on its soil.[17]

Thirty years later, after the United States Drug Enforcement Administration (DEA) hired Mexican nationals to kidnap and bring to the United States a suspect in the torture and murder of a DEA agent,[18] the Mexican government likewise vigorously complained that its sovereignty had been violated. By acting unilaterally rather than abiding by the terms of the extradition treaty between the two countries,[19] the United States government had failed to defer to the sovereignty of a peer in a criminal matter concerning both states.[20] In a less well publicized operation in April 1991 DEA officials hid forty-four kilos of cocaine on a passenger airliner headed from Belize to Honduras without informing Honduran authorities.[21]

16. See Louis Henkin, *How Nations Behave: Law and Foreign Policy*, 2d ed. rev. (New York: Columbia University Press, 1979), pp. 269–77.

17. See *Attorney-General of the Government of Israel v Adolf Eichmann*, 36 *International Law Reports* 5, 6 (Israel, D. Ct. Jerusalem, 1961). A joint communiqué eventually closed the incident (ibid., pp. 6–7). A district court found Eichmann guilty of crimes against the Jewish people, war crimes, crimes against humanity, and membership in enemy organizations. The Israeli Supreme Court rejected his appeal and upheld his death sentence (id. at 14). Israeli authorities executed Eichmann in 1962.

18. See *United States v Alvarez-Machain*, 112 Sup. Ct. 2188 (1991). See also *United States v Verdugo-Urquidez*, 494 US 259 (1990), *United States v Verdugo-Urquidez*, 939 F2d 1341 (9th Cir. 1991), and *United States v Verdugo-Urquidez*, 856 F2d 1214 (9th Cir. 1988). For commentary on the Verdugo-Urquidez case see *Miami Herald* (intl. ed.), 3 May 1990, p. 12A.

19. See U.S. Department of State, "Extradition Treaty, United States–United Mexican States," 4 May 1978, TIAS no. 9656, *United States Treaties and Other International Agreements* [hereafter *UST*], vol. 31, pt. 6, pp. 5,059–78.

20. In fact, in an opinion authored by Chief Justice William Rehnquist over the strong dissent of Justice John Paul Stevens, the United States Supreme Court ruled that the Alvarez-Machain kidnapping did not violate the Extradition Treaty between the two states. See *United States v Alvarez-Machain*.

21. "Incautan 44 kilos de cocaína en avión," *La Prensa* (Honduras), 8 April 1991, p. 2. For analogous, embarrassing incidents involving a German undercover operation in the Netherlands, a DEA–Spanish police operation, and a French customs operation in

After police in San Pedro Sula, Honduras, unwittingly seized the narcotics and wrongfully imprisoned the crew, Honduran officials claimed their sovereignty had been violated by the lack of American consultation over a significant law-enforcement matter.[22] Sovereignty thus continues to be invoked to guide states toward respecting one another's independence by refraining from undertaking unauthorized police activities on another state's soil.[23]

The status of sovereign statehood also signifies a form of legitimacy in international affairs. Sovereign status implies at least some minimal degree of concentrated power, whether in common forms, such as economic weight or military force, or in unusual forms, such as the spiritual influence wielded by the Vatican state.[24] An entity that has achieved sovereign status is thought to be entitled to a substantial degree of deference from other sovereigns. In this sense sovereignty acts as a common denominator among states. A community that proclaims its sovereignty thereby informs the world that an independent government is open for business, one that is similar in important respects to its counterparts around the globe.

To capitalize on the concept's legitimacy, political communities searching for international recognition are naturally attracted to sovereign statehood. As a consequence, sovereignty continues to play a critical role in the creation of states. In 1989 the resolution of clashing territorial claims in southern Africa brought into being

Switzerland, see Ethan A. Nadelmann, *Cops Across Borders: The Internationalization of U.S. Criminal Law Enforcement* (University Park: The Pennsylvania State University Press, 1993), pp. 234, 238, 325.

22. "Discua censura operación de la DEA," *La Prensa* (Honduras), 11 April 1991, p. 4; "E.U. asignó a Honduras 315 mil dólores para combatir narcos," *La Prensa* (Panama), 8 May 1991, p. 10A; and "Pilot and Crew of Belize Air International Get Ready to Sue Drug Enforcement Agency," *The Reporter* (Belize), 14 February 1993, p. D. See also "Suit: Drug Sting Put 6 Through Torture," *Miami Herald*, 23 January 1995, p. 1B.

23. For the historical development of police activities abroad, see Nadelmann, *Cops Across Borders.*

24. For particularly interesting theories of power see Karl Deutsch, "On the Concepts of Politics and Power," *Journal of International Affairs* 21 (1967): 232–41; K. J. Holsti, "The Concept of Power in the Study of International Relations," *Background* 7 (1964): 179–94; John Kenneth Galbraith, *The Anatomy of Power* (Boston: Houghton Mifflin, 1985), especially pp. 140–60; Joseph S. Nye, "Soft Power," *Foreign Policy* 80 (1990): 153–71; and Evan Luard, *The Blunted Sword: The Erosion of Military Power in World Politics* (New York: New Amsterdam Books, 1989), especially pp. 7–55.

the new sovereign state of Namibia. In the early 1990s numerous seccessionist movements set their sights on sovereign statehood, including those in Croatia, Serbia, Bosnia, Macedonia, and Eritrea. The splintering of the Soviet Union brought forth repeated declarations of sovereignty: re-created sovereignty in the case of the Baltic states and Russia and newly created sovereignty in the case of other republics. In 1993 the Palestinian nation took long-awaited steps toward claiming its own sovereign status.

Since sovereignty confers a special degree of legitimacy and is associated with certain critical rights and duties,[25] Kurds[26] and Quebecois, the people of Timor and the Western Sahara, and various other nations lacking sovereignty are keenly aware of the benefits of entry into the private club of sovereign states. Indeed, the attractions of sovereignty are sufficiently compelling that a people need not foresee complementary economic benefits to pursue sovereign statehood. Certainly, many separatist groups, such as those in Biafra in Nigeria, in the Basque area of Spain, and in the Punjab portion of India, have believed that their economic conditions would improve in a new sovereign state.[27] However, sovereignty movements have also persisted in areas likely to suffer economic decline should they suddenly attain sovereign status, such as Quebec,[28] Northern Ireland,[29] or Puerto Rico. The people of Eritrea sought and obtained sovereignty despite an immediate decline in an already marginal standard of living.

While sovereign status exerts a magnetic attraction for many today, quests for sovereign statehood are by no means a contemporary development. For better or for worse, from the American Revolution to the microstates emerging during the final phase of

25. Richard A. Falk, "Evasions of Sovereignty," in Contending Sovereignties: Redefining Political Community, ed. R.B.J. Walker and Saul H. Mendlovitz (Boulder, Colo.: Lynne Reinner, 1990), pp. 61–62.

26. See Hurst Hannum, Autonomy, Sovereignty, and Self-Determination: The Accommodation of Conflicting Rights (Philadelphia: University of Pennsylvania Press, 1990), pp. 178–202.

27. Ibid. For information on Basque separatism, see ibid., pp. 263–79.

28. See Patrick Grady, The Economic Consequences of Quebec Sovereignty (Vancouver: Fraser Institute, 1991), especially pp. 154–57. See also Adalbert Lallier, Sovereignty Association: Economic Realism or Utopia? (New York: Mosaic Press, 1991).

29. See Hannum, Autonomy, Sovereignty, and Self-Determination, p. 8.

decolonization, most anticolonial movements have claimed sovereign statehood to be their objective.[30] And sovereignty's allure extends well beyond those oppressed by imperialism. In 1929 even the pope succeeded in becoming a sovereign leader when the Holy See gained sovereign status as the Vatican state.[31]

Of course, the importance of sovereignty in international affairs should not be overstated. To say that the Maldives and Brazil are both sovereign states is to say that two political entities, dissimilar in most respects, share the lone characteristic of sovereignty.[32] Moreover, many of the most significant current international actors are not territorial entities and never attain sovereign status.[33] The activities of such nonsovereign actors, like skate tracks on a heavily used ice hockey rink, cross and recross one another without much heed for underlying boundary lines. In fact, the dramatic progress in global communications and transportation and the simultaneous rise of

30. Should sovereign statehood be the objective of Third World peoples? See Lester Edwin J. Ruiz, "Sovereignty as Transformative Practice," in *Contending Sovereignties: Redefining Political Community*, ed. R.B.J. Walker and Saul H. Mendlovitz (Boulder, Colo.: Lynne Reinner Publishers, 1990), pp. 79–96. Two of the finest works on anticolonial movements are Rupert P. Emerson, *From Empire to Nation: The Rise to Self-Assertion of Asian and African Peoples* (Cambridge, Mass.: Harvard University Press, 1960), and Tony Smith, *The Patterns of Imperialism: The United States, Great Britain, and the Late-Industrializing World Since 1815* (Cambridge: Cambridge University Press, 1981). See also Peter Lyon, "New States and International Order," in *The Bases of International Order: Essays in Honor of C.A.W. Manning*, ed. Alan James (New York: Oxford University Press, 1973), pp. 24–59.

31. The Vatican City-State immediately took on a neutralized status guaranteed by Italy. Thus, the Vatican steers clear of the political and military ties common to many sovereign states. See Cyril E. Black et al., *Neutralization and World Politics* (Princeton: Princeton University Press, 1968), p. 32. See also F. A. Váli, *Servitudes of International Law: A Study of Rights in Foreign Territories*, 2d ed. rev. (New York: Praeger, 1958), pp. 193–98.

32. See Inis L. Claude, Jr., "The Tension Between Principle and Pragmatism in International Relations," *Review of International Studies* 19 (1993): 218. See also Barry Buzan, *People, States, and Fear: The National Security Problem in International Relations* (Chapel Hill: University of North Carolina Press, 1983), p. 42.

33. For an essay on the process by which political systems have been penetrated by entities outside of the national society see James N. Rosenau, "Pre-Theories and Theories of Foreign Policy," in *Approaches to Comparative and International Politics*, ed. R. Barry Farrell (Evanston: Northwestern University Press, 1966), especially p. 65. For a more general work see Richard W. Mansbach, Yale H. Ferguson, and Donald E. Lampert, *The Web of World Politics: Nonstate Actors in the Global System* (Englewood Cliffs, N.J.: Prentice-Hall, 1976).

international banks and multinational enterprises[34] have created un-precedented flows of goods and capital across boundaries. While sovereign states continue to coin and control currencies, oversee and regulate markets, and contribute funds to international institutions engaged in trade and finance, regional and global nonstate actors have taken on, and continue to take on, new and enterprising roles, particularly in lending money to developing states.

During this same era notable subnational or cross-national private groups have proliferated, ranging in form and function from potentially sweeping social movements like pan-Islam to issue-oriented watchdog groups like Amnesty International to terrorist gangs like Islamic Jihad. Today, labor unions, charitable organizations, religious organizations, grass-roots gatherings, even bands of volunteer soldiers and mercenaries, can exercise considerable influence across state borders and should thus be counted among the ranks of international actors, at least under some circumstances.[35] Scholars of international politics, who might once have conceived of their subject as a neat checkerboard marked by identical chips, now confront a murkier and messier phenomenon—perhaps a more suitable metaphor would be a slippery mass of intertwined ropes heaped in the dark, damp hold of a ship.

Since World War II many notable supranational public organizations have also come into being. This class of influential nonstate actors includes both institutions with virtually universal state membership like the United Nations and much more selective institutions[36] like the Organization of Petroleum Exporting Countries, the Association of Southeast Asian Nations, or even the Organization of Eastern Caribbean States (OECS),[37] a key participant in the events

34. See generally Raymond Vernon, *Sovereignty at Bay: The Multinational Spread of U.S. Enterprises* (New York: Basic Books, 1971), and Raymond Vernon, "Sovereignty at Bay: Ten Years After," *International Organization* 35 (1981): 517–29.

35. See Hans Blix, *Sovereignty, Aggression, and Neutrality* (Stockholm: Amquist & Wiksell, 1970). For a historical view, see Janice E. Thomson, *Mercenaries, Pirates, and Sovereigns: State-Building and Extraterritorial Violence in Early Modern Europe* (Princeton: Princeton University Press, 1994).

36. See generally Ivo D. Duchacek, Daniel Latouche, and Garth Stevenson, eds., *Perforated Sovereignties and International Relations: Trans-Sovereign Contacts of Sub-national Governments* (New York: Greenwood Press, 1988).

37. For an article tracing the development of the OECS, see W. Marvin Will, "A Nation

that led to the American invasion of Grenada in 1983.[38] All this is to say that sovereignty, while an important concept in international relations, is by no means all-important. In carrying on a wide range of international activities nonsovereign actors may be wholly oblivious to, or even consciously adverse to, the implications of sovereign status.

Nevertheless, even at a time when many other actors have joined sovereign states in engaging in international relations, the ability to distinguish sovereigns from other entities remains a matter of considerable weight. Viewed as an organizing principle, the status of sovereignty clarifies whether the international society recognizes that a political community has attained a particular standing. And although nonsovereign actors may seem to be crowding the stage, the sovereign states remain the chief protagonists in the international drama. Sovereignty separates a set of principal actors—the sovereign states—from other territorial and nonterritorial entities, less significant in certain respects. Thus, sovereignty's continued prominence may be principally attributed to the fact that it usefully expresses status in international relations.

Sovereignty and Political Rhetoric

Sovereignty should not be thought of merely as a helpful scorecard identifying the star players in the game of international politics. The rights and duties and implications that attend the status of sovereignty have come to serve as a potent political weapon, one

Divided: The Quest for Caribbean Integration," *Latin American Research Review* 26 (1991): 3–37.

38. For contrasting views on the Grenada invasion and the role of the OECS, see John Norton Moore, *Law and the Grenada Mission* (Charlottesville: University of Virginia, Center for Law and National Security, 1984), especially pp. 45–51; John Norton Moore, "Grenada and the International Double Standard," *American Journal of International Law* (hereafter *AJIL*) 78 (1984): 145–68; Christopher C. Joyner, "Reflections on the Lawfulness of Invasion," *AJIL* 78 (1984): 131–44; Detlev Vagts, "International Law under Time Pressure," *AJIL* 78 (1984): 169–72; and Francis Boyle et al., "International Lawlessness in Grenada," *AJIL* 78 (1984): 172–75. For yet another perspective, see M. Shahabuddeen, *The Conquest of Grenada: Sovereignty in the Periphery* (Georgetown: Guyana: University of Guyana, 1986).

that commands virtually worldwide respect. In keeping with the concept's close link to domestic notions of private property sovereignty is often used as a "No Trespassing" sign to defend independence.[39] Accordingly, the relevance of the status of sovereignty has long encompassed matters of political rhetoric.

One might also note that as the structure and problems of international politics have changed, the objectives of those employing the term have also evolved. And the varied meanings that have gathered under the broad rubric of "sovereignty" have permitted states to apply the concept toward different purposes under different circumstances. As Quincy Wright observed, for all the dynamism of the concept of sovereignty, its "intellectual content, fitted to each particular purpose for which it is employed, has been variable and vague. Thus it has been of more value for purposes of oratory and persuasion than of science and law."[40]

Over the centuries leaders have repeatedly relied upon the concept of sovereignty to defend their state's independence. Though popular references to the term sovereignty may be traced to the works of French philosopher Jean Bodin in the late sixteenth century, the concept existed well before scholars attempted to define and describe it.[41] Indeed, as long ago as the year 607 Prince Shotoku of Japan sent a note to the Sui emperor of China that might best be translated: "From the sovereign of the land of the rising sun to the sovereign of the land of the setting sun."[42] Although this declaration of independence insulted China and the emperor refused to reply, the Japanese crown prince had effectively made the

39. See John Gerard Ruggie, "Continuity and Transformation in the World Polity: Toward a Neorealist Synthesis," in Neorealism and Its Critics, ed. Robert O. Keohane (New York: Columbia University Press, 1986), p. 143.

40. Quincy Wright, Mandates Under the League of Nations (New York: Greenwood Press, 1968), pp. 277–78.

41. Joseph R. Strayer, On the Medieval Origins of the Modern State (Princeton, N.J.: Princeton University Press, 1970), p. 9 ("Sovereignty existed in fact long before it could be described in theory"). See also ibid., pp. 44, 53, 91.

42. H. Paul Varley, Japanese Culture: A Short History (New York: Holt, Rinehart and Winston, 1977), p. 15. Despite the common association of sovereignty with European philosophers, the term has been applied to early states in other cultures. For a discussion of sovereignty within South America before and during the Spanish Conquest, see Charles Gibson, The Inca Concept of Sovereignty and the Spanish Administration in Peru (Austin: University of Texas Press, 1948).

point "that Japan intended to uphold its independence and would not accept the status of humble subordination usually expected of countries that sent tribute to mighty China."[43]

In recent years such rhetorical uses of sovereignty have multiplied. For example, until the issue was settled in 1992, Guatemala claimed title to and refused to recognize its eastern neighbor Belize, a member of the British Commonwealth. The Belizeans defended against their neighbor's threatened encroachment by hosting British troops on training missions and by vigorously asserting their sovereign statehood based on self-government since at least the eighteenth century. By invoking its sovereignty Belize successfully appealed to the international community to pressure Guatemala not to trespass on a neighboring sovereign state. As in the case of Argentina's designs on the Falklands, Belize could garner international support in part because Guatemala appeared more intent on gaining territory than on promoting the welfare of the people of Belize.

Yet while the Belizeans and others have employed sovereignty defensively, various leaders have used the term to rally their people toward offensive action. In 1967 Gamel Abdel Nasser cited Egyptian sovereignty to compel the withdrawal of the United Nations Emergency Force (UNEF) interposed between Israeli and Egyptian forces.[44] In 1982 the Argentine Armed Forces promoted their attempt to reclaim the Falkland Islands as a necessary reassertion of Argentina's sovereign authority.[45] That states explain offensive and

43. Varley, *Japanese Culture*, p. 15. For a study of the sovereignty concept in Japan, see Kotaro Tanaka, "Japanese Law," in *Sovereignty Within the Law*, ed. Arthur Larson and C. Wilfred Jenks (Dobbs Ferry, N.Y.: Oceana Publications, 1965), pp. 223–41.

44. See Joseph Frankel, *International Politics: Conflict and Harmony* (Baltimore: Penguin Books, 1973), p. 212. After receiving Egypt's formal request for withdrawal of UNEF on May 18, 1967, Secretary-General U Thant hastily convened the UNEF Advisory Committee and informed its members that "he had no choice in the matter but to withdraw . . . [the UNEF] as soon as possible." See John F. Murphy, *The United Nations and the Control of International Violence: A Legal and Political Analysis* (Totowa, N.J.: Allanheld, Osmun Publishers, 1982), p. 103. For the background of the UNEF withdrawal, see E.L.M. Burns, "The Withdrawal of UNEF and the Future of Peacekeeping," *International Journal* 23 (1967–68): 1–17, especially p. 4.

45. For works on the Falkland Islands conflict that consider the sovereignty issue, see Lowell S. Gustafson, *The Sovereignty Dispute over the Falkland (Malvinas) Islands* (Oxford: Oxford University Press, 1988); Lawrence Freedman, *Britain and the Falklands War* (Cambridge: Basil Blackwell, 1988); and Fritz L. Hoffmann and Olga Mingo Hoffmann, *Sovereignty in Dispute: The Falklands/Malvinas, 1493–1982* (Boulder, Colo.:

defensive maneuvers in the name of sovereignty illustrates the term's versatility as well as its ambiguity.[46] As one prominent international relations theorist remarked, "[S]overeignty is a catchword which can be used by all, with very different tactical meanings."[47]

In an era of unprecedented global communication, when the spotlight of public attention can be brought to focus on the behavior of states as never before, the concept of sovereignty can also lend emphasis to political arguments or even support propaganda efforts. Many politicians and diplomats use the substantial rhetorical power of the term to provide additional force to their country's diplomatic position or to express outrage at some injustice their people may have suffered. Leaders claim, perhaps with increasing frequency, that their country's sovereign rights are being trampled by an interested power, an international organization, a multinational company, a meddlesome neighbor, or some real or imagined aggressor. For example, in denouncing the actions of the United States Information Agency in beaming television signals into Cuba, Fidel Castro argued that Televisión Martí violated his country's sovereignty.[48] Increasingly, one might say, the notion of violated

Westview Press, 1984). Two of the most interesting articles are Michael P. Socarras, "The Argentine Invasion of the Falklands: International Norms of Signaling," in *International Incidents: The Law That Counts in World Politics*, ed. W. Michael Reisman and Andrew R. Willard (Princeton: Princeton University Press, 1988), pp. 115–43; and Edward E. Azar and Anthony F. Pickering, "The Problem-Solving Forums: The Falklands/Malvinas Islands," in *The Management of Protracted Social Conflicts: Theory and Cases*, ed. Edward E. Azar (Hanover, N.H.: Dartmouth College Press, 1990), pp. 82–108. See also Wayne S. Smith, ed., *Toward Resolution? The Falklands/Malvinas Dispute* (Boulder, Colo.: Lynne Reinner Publishers, 1991).

46. Richard W. Mansbach and John A. Vasquez, *In Search of Theory: A Paradigm for Global Politics* (New York: Columbia University Press, 1981), p. 10.

47. Stanley Hoffmann, "In Search of a Thread: The UN in the Congo Labyrinth," in *United Nations Political Systems*, ed. David A. Kay (New York: John Wiley and Sons, 1967), p. 257.

48. See *Granma Weekly Review* (Cuba), 11 February 1990, p. 11. The line between free exchange of ideas and subversive propaganda may be difficult to draw. See Blix, *Sovereignty, Aggression, and Neutrality*, pp. 16–17, and John B. Whitton, "Hostile International Propaganda and International Law," in *National Sovereignty and International Communication*, ed. Kaarle Nordenstreng and Herbert I. Schiller (Norwood, N.J.: Ablex Publishing Co., 1979), pp. 217–29. See also Sei Kageyama, "International Cooperation and National Sovereignty—Unchanged Role of National Sovereignty in the Provision of International Telecommunications Services," *Case Western Reserve Journal of International Law* 16 (1984): 265–85; Kaarle Nordenstreng and Herbert Schiller, eds.,

sovereignty is to diplomacy as the exclamation point is to sloppy writing.

In sum, the astute observer might conclude that a political community that continually reminds others of its sovereignty may well be engaged in a bit of chest-thumping. As one scholar perceptively observed: "All this is part of the stuff of politics. Here some imprecision of language is to be expected, some stretching of terms, a rather hasty grabbing for any semantic ammunition which can plausibly be pressed into service."[49] The rhetoric of sovereignty reminds us that the concept has retained its importance over time not just as a dry expression of legal status in the society of states but as a handy tool regularly put to use in the tasks of international politics.

Sovereignty and Power

The connection between sovereignty and power within the system of states extends well beyond the merely rhetorical. The question of who is sovereign in a particular territory retains vital significance in international politics. States take quite seriously questions regarding territorial sovereignty, whether the questions concern "boundary disputes" (that is, issues regarding where the property lines between states ought to be drawn) or "title disputes" (that is, issues regarding whether a state has acquired and maintained legal ownership of the territory in question).[50]

Indeed, the reach of a state's sovereign jurisdiction—the extent of territory under its sovereign control—can bear quite directly on its economic or military power. The population of a territory, its strategic location, its natural resources (whether it has oil or timber or minerals or the potential for hydroelectric power)—such factors

---

Beyond National Sovereignty: International Communication in the 1990s (Norwood, N.J.: Ablex Publishing Co., 1992); and David I. Fisher, *Prior Consent to International Direct Satellite Broadcasting* (Boston: Kluwer Academic Publishers, 1990), especially pp. 118–23.

49. James, *Sovereign Statehood*, p. 2.

50. See Friedrich V. Kratochwil, Paul Rohrlich, and Harpreet Mahajan, *Peace and Disputed Sovereignty: Reflections on Conflict over Territory* (Lanham, Md.: University Press of America, 1985), p. 3.

have raised the stakes in many clashes over territorial sovereignty. Even in an era marked by relatively few military conflicts, the extent of a state's territorial jurisdiction can be a source of continuing tension.[51] In the military clashes during the 1980s between Britain and Argentina,[52] Ethiopia and Somalia, and Chad and Libya,[53] and in the Iraqi invasion of Kuwait and the Gulf War of 1992,[54] a political conflict over sovereignty rapidly spiraled into a matter of war and peace.

The concept of sovereignty has thus framed recent disputes of regional significance, such as the territorial claims made by the People's Republic of China to the British colony of Hong Kong,[55] by India and Pakistan to the territory of Kashmir, by Japan to the Northern Territories,[56] by Bahrain and Qatar to the Hawar Islands,

51. See generally ibid. For an interesting theoretical perspective on boundary disputes, focusing on several case studies, see Ian S. Lustick, *Unsettled States, Disputed Lands: Britain and Ireland, France and Algeria, Israel and West Bank–Gaza* (Ithaca: Cornell University Press, 1993).

52. Apparently, the diplomatic mission by Secretary-General Javier Pérez de Cuellar nearly brought about a peaceful resolution to the dispute. However, according to the secretary-general's report, Argentina demanded that Britain recognize its sovereignty on the islands before Argentine troops would withdraw and leave the islands temporarily under a proposed United Nations administration. See Murphy, *The United Nations and the Control of International Violence,* p. 108.

53. The violent dispute over the Aouzou Strip is examined in Matthew M. Ricciardi, "Title to the Aouzou Strip: A Legal and Historical Analysis," *The Yale Journal of International Law* 17 (1992): 301–488.

54. For a historical account of Iraq's claims to Kuwait, see Majid Khadduri, "Iraq's Claim to the Sovereignty of Kuwayt," *New York University Journal of International Law and Politics* 23 (1990): 5–34. See also David Campbell, *Politics Without Principle: Sovereignty, Ethics, and the Narratives of the Gulf War* (Boulder, Colo.: Lynne Reinner Publishers, 1993).

55. In 1997 China will obtain sovereignty over Hong Kong pursuant to the "Joint Declaration of the Government of the United Kingdom of Great Britain and Northern Ireland and the Government of the People's Republic of China on the Question of Hong Kong, initialed at Peking, 26 September 1984," *International Legal Materials* (hereafter *ILM*) 23 (1984): 1371–81. For commentary, see especially William H. Overholt, "Hong Kong and the Crisis of Sovereignty," *Asian Survey* 24 (1984): 471–84, and Kevin P. Lane, *Sovereignty and the Status Quo: The Historical Roots of China's Hong Kong Policy* (Boulder, Colo.: Westview Press, 1990). See also the collection of essays entitled "Hong Kong: Transfer of Sovereignty," *Case Western Reserve Journal of International Law* 20 (1988): 1–278; 301–68; Ming K. Chan and David J. Clark, eds., *The Hong Kong Basic Law: Blueprint for "Stability and Prosperity" under Chinese Sovereignty?* (Armonk, N.Y.: M. E. Sharpe, 1991).

56. This dispute concerns the islands of Kunashiri, Etorofu, and Shikotan, and the Habomai group of islands, all located to the northeast of Hokkaido, Japan. Although the Soviet Union agreed to return Habomai and Shikotan to Japan in a 1956 Joint Declaration,

by Iraq and Iran to land bordering the Shatt-al-Arab River,[57] by the United States, Colombia, and Honduras to the Rock of Quintasueño and the Swan Islands,[58] by Australia and Papua New Guinea to islands in the Torres Strait,[59] by various states to portions of Antarctica[60] and the Arctic,[61] and by six neighboring countries to the Spratly Islands in the South China Sea.[62] Sovereignty has also

the Soviets reneged after the Japanese signed a security agreement with the United States in 1960. See United Nations, Treaty Series, "Joint Declaration by the Union of Soviet Socialist Republics and Japan, signed at Moscow," 19 October 1956, *Treaties and International Agreements Registered or Filed and Reported with the Secretariat of the United Nations* (hereafter UNTS), vol. 263, no. 3768 (1957), pp. 112–16; United Nations, Treaty Series, "Treaty of Mutual Co-operation and Security Between Japan and the United States of America, signed at Washington," 19 January 1960, UNTS, vol. 373, no. 5320 (1960), pp. 186–204. For a synopsis of the dispute see Kratochwil et al., *Peace and Disputed Sovereignty*, pp. 65–70. Japan has also disputed ownership of the Takeshima islands with Korea. See Philip C. Jessup, *The Price of International Justice* (New York: Columbia University Press, 1971), p. 36.

57. See Kaiyan Homi Kaikobad, *The Shatt-al-Arab Boundary Question: A Legal Reappraisal* (Oxford: Clarendon Press, 1988). See also Jessup, *The Price of International Justice*, pp. 37–39.

58. See Jessup, *The Price of International Justice*, pp. 31–33.

59. See K. W. Ryan and M.W.D. White, "The Torres Strait Treaty," *The Australian Year Book of International Law* 7 (1981): 87–113.

60. See Gillian D. Triggs, *International Law and Australian Sovereignty in Antarctica* (Sydney: Legal Books, 1986). For a synopsis of the sovereignty dispute in the polar regions, see Kratochwil et al., *Peace and Disputed Sovereignty*, pp. 101–14. The authors pointed out that sovereignty over the Arctic and Antarctic raises different questions in part because the Arctic is an ice shelf while the Antarctic is an ice-covered land mass.

61. For insights on government policy toward the Arctic, see Shelagh D. Grant, *Sovereignty or Security? Government Policy in the Canadian North, 1936–1950* (Vancouver: University of British Columbia Press, 1988), especially pp. 157–87, and Finn Sollie, "Nordic Perspectives on Arctic Sovereignty and Security," in *Sovereignty and Security in the Arctic*, ed. Edgar J. Dosman (New York: Routledge, 1989), pp. 194–210. Among the best articles on Arctic sovereignty are Donald W. Greig, "Sovereignty, Territory, and the International Lawyer's Dilemma," *Osgoode Hall Law Journal* 26 (1988): 163–69; Donat Pharand, "Sovereignty in the Arctic: The International Legal Context," in *Sovereignty and Security in the Arctic*, ed. Edgar J. Dosman (New York: Routledge, 1989), pp. 145–58; and David Lenarcic and Robert Reford, "Sovereignty versus Defense: The Arctic in Canadian-American Relations," in *Sovereignty and Security in the Arctic*, ed. Edgar J. Dosman (New York: Routledge, 1989), pp. 159–75. See also the remarks of the panel of international lawyers (Elliot Richardson, chair), "Legal Regimes of the Arctic," *American Society of International Law Proceedings* 82 (1988): 315–34.

62. See Michael Bennett, "The People's Republic of China and the Use of International Law in the Spratly Islands Dispute," *Stanford Journal of International Law* 28 (1992): 425–50; Geoffrey Marston, "Abandonment of Territorial Claims: The Cases of Bouvet and Spratly Islands," *The British Year Book of International Law* 57 (1986): 337–56; John K. T. Chao, "South China Sea: Boundary Problems Relating to the Nansha and Hsisha Islands," *Chinese Yearbook of International Law and Affairs* 9 (1989–90):

dominated discussions in conflicts of global importance, such as the clashing territorial claims of the Palestinians and Israelis, the Egyptians and Israelis, the Chinese and Taiwanese, and the Iraqis and Kuwaitis.

When states have quarreled over the reach of their sovereignty in territories often less vital to their interests, they have repeatedly taken their disputes to court.[63] In 1992 El Salvador and Honduras resolved their frontier dispute in a proceeding before the International Court of Justice (ICJ).[64] Over the years international courts and arbitrators have handed down decisions, arbitral awards, or advisory opinions on numerous sovereignty disputes, including those between Mali and Burkina Faso in 1986,[65] Argentina and Chile in 1977 and 1966,[66] Morocco and Mauritania in 1975,[67] India and Pakistan in 1968,[68] Cambodia and Thailand in 1962,[69] Honduras and Nicaragua[70] as well as Portugal and India in 1960,[71] Belgium and the Netherlands in 1959,[72] France and the United

---

66–156; and Steven Kuan-Tsyh Yu, "Who Owns the Paracels and Spratlys?—An Evaluation of the Nature and Legal Basis of the Conflicting Territorial Claims," *Chinese Yearbook of International Law and Affairs* 9 (1989–90): 1–28.

63. See A.L.W. Munkman, "Adjudication and Adjustment—International Judicial Decision and the Settlement of Territorial and Boundary Disputes," *The British Year Book of International Law* 46 (1972–73): 1–116.

64. *Land, Island, and Maritime Frontier Dispute* [El Sal./Hond.], 1992 ICJ 351 (Judgment).

65. *Frontier Dispute* [Burkina Faso v Mali], 1986 ICJ 554 (Judgment).

66. The 1977 dispute involved three islands in the Beagle Channel. See *Beagle Channel Arbitration Award of 18 April 1977* [Arg./Chile], ILM 17 (1978): 634–79. For a synopsis of the dispute see Kratochwil et al., *Peace and Disputed Sovereignty*, pp. 71–77. The 1966 dispute involved certain portions of the boundary between Argentina and Chile. See *Frontier Case* [Arg./Chile], R. Intl. Arb. Awards 109 (1966).

67. *Western Sahara*, 1975 ICJ 3 (Adv. Op.—Order of 3 January 1975). See also Thomas M. Franck, "The Stealing of the Sahara," *AJIL* 70 (1976): 694–721; Tony Hodges, *Western Sahara: The Roots of a Desert War* (Westport, Conn.: Lawrence Hill & Co., 1984); and John Damis, *Conflict in North West Africa: The Western Sahara Dispute* (Stanford, Calif.: Hoover Institution Press, 1983).

68. The Tribunal was constituted pursuant to the Agreement of June 30, 1965. *Indo-Pakistan Western Boundary (Rann of Kutch)*, 17 R. Intl. Arb. Awards 1 (1968).

69. *Temple of Preah Vihear* [Cambodia v Thailand], 1962 ICJ 6 (Judgment). See also Jessup, *The Price of International Justice*, pp. 13–20.

70. *Arbitral Award Made by the King of Spain on 23 December 1906* [Hond. v Nicar.], 1960 ICJ 192 (Judgment). See also Jessup, *The Price of International Justice*, pp. 17–20.

71. *Right of Passage over Indian Territory* [Port. v India], 1959 ICJ 3 (Order). For commentary see Chapter 4.

72. *Sovereignty over Certain Frontier Land* [Belg./Neth.], 1959 ICJ 209 (Judgment).

Kingdom in 1953,[73] Denmark and Norway in 1933,[74] the United States and the Netherlands in 1928,[75] and the United States and Mexico in 1911.[76]

Among various international leaders involved in mediating sovereignty disputes, in 1885 Pope Leo XIII settled the sovereignty dispute between Spain and Germany regarding the Caroline Islands in the South Pacific east of the Philippines.[77] In 1902 King Edward VII of Great Britain determined much of the Andean border between Chile and Argentina, and in 1966 a Court of Arbitration acting in the name of Queen Elizabeth II resolved a dispute that had arisen regarding the 1902 Award.[78] In 1931 the king of Italy awarded sovereignty over Clipperton Island to the French rather than the Mexicans.[79]

In 1963, in the only instance to date in which a United Nations

---

73. *Minquiers and Ecrehos Case [Fr./UK]*, 1953 ICJ 47 (Judgment).

74. *Legal Status of Eastern Greenland [Den. v Nor.]*, 1933 *Permanent Court of International Justice Publications* (Ser. A/B), No. 53, at 21 (5 April 1933).

75. See *Island of Palmas*. In 1928 the Americans and Dutch contested the sovereignty of the Island of Palmas located between the Philippines and the Dutch East Indies. The United States claimed title since it inherited Spanish rights in the Philippines after the Spanish-American War. The Dutch did not dispute Spanish discovery of the island but claimed title on the grounds that the Dutch government had exercised sovereign rights on the island since 1677. The Permanent Court of Arbitration ruled in favor of the Netherlands. Swiss arbiter Max Huber reasoned that although Spain may have had an inchoate title based on discovery, the Spanish and their heirs did not effectively occupy the territory within a reasonable period of time. "The continuous and peaceful display of territorial sovereignty," the arbiter wrote, "is as good as title."

76. The arbitral tribunal's award concerning the Chamizal tract near El Paso favored Mexico. The United States, however, refused to comply with the decision until a 1967 agreement between the governments. For a history of the dispute see John Bassett Moore, ed., *A Digest of International Law*, 8 vols. (Washington, D.C.: U.S. Government Printing Office, 1906), 1:753–66. For the decision of the International Boundary Commission see Green Haywood Hackworth, ed., *Digest of International Law*, 8 vols. (Washington, D.C.: U.S. Government Printing Office, 1940), 1:411–20. For the agreement settling the controversy see U.S. Department of State, "Demarcation of the New International Boundary (Chamizal), signed at Washington, D.C." 27 October 1967, TIAS no. 6372, UST, vol. 18, pt. 3 (1967), pp. 2,836–44. See also Jessup, *The Price of International Justice*, pp. 51–52.

77. See James Brown Scott, *Sovereign States and Suits Before Arbitral Tribunals and Courts of Justice* (New York: New York University Press, 1925), pp. 95–97.

78. See Jessup, *The Price of International Justice*, p. 43.

79. *Arbitral Award on the Subject of the Difference Relative to the Sovereignty over Clipperton Island [Fr./Mex.]*, AJIL 26 (1932): 390–99.

official has been empowered to serve as a binding arbitrator,[80] Secretary-General U Thant resolved the dispute among Malaya, the Philippines, and Indonesia regarding sovereignty over Sarawak and North Borneo by deciding that both belonged in the Federation of Malaysia.[81] And in 1980 Pope John Paul II resolved the long-standing dispute between Argentina and Chile regarding the Beagle Channel, connecting the Atlantic and Pacific Oceans at the tip of South America.[82] Conflicts over territorial sovereignty claims have thus occurred on every continent. Indeed, sovereignty disputes have encircled the globe: from the Western Sahara to Eastern Greenland, from the low countries of Europe to Southeast Asia, from islands in the South Pacific to islands in the English Channel.

Once again, the importance of the concept of sovereignty should not be overdrawn. The association of sovereignty with power is not always as direct or consistent as might appear at first glance. Some states without much military or economic influence at all enjoy charmed lives in the international community, their territory and frontiers rarely if ever challenged by greedy, or voracious, neighbors. At the same time, even an extraordinarily powerful sovereign state, like the Soviet Union, can suddenly vanish from the international scene, replaced by a handful of its component parts.

And during the post–World War II era, the goal of increasing territorial holdings has claimed a preeminent position in a state's foreign policy only on isolated occasions. Today numerous states scarcely consider acquiring territory a worthwhile objective at all. After experiencing difficult decolonization eras, former imperial powers often seem more intent on distancing themselves from historical territorial claims than on acquiring new land and peoples to administer.[83] Certain states have even quelled the urge to reac-

80. See Murphy, *The United Nations and the Control of International Violence*, p. 103. In the early 1980s Venezuela and Guyana asked the secretary-general to mediate their border dispute. See Kratochwil et al., *Peace and Disputed Sovereignty*, p. 42.

81. The secretary-general sent a mission of senior diplomats to the British territories of Sarawak and North Borneo to verify that votes by their legislatures represented the freely expressed wishes of the people for federation with Malaya. See Franck, "The Stealing of the Sahara," p. 700. See also Murphy, *The United Nations and the Control of International Violence*, p. 103; June Bingham, *U Thant: The Search for Peace* (New York: Alfred A. Knopf, 1970), p. 275.

82. See Kratochwil et al., *Peace and Disputed Sovereignty*, p. 73.

83. See generally Marston, "Abandonment of Territorial Claims," pp. 337–56.

quire disputed territory. For instance, after the military coup in Portugal in 1974 Chinese diplomats rebuffed the Portuguese offer to return the territory of Macao to the People's Republic.[84]

Moreover, the frequency of the territorial disputes that have occurred should not be taken to imply that every corner of the globe lies under the control of a sovereign. The community of states has agreed under international law that certain areas, such as the high seas and outer space, are res communis and cannot be possessed by sovereigns. Other territories—not all under a particular sovereign's control—have at times been neutralized or demilitarized.[85] To help keep the peace between hostile neighbors, buffer zones have been established from colonial times, as in the buffer between Togo and the Gold Coast in Africa or between Siam and French Indochina along the Mekong River. This century the Rhineland was demilitarized from 1919 to 1935, as was the buffer between Saudi Arabia and Iraq, eventually divided between the countries in 1981.[86]

Governments occasionally have extended the notion of a "right of passage" to create a zone of land under dual or international administration in order to allow a state access to the sea or to isolated territory.[87] The Boxer Protocol of 1901 demilitarized and placed under foreign police control an access zone from Peking to the sea.[88] The Free City of Danzig, under League of Nations supervi-

---

84. Jaw-ling Joanne Chang, "Settlement of the Macao Issue: Distinctive Features of Beijing's Negotiating Behavior," Case Western Reserve Journal of International Law 20 (1988): 257. After more than fifteen additional years of Portuguese administration China and Portugal agreed that Macao would be restored to China in 1999, two years after the British return Hong Kong and the New Territories to Chinese control. See ibid., pp. 253–78, and "The Sino-Portuguese Joint Declaration on the Question of Macao, Signed April 13, 1987," Beijing Review 30 (6 April, 1987), special insert.

85. See generally Black et al., Neutralization and World Politics.

86. The examples of buffers are drawn from Kratochwil et al., Peace and Disputed Sovereignty, pp. 16, 37. See also Quincy Wright, The Existing Legal Situation as it Relates to the Conflict in the Far East (New York: Institute of Pacific Relations, 1939), pp. 73–74, and Friedrich V. Kratochwil, "Of Systems, Boundaries, and Territoriality: An Inquiry into the Formation of the State System," World Politics 39 (1986): 40. One might also recall the demilitarized zone in the Sinai, arranged at the Camp David negotiations between Israel and Egypt, that remained under Egyptian sovereignty.

87. For majority and dissenting legal opinions concerning the creation of such a right, see Right of Passage over Indian Territory, at 4–143. Analogous to such rights of passage were the railway zones extracted from China by Japan and various western states. See Wright, Existing Legal Situation, pp. 74, 76.

88. Wright, Existing Legal Situation, pp. 36, 38.

sion, allowed the reborn state of Poland access to the Baltic Sea,[89] and the Alcan Highway still connects the United States with Alaska across formerly Canadian soil.[90] Finally, certain out-of-the-way territories, such as small islets or emerging volcanic or coral islands[91] or so-called waste land,[92] have not yet been sullied by the sovereign claims of any state and under international law are termed res nullius or terra nullius.[93]

Nevertheless, since the extent of territory under a state's control can directly affect its economic prowess and its national security, much of the earth's territory has been divided up so that the sovereigns may control ever larger chunks of it.[94] Moreover, when governments perceive the current configuration of sovereign lands to be unjust or illegitimate for legal, historical, or political reasons, their leaders have regularly attempted to redivide disputed territory on more favorable terms. Because of the link between sovereignty and power reflected in this ongoing competition, neutral or unclaimed territories rarely remain neutral or unclaimed for long periods.

89. See Hannum, Autonomy, Sovereignty, and Self-Determination, pp. 375–79.

90. See United Nations, Treaty Series, "Exchange of Notes Constituting an Agreement between the United States of America and Canada Relating to the Construction and Maintenance of a Highway to Alaska, signed at Ottawa," 18 March 1943, UNTS, vol. 101, no. 294 (1951), p. 208. See also David Mitrany, A Working Peace System (Chicago: Quadrangle Books, 1966), p. 158.

91. See Jon M. Van Dyke and Robert A. Brooks, "Uninhabited Islands: Their Impact on the Ownership of the Oceans' Resources," Ocean Development and International Law Journal 12 (1983): 265–300. See also Mark Dingley, "Eruptions in International Law: Emerging Volcanic Islands and the Law of Territorial Acquisition," Cornell International Law Journal 11 (1978): 121–35.

92. For an explication of the notion of "waste land" in international law see Ya'akov Meron, "Waste Land (Mewat) in Judea and Samaria," Boston College International and Comparative Law Review 4 (1981): 1–37.

93. See Brownlie, Principles of Public International Law, p. 109. For an interesting historical study of how European maritime states attempted to acquire dominion over terra nullius by virtue of various symbolic acts see Arthur S. Keller, Oliver J. Lissitzyn, and Frederick J. Mann, Creation of Rights of Sovereignty Through Symbolic Acts, 1400–1800 (New York: Columbia University Press, 1938). For an example of a 1931 terra nullius dispute see Legal Status of Eastern Greenland. The ongoing disputes over the Spratly Islands chain in the South China Sea also raise terra nullius considerations. For commentary, see Chapter 2.

94. For a recent example of this competition see the differing positions held by the United States and Canada on the issue of sovereignty and the Northwest Passage. See Donat Pharand, "Canada's Sovereignty over the Northwest Passage," Michigan Journal of International Law 10 (1989): 653–78.

Conclusion

The persistence of the academic view that sovereignty discussions will soon be absolutely obsolete invites the skeptic "to question the absoluteness of its obsoleteness."[95] In our view sovereignty remains directly relevant to the conduct of foreign relations for several reasons. It helps the international community to order itself by serving as a guide to an entity's international status. It remains a significant rhetorical device, and hence a potent political weapon, in disputes between states. And the reach of a state's sovereignty over people and territory can contribute to that state's power.

From the gathering momentum toward a united Europe to the splintering of the former Soviet Union to the budding secessionist movements in other established states, the idea of sovereignty seems to arise in international discussions rather frequently for a term that so many believe is so outmoded. Yet despite its regular use, sovereignty remains a somewhat misty concept clouded by a fog of contested assumptions and unresolved questions. In the following chapter we ask what precisely constitutes sovereign status? What must an entity possess if it seeks to be accepted as a member of the club of sovereign states? Thereafter we explore several other outstanding issues related to the current prominence of the concept of sovereignty. Despite repeated references to sovereignty, indeed perhaps in part on account of them, answers to fundamental questions about this familiar yet slippery term are far from self-evident.

95. Charles Burton Marshall, *The Exercise of Sovereignty: Papers on Foreign Policy* (Baltimore: Johns Hopkins University Press, 1965), p. 4.

2

What Constitutes a Sovereign State?

If one supposes . . . that states are the most significant actors on the international scene, the first question to ask about them is how they—and not others—came to get there.

—Alan James[1]

One might try to determine just what constitutes a sovereign state empirically, by examining the characteristics of states whose sovereignty is indisputable. All sovereign states, it might be observed, have territory, people, and a government. Curiously, however, cogent standards do not seem to exist either in law or in practice for the dimensions, number of people, or form of government that might be required of a sovereign state. Indeed, a United Nations General Assembly Resolution declared that neither small size, nor remote geographical location, nor limited resources constitute valid objections to sovereign statehood.[2]

1. Alan James, *Sovereign Statehood: The Basis of International Society* (London: Allen & Unwin, 1986), p. 20. James further observed: "It is indeed remarkable that there has been a widespread failure by writers on international relations to ask . . . [what it is about a sovereign state that enables it to participate in the international system alongside others of its kind]. For it is in a very real sense the most basic which can be asked about their subject."

2. United Nations, General Assembly, "Question of American Samoa, Bahamas, Brunei, Cayman Islands, Cocos (Keeling) Islands, Gilbert and Ellice Islands, Guam,

Plainly, sovereign states differ dramatically in expanse from the vast reaches of Russia, India, or Canada to the tiny specks of Malta, Tuvalu,[3] and the Maldives. Their borders range from the uncontroversial boundary lines encircling an isolated island chain to the sometimes dubious logic of geographical landmarks to the wholly artificial divisions erected by colonial conquerors. Since the rationale for particular borders is frequently open to dispute, the boundaries of sovereign states do not often remain fixed over the generations.[4] Even more astonishing, after long periods of dormancy a sovereign state may suddenly spring back to life, as Poland did after 123 years when it contained neither territory, nor a government, nor the formal allegiance of its people.[5] More recently, the Baltic states of Estonia, Latvia, and Lithuania, and the Balkan states of Macedonia, Croatia, Serbia, and Bosnia-Herzegovina have reappeared in similar fashion. Sovereign states thus differ sharply in size; their boundaries exhibit a remarkable elasticity over time; and the nationalism that is their vital life force may, in effect, be freeze-dried such that fallen sovereign states later exhibit exceptional regenerative qualities.

Sovereign states also vary considerably in population: witness the multitudes of Chinese versus the relative handfuls of citizens on St. Kitts and Nevis in the Caribbean. Obscuring matters further still, even a very large nation desiring self-government, such as the Kurds, has long been denied sovereign statehood,[6] while a very small nation, such as Nauru in the South Pacific,[7] was granted sovereignty as a

---

Montserrat, New Hebrides, Pitcairn, St. Helena, Seychelles, Solomon Islands, Turks and Caicos Islands, and the United States Virgin Islands," *United Nations Resolutions: Resolutions of the General Assembly*, ser. 1, vol. 13, 1970–71, pp. 180, 459–60.

3. The ten square miles that make up the South Pacific microstate of Tuvalu (formerly the Ellice Islands in the Gilbert and Ellice chain) are at their highest point only three feet above sea level. Conceivably, a typhoon could submerge the entire sovereign state of nine thousand people.

4. One authority went so far as to note: "In the world as we know it in the 1990s, no fact about states is more obvious than the impermanence of their boundaries." Ian S. Lustick, *Unsettled States, Disputed Lands: Britain and Ireland, France and Algeria, Israel and the West Bank–Gaza* (Ithaca: Cornell University Press, 1993), p. 1.

5. See Quincy Wright, *The Existing Legal Situation as it Relates to the Conflict in the Far East* (New York: Institute of Pacific Relations, 1939), 45 n. 1.

6. See ibid., pp. 178–79, 199. The Kurdish nation comprises between sixteen and twenty million people.

7. The wealthy island of Nauru encompasses eight square miles and contains a population of about 8,400. Although the smallest republic in the world, Nauru has parlayed its

matter of course. A population's quest for a sovereign state may cover generations, as in the case of Israel, or a mere decade or two, as in the case of Pakistan.[8] A sovereign state like the Sudan illustrates that the population need not exhibit much unity in culture, politics, or economics.[9] Indeed, the case of the Bedouin in Mauritania may demonstrate that a political entity can gain sovereignty even when a substantial percentage of its citizens fails to comprehend their own state's sovereign existence.[10] Thus, while all sovereign states contain a population, sovereign status seems to depend neither on the population's size[11] nor on its particular characteristics.

Determining what constitutes a sovereign state by examining the most salient features of the governments of states widely recognized as sovereign is similarly frustrating, at least at first blush. Not only do the forms of government and the political ideologies of sovereign states vary widely, but their governments differ markedly in power, objectives, and bureaucratic sophistication. Whether large or small, a sovereign state may be blessed with staggering quantities of natural resources, such as the phosphate of Nauru, the timber, mineral, and hydroelectric potential of Canada or Russia, or the oil of Qatar, Kuwait, Saudi Arabia, and the United Arab Emirates. Like Japan and Costa Rica, a sovereign state may overcome deficiencies in natural resources by developing industrial output and technological capability. Or, like Chad and Somalia, it may be cursed with such negligible quantities of resources, industry, and technology as

---

extraordinary deposits of phosphate to become one of the richest per capita states. About 45,000 people live on St. Kitts and Nevis, the least populated sovereign state in the Western Hemisphere. For an account of the problems St. Kitts has faced in having Great Britain respect its sovereignty see Francis Alexis, "British Intervention in St. Kitts," *New York University Journal of International Law and Politics* 16 (1983–84): 581–600.

8. Dr. Muhammad Iqbal proposed the creation of a separate state for Muslims in 1930, only seventeen years before the British transferred sovereignty to India and Pakistan.

9. See Hurst Hannum, *Autonomy, Sovereignty, and Self-Determination: The Accommodation of Conflicting Rights* (Philadelphia: University of Pennsylvania Press, 1990), p. 327.

10. In disputing the independence of Mauritania, Moroccan diplomat Ben Aboud argued: "The population of that area does not even know the word 'Mauritania.' If you tell a Bedouin of so-called Mauritania that you are in Mauritania, he will not understand what you are talking about." See Thomas M. Franck, "The Stealing of the Sahara," *American Journal of International Law* 70 (1976): 694 n. 5.

11. For a different approach to this issue see Barry Buzan, *People, States, and Fear: The National Security Problem in International Relations* (Chapel Hill: University of North Carolina Press, 1983), pp. 40–41.

to cast grave doubts on its ability to support any sizable population in minimal comfort.[12]

Moreover, while all sovereign states have governments, the ease with which their societies are governed varies dramatically. Some relatively docile populations are culturally homogeneous—or, as in Japan, at least believe in a popular myth of their own homogeneity—while others are wracked by age-old schism, antagonism, and violence. Not only do governments differ markedly in ideology, composition, and constitutional framework, they also appear exceptionally diverse in the strength of their central and local government branches. Few observers could have predicted that in the several decades since decolonization some of the very weakest governments in Africa have neither splintered into multiple sovereign states nor been absorbed into larger ones.[13] Thus, the obvious characteristics of the governments of sovereign states do not seem to help us distinguish sovereign from nonsovereign entities.

One must conclude that although a sovereign state is fundamentally composed of territory, people, and a government, this statement is a partial description, not a definition. Macau, Gibraltar, Okinawa,[14] Hong Kong, Puerto Rico, the Falkland Islands, the District of Columbia, and many other political entities have territory, people, and a government, yet no one considers them to be sovereign states. How then is sovereign statehood gained? What precisely constitutes sovereignty? What missing elements transform a territory with people and a government into a sovereign state?

The Requirement of De Facto Autonomy

It is often said that to attain sovereignty a territorial entity must demonstrate internal supremacy and external independence.[15]

12. See Inis L. Claude, Jr., "The Tension Between Principle and Pragmatism in International Relations," Review of International Studies 19 (1993): 215–26.

13. See Robert H. Jackson and Carl G. Rosberg, "Why Africa's Weak States Persist: The Empirical and Juridical in Statehood," World Politics 35 (1982): 1.

14. See James, Sovereign Statehood, pp. 13–15. For the postwar history of Okinawa see Akio Watanabe, The Okinawa Problem: A Chapter in Japan-U.S. Relations (Melbourne: Melbourne University Press, 1970).

15. In 1577 in Six livres de la republique Jean Bodin, perhaps the first recognized authority on sovereignty, noted that sovereignty has internal and external dimensions.

First, a sovereign state is able to show actual political supremacy in its own territory. The government must convincingly maintain its supremacy over all other potential authorities within that territory and population. Second, the state must demonstrate actual independence of outside authority, not the supremacy of one state over others but the independence of one state from its peers. A sovereign state is said to be in fact politically and juridically independent of any superior.[16] From this perspective a sovereign state must do more than merely claim to be autonomous. A truly sovereign state is able to assert its de facto internal supremacy and external independence in practice.

De Facto Internal Supremacy

The early doctrine of sovereignty envisaged absolute monarchy, that is, supreme power by the Crown unchecked except perhaps by God. However, as monarchical government yielded to constitutional government, the content of the notion of domestic political supremacy gradually evolved toward an expectation of self-government of one form or another. By the early twentieth century the Covenant of the League of Nations presumed that a sovereign state's system of government would be generated internally rather than imposed from abroad: sovereign states would be "fully self-governing."[17] A sovereign state, then, had demonstrated its ability to establish and maintain its own government rather than be ruled by a government of outsiders or by a different government of fellow citizens.

Thus, notions of supremacy long retained prominence in scholarly discussions of the meaning of sovereignty. For instance, Hedley Bull explained internal supremacy in the following terms: "[S]tates assert, in relation to [their] territory and population, what may be called internal sovereignty, which means supremacy over all other authorities within that territory and population."[18] F. H. Hinsley

See Ingrid DeLupis, *International Law and the Independent State* (New York: Crane, Russak and Co., 1974), p. 3. For a recent translation of Bodin's chief work on sovereignty, see Jean Bodin, *On Sovereignty: Four Chapters from the Six Books on the Commonwealth*, ed. and trans. Julian H. Franklin (New York: Cambridge University Press, 1992).

16. Martin Wight, *Systems of States*, ed. Hedley Bull (Leicester: Leicester University Press, 1977), p. 30.

17. See Article 1(2) of the Covenant of the League of Nations. *The Covenant of the League of Nations* (New York: World Peace Foundation, 1936), p. 2.

18. Hedley Bull, *The Anarchical Society* (London: Macmillan, 1977), pp. 8–9.

generally concurred: "[T]he idea of sovereignty was the idea that there is a final and absolute political authority in the political community . . . and no final and absolute authority exists elsewhere."[19] Another authority defined sovereignty as "[t]he supreme, absolute, and uncontrollable power by which any independent state is governed."[20]

In our view such declarations seem overstated—evidence of scholars turning conditional thoughts into absolute standards.[21] Certainly, as the notion of "absolute domestic political supremacy" has evolved, quite different approaches have been proposed to determine when a state's control meets this standard. Charles Burton Marshall suggested, "Sovereignty is the situation of being in charge of a domain."[22] Raymond Aron observed that sovereignty is actually the "supreme power of deciding in a case of crisis."[23] Indeed, Aron and other scholars attempted to add yet another critical requirement—legitimacy.[24] Aron claimed: "Sovereignty belongs to the authority that is both *legitimate* and *supreme*. Thus the search for sovereignty is, at the same time or alternately, *the search for conditions in which an authority is legitimate and of the place, men and institutions in which it resides*."[25] Thus, for Aron's followers a legitimate government that constitutes the supreme power in a moment of crisis has fulfilled a vital prerequisite to sovereign statehood.

19. F. H. Hinsley, *Sovereignty* (New York: Basic Books, 1966), p. 26.

20. *Black's Law Dictionary: Definitions of Terms and Phrases of American and English Jurisprudence, Ancient and Modern*, 5th ed. rev. (St. Paul, Minn.: West Publishing, 1979), p. 1,252.

21. Inis Claude observed: "Most people are addicted to the overstatement of their favorite propositions, the exaggeration of the scope of their generalizations. We say 'always' when we mean 'sometimes,' and 'certainly' when we mean 'perhaps'; we tend to convert conditional thoughts into absolute standards." Claude, "The Tension between Principle and Pragmatism," p. 219.

22. Charles Burton Marshall, *The Exercise of Sovereignty: Papers on Foreign Policy* (Baltimore: Johns Hopkins University Press, 1965), p. 4.

23. Raymond Aron, *Peace and War: A Theory of International Relations*, trans. Richard A. Howard and Annette Baker-Fox (New York: Frederick A. Praeger, 1967), p. 746.

24. Ibid., p. 739. James likewise claimed: "What sovereignty refers to . . . is the presence, within a governed community, of supreme legal authority—so that such a community can be said to possess sovereignty, or to be sovereign, if it does not look beyond its own borders for the ultimate source of its own legitimacy." James, *Sovereign Statehood*, p. 3.

25. Aron, *Peace and War*, p. 739 (italics in original).

Yet whether a claim to domestic political supremacy is considered legitimate has itself changed over time. During twentieth-century decolonization movements, Third World leaders declared former colonies to be new sovereign states. Over time much of the international community accepted, indeed hailed, such declarations.[26] The imperial powers thereby lost what had previously been widely regarded as legitimate sovereignty over their colonies. Legitimate domestic political supremacy within colonial lands moved from the imperial powers to governments composed of native leaders.

In various states, assessing legitimacy is likely to be fraught with historical and ideological problems. For instance, the international community generally recognized as legitimate and sovereign the Marxist government led by Maurice Bishop in Grenada. However, after Bishop's assassination by extremists many countries refused to recognize the legitimacy or sovereignty of the successor regime eventually overthrown in the American invasion of the island. On account of such difficulties, some prefer to assess domestic political supremacy by simply examining whether a government actually controls the territory in question. If a political entity is the sole authority within a particular territory, if no other authority exercises actual control over the people who reside within the entity's boundaries, then, one might argue, the political community has established its domestic political supremacy. From this perspective, determining sovereignty should not be a matter of conferring compliments on politically correct regimes; rather, it should be a matter of describing reality.

For example, during the War of 1812 Great Britain seized much of the state of Maine. During the occupation, British troops compelled payment of import duties on goods entering the port of Castine. After the fighting, U.S. Customs tried to collect duties again on the theory that the goods had been imported into the United States but that no duty had been paid to the federal government. The Supreme Court held that the federal authorities could not re-collect the duties because Castine, Maine, had not been a part of the sovereign

26. The newly independent states first pressed this course of action in the United Nations and obtained a series of sweeping declarations against colonialism. See Inis L. Claude, Jr., *The Changing United Nations* (New York: Random House, 1967), pp. 96–97.

territory of the United States at the time the goods were imported. Justice Joseph Story wrote:

> [W]e are all of the opinion, that the claim for duties cannot be sustained. By the conquest and military occupation of Castine, the enemy acquired that firm possession which enabled him to exercise the fullest rights of sovereignty over that place. The sovereignty of the United States over the territory was, of course, suspended, and the laws of the United States could no longer be rightfully enforced there, or be obligatory upon the inhabitants who remained and submitted to the conquerors.[27]

One commentator later observed: "Now, the United States had never said or admitted through the Department of State that Britain, and not it, was sovereign in Castine. There was nothing equivalent to a recognition. Sovereignty, says the Court, is merely equivalent to possession and ability to enforce the law. . . . [T]he case is grounded solidly in the conception that 'sovereignty' is a function of political control as it exists in fact."

This pragmatic approach, however, raises other questions. To what degree must the entity be separate from all other sovereign states, including former colonial powers[28] or ideological allies that

27. *United States v Rice*, 15 US (4 Wheat.) 391, 392 (1819). Justice Story concluded: "By the surrender, the inhabitants passed under a temporary allegiance to the British government, and were bound by such laws, and such only, as it chose to recognize and impose. From the nature of the case, no other laws could be obligatory upon them; for where there is no protection, or allegiance, or sovereignty, there can be no claim to obedience. Castine was, therefore, during this period, so far as respected our revenue laws, to be deemed a foreign port; and goods imported into it by the inhabitants were . . . , in no correct sense, imported into the United States" (ibid., pp. 393–94). See also *Keene v McDonough*, 33 US (8 Pet.) 110, 113 (1834) (the decree of a Spanish court in Louisiana was held to be binding, although it occured after the date at which Louisiana was ceded to the United States, since it occurred before the date of delivery of possession to the United States). But see *Davis v Policy Jury of the Parish of Concordia*, 50 US (9 How.) 139, 148 (1850) (exclusive ferry franchise granted by Spanish governor held void since, prior to delivery, the ceding state cannot exercise sovereignty other than regarding matters necessary for social order or commercial purposes).

28. Similarly, to this day under the Constitution of the Cook Islands, a range of critical decisions made by the Cook Islands cabinet cannot come into effect immediately unless the decisions are approved by the high commissioner, appointed by New Zealand's

might wish to influence, or even perhaps to dictate, decisions on domestic matters?[29] To what degree must the entity be able to demonstrate its supreme power throughout the political community? For instance, to what extent should the authorities be capable of controlling the movements of people, objects, or ideas across the state's borders?[30] Has not absolute domestic political supremacy regularly been beyond the grasp of many governments? Should not scholars speak of adequate, rather than absolute, domestic political supremacy? What precisely would constitute such a standard of adequate domestic supremacy?

Some might argue that the course of the twentieth century has subtly altered the way people think about de facto internal supremacy. One might wonder in what sense the governments of Peru, Cyprus, or Nicaragua, or Lebanon, Afghanistan, or Sri Lanka, or Chad, Somalia, or Ethiopia, or Angola, Nigeria, or Zaire truly possessed "final and absolute political authority in the political community" in recent years? Does not the claim to political authority by a state appear audacious if its government cannot elicit allegiance, or even much compliance, within a substantial portion of its territory?[31]

The current prevalence of limited and civil wars, as well as powerful guerrillas, terrorists, and narcotics traffickers, may be eroding the extent to which a territorial entity must be supreme throughout its territory in order to qualify as a sovereign state. Or

---

governor-general and the leader of the executive council. See Cook Islands Constitution Act of 1964, *Statutes of New Zealand* 3, no. 69 (1966), pp. 2,033, 2,040–41. See also Alexis, "British Intervention in St. Kitts," 586 n. 29.

29. James Rosenau argued: "[T]he autonomous capacity of states to be effective at home can be seen as increasingly dependent on either favorable circumstances abroad or the cooperation of foreign actors." James N. Rosenau, "The State in an Era of Cascading Politics: Wavering Concept, Widening Competence, Withering Colossus, or Weathering Change?" in *The Elusive State: International and Comparative Perspectives*, ed. James A. Caporaso (Newbury Park, Calif.: Sage Publications, 1989), p. 23.

30. Stephen Krasner noted: "The claims that states have made with regard to the authoritative control of movements of people, commodities, investments, and information, ideas, or culture across their international boundaries have changed across time and over countries." Stephen D. Krasner, "Sovereignty: An Institutional Perspective," in *The Elusive State: International and Comparative Perspectives*, ed. James A. Caporaso (Newbury Park, Calif.: Sage Publications, 1989), p. 90.

31. For a similarly phrased observation, see Lustick, *Unsettled States, Disputed Lands*, p. 443.

perhaps absolute domestic political supremacy was always a legal fiction of sorts. Did Belgium really exercise anything approaching absolute supremacy throughout the colonial Congo?[32] Were the forces of the German Republic in any sense absolutely supreme when the Brownshirts also were using force to coerce citizens?[33]

Here, as elsewhere, the actual behavior of states helps to shape the meaning of sovereignty. Despite the doubt cast upon the "absolute" authority of the states noted above in certain portions of their territories, the international community typically treated these countries as sovereign states. This perhaps suggests that once a state is duly baptized and confirmed as a sovereign the international community relaxes, or perhaps even ignores, the requirement of absolute domestic political supremacy. With infrequent exceptions,[34] other sovereign states treat a peer as sovereign even though its hold on power may be quite tenuous, or even nonexistent, in particular areas within its formal boundaries.[35]

Certainly, when the central government of the state of Lebanon lost control over warring factions within its borders during the late 1980s, the international community continued to recognize Lebanon as having maintained sovereign status. Despite the Lebanese government's highly questionable domestic political supremacy in many parts of the country, including the capital of

32. Charles Burton Marshall counselled: "For simplicity and clarity, the absolute modifier *absolute* applied to sovereignty can well be disposed of at once. . . . I can scarcely imagine any faculty or endeavor wholly untrammeled, infinite, or . . . beyond contingency. . . . [S]overeignty, . . . at root, . . . merely denotes superiority. . . . Applied to a finite government, sovereignty merely is a term implicit of ascendancy established with respect to . . . the government's capacity to function as a going concern." Marshall, *The Exercise of Sovereignty*, p. 4 (italics in original).

33. Stanley I. Benn, "The Uses of 'Sovereignty,' " in *In Defense of Sovereignty*, ed. W. J. Stankiewicz (New York: Oxford University Press, 1969), pp. 80–81.

34. One such exception might be Somalia in the early 1990s, which in the midst of political chaos and famine may have lost its sovereignty. However, as the following chapter suggests, some theorists would argue that a state experiencing such a severe internal crisis is not stripped of sovereign status but instead is accorded a lesser basket of sovereign rights than that enjoyed by many of its peers.

35. Robert Jackson observed: "Ramshackle states today are . . . not allowed to disappear juridically—even if for all intents and purposes they have already fallen or been pulled down in fact. They cannot be deprived of sovereignty as a result of war, conquest, partition, or colonialism such as frequently happened in the past. The juridical cart is now before the empirical horse." Robert H. Jackson, *Quasi-States: Sovereignty, International Relations, and the Third World* (New York: Cambridge University Press, 1990), pp. 23–24.

Beirut, no group of states seems to have seriously considered mounting a campaign to revoke Lebanese sovereignty. In fact, other members of the international community do not routinely withdraw recognition of a government on the grounds that its sovereign status has been forfeited through loss of domestic control.[36]

One might also note that the international community has often not permitted states to justify outrageous domestic behavior on the grounds of sovereign independence. In practice absolute domestic political supremacy is not so unlimited as some scholars might imply. Since sovereignty expresses responsibility as well as authority, all the talk of absolute supremacy has not been taken by the international community to excuse genocide or other extraordinary violations of human rights, even should they occur at the instigation of a sovereign state within its own borders. Ivo Duchacek noted: "A sovereign but defeated nation-state, Germany, was held accountable, among other things, for its actions directed against its own citizens of Jewish faith before an International War Crimes Tribunal at Nuremberg. If sovereignty really meant the supreme authority to give and enforce law within the national territory, the Nazi atrocities in Germany proper could hardly be a matter for other than national preoccupation and trial."[37] Similarly, with regard to race relations in South Africa the international community long overlooked the supposedly absolute domestic supremacy of a sovereign state and treated apartheid as a matter of legitimate international concern.[38]

Increasing the ambiguity of internal sovereignty still further, many would maintain that in the current era absolute domestic supremacy is most often viewed as an evil to be avoided rather than as an ideal to be pursued.[39] Truly absolute domestic political

36. See ibid., p. 24. For information on sovereignty and Lebanon, see Wade R. Goria, *Sovereignty and Leadership in Lebanon, 1943–1976* (London: Ithaca Press, 1985), and Sandra M. Saseen, "The Taif Accord and Lebanon's Struggle to Regain Its Sovereignty," *American University Journal of International Law and Policy* 6 (1990): 57–75.

37. Ivo D. Duchacek, *Nations and Men: International Politics Today* (New York: Holt, Rinehart and Winston, 1966), p. 48.

38. See Louis Henkin, *How Nations Behave: Law and Foreign Policy*, 2d ed. rev. (New York: Columbia University Press, 1979), p. 17.

39. David Mitrany wryly observed: "It is curiously true that after trouncing the claim to 'divine right' of the absolute monarchs, political theory allowed it to be transferred to the absolute State, and we have suffered it to persist to our own day, though our culture

supremacy is often associated with dictatorship and totalitarianism. Indeed, the experience of the Soviet bloc and of various authoritarian regimes in Latin America suggests that repression at home may well "diminish a state's capacity to cope with its internal and external challenges."[40] Thus, to qualify for sovereign status, a government may need to be less supreme today than in past eras precisely because notions of democracy, popular liberty, and limited and checked government are ascendant. From this perspective, too, the notion of "absolute and final political authority" smacks of overstatement.

One might also observe that the concept of sovereignty itself limits the supposedly absolute supremacy of states in domestic matters.[41] A sovereign is not supposed to act, even at home, so as to infringe upon the sovereign prerogatives of other states. For instance, in order to enjoy protection for its citizens when abroad, a sovereign state accepts limitations on its powers over foreigners within its boundaries.[42]

In outlining the notion of sovereign immunity in 1812 Chief Justice John Marshall similarly observed that a state's jurisdiction within its own borders is not wholly absolute:

> The world being composed of distinct sovereignties, possessing equal rights and equal independence, whose mutual benefit is promoted by intercourse with each other, and by an interchange of those good offices which humanity dictates and its wants require, all sovereigns have consented to a relaxation in practice, in cases under certain peculiar circum-

---

rejects the absolute and our outlook discounts the divine in politics." David Mitrany, *The Progress of International Government* (New Haven: Yale University Press, 1933), p. 71.

40. Rosenau, "The State in an Era of Cascading Politics," p. 23.

41. See K.W.B. Middleton, "Sovereignty in Theory and Practice," in *In Defense of Sovereignty*, ed. W. J. Stankiewicz (New York: Oxford University Press, 1969), pp. 140–41. Middleton later noted: "Unlimited legal supremacy is, indeed, a self-contradictory notion, for any ruler who claims to possess legal authority admits by doing so that there is some legal justification for his rule, and accordingly that there must be some limit to what he is entitled to do. To argue the contrary involves the strange contradiction that law can confer on a man the right to act as if law did not exist." Ibid., pp. 146–47.

42. Quincy Wright, *Mandates Under the League of Nations* (New York: Greenwood Press, 1968), p. 274.

stances, of that absolute and complete jurisdiction within their respective territories which sovereignty confers.[43]

Nationality laws also nicely illustrate how sovereignty itself limits absolute domestic supremacy. Generally, a state may settle issues concerning who gains and loses its national citizenship by applying whatever nationality laws the government has chosen to adopt.[44] However, a state may not lawfully encroach on the sovereignty of another state by an act such as conferring its nationality on all foreigners entering its territory.[45] In reality, the absolute domestic supremacy of which scholars often write does not even extend to certain legislative matters that might infringe upon another sovereign.

The notion that sovereignty means de facto authority thus masks sharp disagreements on fundamental theoretical questions concerning domestic political supremacy. How supreme must an entity be to qualify as a sovereign? Is control in daily affairs or in crisis the test of sovereignty? Is legitimacy a prerequisite to a claim to sovereignty? To what degree must domestic supremacy be eroded before the international community considers revoking the sovereign status of a state? Various qualifications cast into doubt the "absolute" quality of internal supremacy. Perhaps for many observers today domestic political supremacy amounts to little more than occupying the recognized seat of government.

Certainly, while de facto internal independence is frequently thought to be a prerequisite to sovereign status, many people disagree on the elements that constitute such independence. Never-

43. *Schooner Exchange v M'Faddon & Others*, 11 US (7 Cranch) 116, 136 (1812). Chief Justice Marshall pointed out that the notion of diplomatic immunity also represents a waiver of the absolute independence of sovereigns (ibid., pp. 138).

44. See League of Nations, Treaty Series, "Convention on Certain Questions relating to the Conflict of Nationality Laws, signed at The Hague" 12 April 1930, *Société des Nations* 179, no. 4137 (1937), pp. 91–137. Article I states: "It is for each State to determine under its own law who are its nationals" (ibid., p. 99). See also *Nationality Decrees Issued in Tunis and Morocco* [Gr. Br./Fr.], *Permanent Court of International Justice Publications* (hereafter *PCIJ*) (Ser. B), No. 4, at 6 (1923) (Adv. Op.).

45. The German government acknowledged this principle in a statement prepared for a 1929 League of Nations Conference for the Codification of International Law convened prior to the 1930 Hague Convention on Nationality Laws. See Ian Brownlie, *Principles of Public International Law* (Oxford: Clarendon Press, 1979), p. 370.

theless, the fact that sovereign status is often conceived as de facto internal supremacy is underscored by the behavior of states. Neither the island of Timor nor the Western Sahara region has succeeded in attaining sovereign status in the face of determined and forcible opposition by Indonesia and Morocco.

In fact, even states whose sovereignty is beyond dispute typically view the goal of retaining actual freedom of action at home as a vital foreign policy objective. They jealously guard their de facto internal supremacy even at significant costs to other domestic and international goals. To take one notable instance, the Colombian government has resisted various American offers to assist Colombia in its efforts against narcotics traffickers. In accounting for their opposition to American military assistance within Colombian territory or territorial waters and their opposition to the extradition of Colombian drug lords to face prosecution within the American criminal justice system, Colombian leaders point to their state's sovereignty. They fear that an active role for the United States in juridical and law enforcement matters widely viewed within Colombia as domestic affairs would curtail their government's de facto internal independence of action, or sovereignty.[46]

Just as Colombia has rejected offers of American assistance in coping with law and order matters within its sovereign territory, so have other states proved sensitive to more powerful countries becoming too intimately involved in national security matters. For instance, in rejecting the argument that an American military presence in France amounted to an intelligent use of French sovereignty, Charles de Gaulle maintained that U.S. troops and bases in

46. See, for example, Rensselaer W. Lee, "Why the U.S. Cannot Stop South American Cocaine," *Orbis* 32 (1988): 513–19. For an interesting account of Americans reacting similarly after U.S. officials authorized Mexican police to search streetcars leaving El Paso, Texas, for Juárez, Mexico, see Ethan A. Nadelmann, *Cops Across Borders: The Internationalization of U.S. Criminal Law Enforcement* (University Park: The Pennsylvania State University Press, 1993), p. 79. An active American role in Colombian juridical and law-enforcement matters might also be viewed as compromising Colombia's de facto external independence as that concept is defined in the following pages of this chapter. Curiously, while Colombians, Hondurans, and others have viewed the extradition of national citizens to a foreign legal system as derogating from their sovereignty, they have often welcomed foreign legal assistance programs, perhaps because of the formal invitation offered by one sovereign to another. See generally Michael Ross Fowler and Julie Marie Bunck, "Legal Imperialism or Disinterested Assistance?: American Legal Aid in the Caribbean Basin," *Albany Law Review* 55 (1992): 815–47, especially 843–47.

France so infringed upon the country's sovereignty that the people would be better off without them. Corazón Aquino eventually arrived at the same conclusion in considering the worth of an American military presence in the Philippines.

De Facto External Independence

In dividing sovereign from nonsovereign entities, scholars and leaders tend to look to international as well as domestic affairs. A formidable group emphasizes that a state must demonstrate not only domestic political supremacy but actual independence of outside authority in foreign affairs. Thus, within the international context the concept of sovereignty is not used to denote the supremacy of one state over other states. Instead, sovereignty denotes what may appear to be quite the opposite: not supremacy but independence. Those who take de facto external independence to be a prerequisite for sovereign status argue that a sovereign state is a political community that does more than merely claim its independence; rather, a sovereign state is able to assert its independence in practice.[47]

The requirement of de facto independence in its external as well as internal dimensions is illustrated by the case of Hyderabad.[48] In 1947 the India Independence Act transferred sovereignty over British India from Great Britain to the Dominion Governments of India and Pakistan. Britain, however, also had long-standing relations with certain, at least nominally sovereign, princely states within the Indian subcontinent. Most of these territorial entities were content to place themselves under the sovereignty of newly independent India. However, the state of Hyderabad balked. Its wealthy prince, the Nizam, claimed that Hyderabad was already a sovereign state.

As Indian troops massed to invade Hyderabad, the Nizam sent three frantic cablegrams appealing to the United Nations Security

47. James, *Sovereign Statehood*, p. 20. James also pointed out that the state need not in fact be active internationally. An isolationist state can be sovereign if it is able to assert itself when it wishes to do so. Ibid., p. 24.

48. See Hannum, *Autonomy, Sovereignty, and Self-Determination*, p. 152. Those unfamiliar with the geography of the Indian subcontinent might confuse Hyderabad, Pakistan, a city of one million inhabitants, with Hyderabad, India, a city of more than four million. The following account refers to Hyderabad, India.

Council to compel India to desist.[49] Before the Security Council had done much of anything other than agree to hear the dispute,[50] the Indian army overwhelmed the small state. The Nizam thereupon chose to withdraw his Security Council complaint and accede to the sovereignty of India.[51] Thus, facing determined opposition by India, Hyderabad proved wholly unable to assert its purported independence in practice. The state was unable to make a credible claim to de facto external independence.

The situation confronted by the maharaja of Kashmir in the summer of 1947 offers an instructive parallel case since the maharaja also hoped to create a sovereign state. In Kashmir, however, a Muslim uprising, soon to be supported by Pakistan, led the maharaja to ask for India's military assistance. That aid was not forthcoming until Kashmir agreed to join the Indian Union. After two years of war India and Pakistan divided Kashmir, with the entire former Princely State of Kashmir incorporated into Indian territory. As in Hyderabad, a political entity pursuing sovereign statehood was unable to grasp de facto independence.

The complications evident in examining internal supremacy arise in analogous form in analyzing the requirement of external independence. Once again the notion of de facto independence is confused by a substantial gap between the theory and the reality of international life.[52] Scholars regularly refer to the independent and

49. See United Nations, Security Council, "Cablegram dated 21 August 1948 from the Hyderabad Government to the President of the Security Council," *United Nations Security Council Official Records* (hereafter *UNSCOR*), Suppl. (UN DOC S/986), September 1948, p. 5; United Nations, Security Council, "Cablegram dated 12 September 1948 from the Hyderabad Government to the President of the Security Council," *UNSCOR*, Suppl. (UN DOC S/998), September, 1948, p. 5; United Nations, Security Council, "Cablegram dated 13 September 1948 from the Hyderabad Government to the President of the Security Council," *UNSCOR*, Suppl. (UN DOC S/1000), September 1948, p. 5.

50. United Nations, Security Council, "The Hyderabad Question," *United Nations Resolutions: Resolutions and Decisions of the Security Council*, ser. 2, vol. 2, 1948–50, p. 42.

51. United Nations, Security Council, "Cablegram dated 22 September 1948 from the Nizam of Hyderabad," *UNSCOR*, Suppl. (UN DOC S/1011), September 1948, p. 7.

52. Hans Morgenthau observed: "At the root of the perplexities which attend the problem of the loss of sovereignty there is the divorce, in contemporary legal and political theory, of the concept of sovereignty from the political reality to which the concept of sovereignty is supposed to give legal expression." Hans J. Morgenthau, *Politics Among Nations: The Struggle for Power and Peace* (New York: Alfred A. Knopf, 1948), p. 249.

autonomous sovereign state. Sovereignty is taken to mean "a legal power which is indivisible, unlimited and supreme."[53] Yet while scholars at times speak in ideal theoretical terms of independence and autonomy, the international system is also routinely described as a place of cooperation and competition. One might observe that states reminiscent of town busybodies far outnumber their hermitlike cousins. Large and small states find that to prosper, and at times to survive, in the international community requires a degree of interaction quite different from the scholarly fiction of separateness. As Inis Claude noted, "For all their vaunted sovereignty and independence, states are rarely lone wolves, intent upon going their own way heedless of the actions of other states."[54]

In an international system marked not just by blocs, satellites, and protectorates, but by interlocking economic suppliers, producers, and consumers, the vital interests of states demand that influence be exerted regularly and dramatically on other sovereigns. Should external independence of action ever have approached absolute qualities, it has now been seriously eroded.[55] The constant push and pull of states influencing one another complicates the simplistic criterion that a sovereign state must be free to act as it pleases in international affairs. Despite academic rhetoric, external political independence is a matter of degree, not of bright lines. In a system marked by busily interacting and interdependent actors, the independent status supposedly accorded sovereigns does not appear to be so absolute today as is often pictured in the literature on sovereignty.

Sovereignty as de facto external independence raises significant

53. Herbert A. Wilkinson, *The American Doctrine of State Succession* (Westport, Conn.: Greenwood Press, 1975), p. 119. Hans Morgenthau described sovereignty in absolute terms as follows: "[E]ach state is free to manage its internal and external affairs according to its own discretion, in so far as it is not limited by treaty or . . . common international law. The individual state has the right to give itself any constitution it pleases, to enact whatever laws it wishes regardless of their effect upon its own citizens, and to choose any system of administration. It is free to have whatever kind of military establishment it deems necessary for the purposes of its foreign policy which, in turn, it is free to determine as it sees fit." Morgenthau, *Politics among Nations*, pp. 245–46.

54. Inis L. Claude, Jr., *American Approaches to World Affairs* (Lanham, Md.: University Press of America, 1986), p. 39.

55. See Geoffrey L. Goodwin, "The Erosion of External Sovereignty?" in *Between Sovereignty and Integration*, ed. Ghita Ionescu (New York: John Wiley and Sons, 1974), pp. 100–117.

theoretical questions. To qualify as sovereign, just how independent must a territorial entity be in conducting its foreign relations? Is a state still fully sovereign when authority over certain vital matters is vested elsewhere, such as in a neighboring great power or perhaps in an international tribunal or organization? Although sovereignty is often taken to mean absolute legislative, executive, and judicial independence, total autonomy is surely an ideal for virtually all members of the current society of states.

Nevertheless, despite the useful qualifications that might be appended to the notions of internal and external autonomy, de facto supremacy and independence is firmly rooted in thinking about sovereignty. For an entity with territory, people, and a government to attain sovereign status, some showing of actual external independence must customarily be made. Indeed, the fighting in Chechnya during its attempt to break away from Russia, or in Croatia, Slovenia, and Bosnia-Herzegovina after the dissolution of Yugoslavia underscores how important it may be for a prospective sovereign state to be able to defend itself against reintegration by a nearby covetous power.

The Requirement of De Jure Independence

The thesis that sovereign status requires internal supremacy and external independence in addition to people, territory, and a government is challenged by another school of thought. These thinkers contend that what actually determines sovereign status is de jure independence. This theory holds that sovereign statehood is determined by focusing on whether a country is legally separate from other states. As one scholar observed years ago: "The general proposition may here be laid down, . . . that the presence or absence of sovereignty in a given political entity depends upon whether or not that entity has such complete control over its own legal competence that it cannot against its own legal will, be legally bound in any way whatsoever by the legal will of another political body. This is the one and final test of sovereignty."[56] From this

56. Westel W. Willoughby, *The Fundamental Concepts of Public Law* (New York: Macmillan, 1924), cited in Vernon A. O'Rourke, *The Juristic Status of Egypt and the Sudan* (Baltimore: Johns Hopkins University Press, 1935), p. 21.

perspective sovereignty means not necessarily actual independence of outside authority but legal, or constitutional, separation from other states.

In this vein Alan James wrote: "[F]or the Solomon Islands and Tuvalu, as for all other internationally active states, the sovereignty on which their international activity is based amounts to constitutional separateness."[57] James continued: "A sovereign state may have all sorts of links with other states and with international bodies, but the one sort of link which, by definition, it cannot have is a constitutional one. For sovereignty . . . consists of being constitutionally apart, of not being contained, however loosely, within a wider constitutional scheme."[58] James later concluded: "A helpful way of envisaging sovereignty is as a kind of shell encasing an appropriately qualified state, but not of the sort which helps to provide a barrier to physical penetration. . . . For what sovereignty entails is not a physical but a constitutional shell. It expresses the lack of any links which place the state concerned in a subordinate constitutional position in relation to another state."[59]

Here, too, the actions of states help to illustrate the prerequisites of sovereign statehood. Consider, for instance, the issue of sovereignty in Cyprus. Since independence in 1960, the sovereign state of Cyprus has witnessed a long-standing battle between the Greek Cypriots, in firm control of the recognized government, and the minority Turkish Cypriots.[60] In 1974 Turkey invaded Cyprus and occupied the northern third of the island. The following year the Turkish Cypriots formed a political entity touted as a "secular and federated State." In 1983 they declared that state to be sovereign:

57. James, *Sovereign Statehood*, p. 24.

58. Ibid., p. 24. James hastened to explain that by defining sovereignty in this manner, he did not mean to imply that constitutionalism—that is, the conduct of a government in accordance with the country's constitution—is a factor in determining whether a political entity qualifies as a sovereign state. Rather, James described sovereignty as primarily determined by whether the entity in question is encumbered by constitutional links to another state. See ibid., p. 25.

59. Ibid., p. 24. James's approach leads to the conclusion that sovereignty is not a concept of international law at all but that international law presupposes sovereignty (ibid., p. 40). For a somewhat similar view, citing the history of political philosophy, see Hinsley, *Sovereignty*, pp. 185–96.

60. See generally Alan James, "The UN Force in Cyprus," *International Affairs* 65, no. 3 (Summer 1989), pp. 481–500, especially p. 483; John Dugard, *Recognition and the United Nations* (Cambridge: Grotius Publications, 1987), pp. 108–11.

the Turkish Republic of Northern Cyprus (TRNC). Shortly thereafter, the government of Turkey recognized the TRNC as a sovereign
equal.

Yet attaining membership in the exclusive club of sovereign
states requires more than a mere invitation to join from a single
current club member. Since the Turkish government's declaration
occurred, the international community has wholly failed to recognize the TRNC's sovereignty. Indeed, the United Nations Security
Council stated firmly that the TRNC's declaration of independence
was null and void.[61] Some states conceivably may have doubted
the Turkish Cypriots' domestic political supremacy or their independence from Turkey; however, the preeminent problem for the
Turkish Cypriots seems to have been their inability to demonstrate
de jure political independence. That is, most states have taken issue
with the Turkish Cypriots' view that they are legally separate from
the government of Cyprus.

Once again, however, the repeated use of sovereignty in a particular sense should not deflect attention from underlying theoretical
disagreements. Legal scholars can attest that constitutional separation can also come in degrees. For instance, until 1982 Great
Britain did not grant to Canada the legal power to amend its own
constitution.[62] Similarly, to this day, under the constitution of the
Cook Islands, a range of critical decisions made by the Cook Islands
cabinet cannot come into effect immediately unless the decisions
are approved by the high commissioner, appointed by New Zealand's governor-general and the leader of the Executive Council.[63]
Since Canada, but not the Cook Islands, has long been considered
a sovereign state, one is tempted to conclude either that some
constitutional links are permissible, while others are not, or that de
jure independence is not the sole criterion for sovereign statehood,
or both.

Moreover, some who use the de jure meaning of sovereignty
ignore the issue of constitutional links and calculate legal indepen-

61. U.N. Security Council Resolution 550 (1984), cited in Alan James, "Unit Veto
Dominance in United Nations Peace-Keeping," in *Politics in the United Nations System*,
ed. Lawrence S. Finkelstein (Durham: Duke University Press, 1988), p. 83.

62. Buzan, *People, States, and Fear*, p. 43.

63. See Cook Islands Constitution Act, pp. 2,033, 2,040–41. See also Alexis, "British
Intervention in St. Kitts," 586 n. 29.

dence by different standards. For instance, before the disintegration of the Soviet Union, Ernst Haas and Alan Whiting concluded: "Our criterion for sovereign statehood is the *pro forma* capacity to enter into diplomatic relations with other states through the existence of a foreign ministry. Thus Outer Mongolia and North Korea are included, while Byelorussia and the Ukraine are not."[64] In determining whether or not a sovereign state exists, Haas and Whiting would not ask whether the entity is constitutionally independent. Instead, they would ask a related, yet slightly different, question: whether—as a matter of form or law—sufficient political institutions exist such that the entity could carry on foreign relations with other states.[65]

Although using sovereignty to mean legal independence can mask telling differences in criteria, the de jure school of thought argues convincingly that a political community that can demonstrate its de jure independence will be well on the way to gaining sovereign status.

Conflict between the De Jure and De Facto Requirements

Although in many cases de facto independence and de jure independence go hand in hand, they need not necessarily accompany

---

64. Ernst B. Haas and Alan S. Whiting, *Dynamics of International Relations* (New York: McGraw-Hill, 1956), 61 n. 3. This approach hearkens back to the words of nineteenth-century international lawyer Sir Robert Phillimore: "International law has no concern with the form, character, or power of a state, if, through the medium of a government, it has such an independent existence as to render it capable of entertaining international relations with other states." See J. A. Andrews, "The Concept of Statehood and the Acquisition of Territory in the Nineteenth Century," *The Law Quarterly Review* 94 (1978): 425.

65. This approach echoes that taken at the 1933 Montevideo Convention on the Rights and Duties of States. Article One of that Inter-American Convention reads: "The state as a person of international law should possess the following qualifications: a) a permanent population; b) a defined territory; c) government; and d) capacity to enter into relations with other states." "Rights and Duties of States (Inter-American) signed at Montevideo, 26 December 1933," *Treaties and Other International Agreements of the United States of America 1776–1949*, ed. C. I. Bevans, vol. 3, 1931–45 (Washington, D.C.: U.S. Government Printing Office, 1969), pp. 145–51.

one another. One might concede the de facto independence of the Turkish Republic of Northern Cyprus yet challenge its de jure independence. Similarly, one might concede that an entity trying to attain sovereign status has a solid claim to de jure independence yet question its claim to de facto independence.

A curious, indeed somewhat whimsical, example of the international community failing to treat an entity as sovereign because it lacked de facto independence concerns the so-called Republic of Morac-Songhrati-Meads. As British sea captain James George Meads sailed through the South China Sea in the 1870s, he created this purported territorial entity by claiming various small islands in the name of the republic. The islands Meads claimed are part of the Spratly Islands, a chain of tiny atolls, islets, and reefs that dot the seas starting several hundred miles off the southern coast of Vietnam and ending about a hundred miles from the coast of Brunei.

Through their republic, which has boasted a foreign minister as well as its own diplomatic stamp, Meads's descendants have continued to stake their claim to certain of the Spratlys. Many of these islands scarcely amount to more than large reefs; indeed, some are even submerged during periods of each year. Nevertheless, since significant marine resources, including minerals and oil and gas, are now suspected to lie under the island chain, their sovereignty has become a matter of serious contention among Brunei, China, Malaysia, the Philippines, Taiwan, and Vietnam. And the Republic of Morac-Songhrati-Meads has continued to file papers complaining about perceived intrusions by these foreign governments in the ongoing sovereignty dispute.[66]

If this strange republic seriously wanted to be considered a sovereign state, it might be able to make a colorable de jure claim to independence. Despite the fact that other states have also claimed its islands, the republic seems to pass at least the Haas-Whiting test of having designated a foreign minister. It may also have created a credible constitution. However, since the republic is not much more than a paper creation, it wholly lacks de facto independence.

66. A recent complaint, signed and stamped by Secretary of Foreign Affairs C. Aran, declared that the Republic would not "tolerate any tampering, trespassing or titillating with any of the sacred island territories of our invincible republic." *Miami Herald* (intl. ed.), 22 January 1992, p. 11A.

The republic can show neither domestic political supremacy nor sufficient power to withstand claims by other states. In short, the republic could not attain sovereign status since it cannot pass the test of de facto independence.

That de jure and de facto independence do not constitute the same test complicates the task of determining the prerequisites of a sovereign state. People tend to differ on whether a particular political community is properly qualified for sovereign statehood depending upon several factors including (i) which criterion the person has in mind—de facto independence or de jure independence; (ii) what criteria to employ in assessing whether an entity is in fact de facto or de jure independent; and (iii) whether a sovereign state must be sovereign in both the de facto and the de jure senses of the word or if one sense will suffice.

Assume, for instance, that Outer Mongolia had never been accorded sovereign status. Assume further that during the Cold War Outer Mongolian leaders attempted to gain sovereign statehood. Was Outer Mongolia during the Cold War properly qualified to be recognized as a sovereign state? If the speaker views sovereign status in terms of de facto independence, the answer is probably no. Although the Outer Mongolian government was surely supreme domestically, its external independence of action at that time is open to serious question. Yet if sovereign statehood is thought of in terms of de jure independence, the answer may well be yes. If the speaker believes that in order for a state to be sovereign it must meet both of the criteria, then the answer would likely be no.

This very process of assessing various factors to determine whether an entity is in fact sovereign is illustrated by a 1937 case before the Permanent Court of International Justice (PCIJ) entitled *Lighthouses in Crete and Samos*.[67] The case involved a contract concluded in 1913 between the Ottoman Sultan and a French business to develop, manage, and maintain a series of lighthouses along the coasts of the Ottoman Empire.[68] Later that year, after the wars in the Balkans, the Treaty of London[69] assigned various for-

---

67. *Lighthouses in Crete and Samos* [Greece v Fr.], *Permanent Court of International Justice Publications* (Ser. A/B), No. 71, at 94 (1937).

68. The term of the contract was from 1924 to 1949, and compensation was to be paid through the collection of shipping dues.

69. "Treaty of Peace between Bulgaria, Greece, Montenegro, Servia, and Turkey,

merly Ottoman territories to Greece. When the Greek government eventually claimed the 1913 contract to be invalid, France and Greece took their dispute to the PCIJ. In an initial judgment in 1934, called *Lighthouses Case between France and Greece*,[70] the court ruled that the French company could enforce the contract against Greece. However, the court added the reservation that it had issued its ruling on the basis of legal principles regarding contracts and had not been called upon to determine whether the contract was operative to all the lighthouses or not.

The parties returned to the World Court three years later with Greece arguing that the contract was not applicable to lighthouses on the islands of Crete and Samos because these territories had already been detached from the Ottoman Empire prior to the signing of the contract. The court then split on how to determine the autonomy of these islands. The majority examined de jure independence, writing:

> [T]he Greek Government has argued that Samos, since 1832, and Crete, since 1899 and in any case since 1907, did in fact enjoy a régime of autonomy which was so wide that those islands must be regarded as having been thenceforward detached from the Ottoman Empire.
>
> No confirmation of this view is obtained by the examination of either of the Cretan Constitutions or of the Organic Statute of Samos. The autonomy of Crete was only recognized by the Constitutions of 1899 and 1907 'under the conditions established by the four Great Powers.' These conditions emphasized 'the supreme rights of the Sultan over Crete' . . . and 'the legitimate rights of the Sultan.' . . .[71]

However, in a powerful dissenting opinion American judge Manley O. Hudson focused on internal supremacy and external independence and thus weighed the factors quite differently in concluding that Crete no longer formed a part of the Ottoman Empire

---

signed at London, 30 May 1913," *The Consolidated Treaty Series*, ed. Clive Parry, vol. 218, 1913 (Dobbs Ferry, N.Y.: Oceana Publications, 1980), pp. 159–61.

70. *Lighthouses Case Between France and Greece* [Greece v Fr.], PCIJ (Ser. A/B), No. 62, at 3 (1934).

71. *Lighthouses in Crete and Samos*, at 104–5.

when the sultan signed the concessions contract with the French company. He wrote:

> [A]fter 1899 the Ottoman Government exercised no governmental powers in Crete, and . . . although the Sultan's flag was ceremoniously flown in Crete until February 1913, the government of the island was entirely in the hands of the High Commissioner and the Cretans themselves, subject in certain respects to the approval of the four European States. In its external relations, the Cretan Government acted independently of the Ottoman Government, also, and it concluded or acceded to various international conventions.

And Judge Hudson concluded: "If it can be said that a theoretical sovereignty remained in the Sultan after 1899, it was a sovereignty shorn of the last vestige of power. He could neither terminate nor modify the autonomy with which Crete had been endowed against his will and with the sanction of the four European States. A juristic conception must not be stretched to the breaking point, and a ghost of a hollow sovereignty cannot be permitted to obscure the realities of the situation."[72] The *Lighthouses* cases thus reveal how pursuing a de facto or a de jure line of argument can lead to conflicting conclusions regarding the status of a potentially sovereign political entity. They also illustrate the practical importance of determining an entity's status in the international community.

The Political Process by Which Sovereign Status Is Conferred

How, then, is sovereign status conferred? The answer is that the international community determines sovereign statehood through an untidy political process that scholars have occasionally noted but have rarely studied.[73] The views of the other sovereigns fre-

72. Ibid., p. 127.
73. The outstanding exception is Quincy Wright, who observed: "[M]ost governments, courts and jurists assumed that a state, whether it had long existed in fact, like Turkey, or had recently become a *de facto* state through successful revolution, like the United

quently are expressed through the act of formal recognition and the consequent establishment of diplomatic relations on the part of a substantial number of states. Quincy Wright noted: "In the case of ancient states of non-European civilization, it has not been assumed that they became equal members of the Family of Nations through entering into formal diplomatic or treaty relations with *a few states.* Recognition of their equality in relations with *a large number* of existing members has usually been considered necessary."[74]

Thus, although sovereignty is sometimes thought to be a prerequisite to recognition, in practice the primacy of the chicken over the egg is not so readily evident.[75] The fact that Turkey recognized the TRNC did not bestow sovereign status on that political community. Yet if Turkey were to convince ten other states each year to establish diplomatic relations with the TRNC as a sovereign equal, the Turkish Cypriots' claim to sovereign status would steadily grow stronger. Once a sufficiently large and influential sector of the international community viewed the TRNC as sovereign, one might conclude that its sovereign statehood in fact existed.[76]

This very process can be seen in the efforts of the Baltic states to gain de jure independence in the waning days of the Soviet Union. To establish that their political communities were legally separate

---

States, could not become a member of the Family of Nations and a state *de jure* except through admission to that circle by the states already in it." Wright, *Existing Legal Situation*, pp. 26–27. Robert Jackson likewise declared: "New statehood therefore springs from international recognition. . . . New states are legally 'posited' by formal actions of international society and the will of states already established." Jackson, *Quasi-States*, p. 78, citing Wight, *Systems of States*, p. 118.

74. Wright, *Existing Legal Situation*, p. 28 (emphasis added).

75. In determining sovereign status by gauging the will of the international community, Quincy Wright observed: "The Family of Nations . . . has not developed procedures through which it clearly manifests the collective will on all occasions. Ordinarily its attitude is manifested only through the consensus of the will of its members expressed in individual acts of recognition over a long period of time." Ibid., p. 44.

76. Here, the constitutive and declaratory theories clash. Constitutive theory holds that the act of recognition actually "creates" the state. Declaratory theory maintains that recognition merely acknowledges a fact: the existence of the state in question. See Mark W. Janis, *An Introduction to International Law* (Boston: Little, Brown and Co., 1988), pp. 127–29; Antonio Cassese, *International Law in a Divided World* (Oxford: Clarendon Press, 1988), pp. 78–79; Richard N. Swift, *International Law: Current and Classic* (New York: John Riley and Sons, 1969), pp. 60–61. In the circumstances here addressed— marginal sense in which sovereign statehood might be disputed—the constitutive theory better describes state practice. See Malcolm N. Shaw, *International Law*, 3d ed. rev. (New York: Cambridge University Press, 1991), p. 246.

from the Soviet Union, Baltic leaders pointed to the acceptance of their sovereignty by many other sovereigns. The international community eventually accepted their claim, as it has many other claims advanced by aspiring political entities over the years.

However, acceptance of the sovereign statehood of a political entity by the international community need not necessarily be expressed in such a manner. Formal recognition is an inherently political act. Governments sometimes bow to wishful thinking and recognize entities that their officials hope will become sovereign. By 1990 seventy-four states had recognized the Saharan Arab Democratic Republic despite Moroccan control of much of the Western Saharan territory.[77] Similarly, by 1988 more than one hundred countries had formally recognized the "state" of Palestine, which also received official acknowledgment by the United Nations General Assembly.[78]

Likewise, governments sometimes bow to domestic or international pressures and fail to recognize entities as sovereign states not so much because they are seriously thought to lack sovereignty but because recognition of the particular regime in question would be distasteful, perhaps even unpalatable, for weighty political constituencies.[79] For instance, while the international community quickly moved to recognize the majority-rule government of Zimbabwe in 1980, the country's prior political incarnation, the white government of Rhodesia, had been denied international recognition.[80]

In February 1994, after two years of delay, the United States finally recognized the former Yugoslav republic of Macedonia as a

77. On 11 June 1990, Namibia became the seventy-fourth state to recognize the Saharan Arab Democratic Republic (SADR). In 1984 SADR became a full member of the Organization of African Unity, causing Morocco to withdraw from the organization in protest. See generally Malcolm N. Shaw, *International Law*, 3d ed. rev. (New York: Cambridge University Press, 1991), p. 164.

78. See Vera Gowlland-Debbas, "Collective Responses to the Unilateral Declarations of Independence of Southern Rhodesia and Palestine: An Application of the Legitimizing Function of the United Nations," *The British Year Book of International Law* 61 (1990): 135–36.

79. Presumably, leaders of the states that failed to recognize the People's Republic of China did not question that China had attained de facto independence. Rather, they feared the political repercussions of acknowledging the sovereignty of what they viewed as an illegitimate Marxist-Leninist regime in China.

80. Gowlland-Debbas, "Collective Responses to the Unilateral Declarations of Independence of Southern Rhodesia and Palestine," pp. 135–36.

sovereign state. The two years of nonrecognition illustrate how a state occasionally fails to recognize another whose sovereign status seems beyond question. In fact, American leaders had stalled to allow time for a futile diplomatic effort aimed at persuading Macedonia to change its name so as to assuage feelings in neighboring Greece, which has a province also called Macedonia. During the months of discussions and deliberations U.S. policymakers seriously considered the Greek reaction to a possible recognition of Macedonia not only because of the Greek-American alliance formalized in the North Atlantic Treaty Organization but because Greek-Americans form a considerable voting constituency in American politics.[81]

Thus, while formal recognition is the typical route through which the international community expresses its views of sovereign status, such views may also surface through the manner in which states treat an aspirant political entity. Is the entity admitted to participate in international conferences? Is it a party to treaties? Do respected scholars and lawyers believe it to be sovereign? For instance, in determining precisely when the People's Republic of China (PRC) gained sovereign status, one might well choose to ignore the roster of states that had formally recognized or established diplomatic relations with the PRC as the postwar era proceeded. One might, instead, focus on behavior rather than pronouncements and evaluate when the international community began to treat the PRC as custodian of the sovereign state of China and, hence, as a sovereign equal.

It is also apparent that in conferring sovereign status the international community by no means functions as a rubber stamp. Various entities claiming sovereignty have not been recognized as such by sufficient numbers of other sovereigns. Because the international community has withheld its blessing, such entities have never attained sovereign status. Despite the efforts of Japanese diplomats to consolidate the army's imperial hold on northern Asia at the beginning of the twentieth century, the Japanese puppet state of Manchukuo gained the formal recognition of only five states.[82]

81. See "U.S. Recognizes Macedonia Over Greek Objections," *Washington Post*, 10 February 1994, p. A23.

82. Manchukuo comprised three eastern provinces of China—Heilungkiang (or Manchuria), Kirin, and Fengtien (or Liaoning)—along with the province of Inner Mongolia known as Jehol. The only states to recognize Manchukuo were Japan, Italy, Germany, Poland, and El Salvador. See Wright, *Existing Legal Situation*, pp. 39, 56–58.

Similarly, the international community as a whole failed to recognize the sovereignty of Biafra, Katanga, and the various "homeland states" in South Africa.[83] One source noted: "The Transkei is not a state because South Africa alone does not have the right to confer statehood, whereas Lesotho is a state because the international community accepted—indeed encouraged—British decolonization in Africa."[84]

The experiences of aspirant states denied sovereign status by other reluctant sovereigns may be contrasted with those of the Baltic states, granted sovereign status by other supportive peers. Thus does the political process work through which sovereignty is conferred.

Conclusion

In closing, then, let us return to the original question posed and offer our thoughts on what central ingredient—aside from territory, people, and a government—is necessary in order for sovereignty to be conferred. In our view, sovereignty, like many other concepts of international law, is useful because the international community tends to act as though the term is valid and important.[85] Although states occasionally violate the sovereignty of others, as the invasion of Kuwait by Iraq in 1990 duly illustrates, sovereign statehood remains a central concept that states generally regard as legitimate. Indeed, the sweeping denunciations of Iraq's actions from virtually every corner of the globe, and the United Nations coalition that came together to reclaim Kuwait from the Saddam Hussein regime, attest to the seriousness with which the international community now views attacks on sovereign statehood.

Since the concepts of international law are indebted to the community of states for their birth and continued existence, sovereignty

---

83. See generally, "Non-Recognition of States and Territorial Acquisitions: The Practice of the United Nations," in Dugard, Recognition and the United Nations, pp. 81–122.

84. Jackson and Rosberg, "Why Africa's Weak States Persist," pp. 16–17.

85. See Charles O. Lerche, Jr., and Abdul A. Said, Concepts of International Politics (Englewood Cliffs, N.J.: Prentice-Hall, 1970), p. 107. The authors correctly observed: "The persistence of states in acting as if sovereignty were a reality gives the doctrine great political significance."

and the consent of states are naturally related. In this sense, becoming an accepted member of the ranks of sovereign states is something like joining an exclusive club. While no formal procedure exists to determine membership status,[86] the other members must voice acceptance in substantial numbers before membership is legitimately obtained. Such acceptance may be derived from a strong showing of de facto or de jure independence, or ideally both, but it is ultimately the international community that determines whether a particular political entity qualifies as a sovereign state.[87]

---

86. Wright, *Existing Legal Situation*, p. 27.

87. In his article "Collective Legitimization as a Political Function of the United Nations" Inis Claude noted: "The United Nations has been heavily involved in matters relating to the question of the ratification and solidification of the status claimed . . . by political entities. Generally, this can be subsumed under the heading of membership business; admission to or seating in the organization has tended to take on the political meaning, if not the legal implication, of collective recognition. New states have been inclined to regard the grant of membership as the definitive acknowledgment of their independence." Claude continued: "Non-admission of the segments of divided states appears to have been motivated in part by the conviction that admission would somehow sanctify existing divisions, thereby diminishing the prospects for future reunification." Inis L. Claude, Jr., *States and the Global System: Politics, Law, and Organization* (New York: St. Martin's Press, 1988), p. 155.

3

How Is Sovereignty Applied in Theory?

The word sovereignty holds various conflicting connotations and by no means arouses identical patterns in the minds of different students.

—Vernon A. O'Rourke[1]

Since determining how a state attains sovereignty can be an elusive matter, one might anticipate that the consequences of gaining sovereign status would be similarly controversial. In fact, not only do thinkers disagree on what confers sovereign status, they also dispute just what sovereign status confers. We next examine issues regarding how, in theory, sovereignty is applied to modern international relations. Is sovereignty principally a legal idea or a political one?[2] Do states by virtue of their sovereign status really possess a set of identical rights and obligations? Or, alternatively, does

1. Vernon A. O'Rourke, *The Juristic Status of Egypt and the Sudan* (Baltimore: Johns Hopkins University Press, 1935), p. 10.

2. Barry Buzan asked: "Can sovereignty exist without being exercised? In other words, is it primarily a legal idea which exists as a right? Or is it primarily a political idea, which comes into being only when exercised?" Barry Buzan, *People, States, and Fear: The National Security Problem in International Relations* (Chapel Hill: University of North Carolina Press, 1983), p. 41.

sovereignty in practice confer somewhat different rights and impose somewhat different duties upon satellites and superpowers, or upon tiny, newly independent states and large, populous powers?

We believe that when leaders and diplomats, judges and arbiters, and others playing an active role in international relations apply the concept of sovereignty, they tend to follow one of two lines of thought. Either sovereignty is viewed as something absolute that may be won or lost or as something variable that may be augmented or diminished.[3] In metaphorical terms, some conceive of sovereignty as a chunk; others take it to be a basket. The theory of the chunk and basket approaches to sovereignty merits our attention next.

The Chunk Approach to Sovereignty

In applying sovereignty to international politics, one important school of thought views the concept in terms that are both deductive and monolithic. One deduces a particular set of sovereign rights from the fact that a state is sovereign,[4] and sovereignty is possessed "in full or not at all."[5] From this perspective one might think of sovereignty as a monolith, like a chunk of stone. Every state has one of these stones, and, as with identical cobblestones, all are exactly alike.

If conceived in these terms, sovereignty cannot be enlarged or diminished. Neither can it be chipped away. When these thinkers

3. Professor Emeritus Inis L. Claude, Jr., of the University of Virginia originally devised the "chunk and basket approach" to clarify discussions of sovereignty. However, Claude never published an exposition of his sovereignty theories, and the first published account of the approach was Michael Ross Fowler and Julie Marie Bunck, "The Chunk and Basket Theories of Sovereignty," in *Community, Diversity, and a New World Order: Essays in Honor of Inis L. Claude, Jr.*, ed. Kenneth W. Thompson (Lanham, Md.: University Press of America, 1994), pp. 137–44.

4. W. J. Stankiewicz observed: "In essence, sovereignty is a declaration that if order is to have certain characteristics, then an ordering body or sovereign having certain qualities must exist." W. J. Stankiewicz, "In Defense of Sovereignty: A Critique and an Interpretation," in *In Defense of Sovereignty*, ed. W. J. Stankiewicz (New York: Oxford University Press, 1969), p. 5.

5. Inis L. Claude, Jr., *National Minorities: An International Problem* (Cambridge, Mass.: Harvard University Press, 1955), p. 32.

refer to sovereignty, they mean "an unalterable and irreducible quantity of rights and immunities which automatically accrue to any state. Either a sovereign state exists or it does not; if the existence of a state is conceded, then no alternative exists but to treat it as the possessor of a standard set of sovereign attributes, identical with that possessed by all other states."[6] In this view sovereignty is something a political community either has and is thus a sovereign state or lacks and is thus some entity other than a sovereign state.

The rhetoric of the chunk theory of sovereignty may be traced back to the Peace of Westphalia of 1648, concluding the Thirty Years' War, and to the writings of the early philosophers of international law in the prior century. The conference at Westphalia helped to establish a European system of sovereign states. Each of these states considered itself equal to its regional peers insofar as a handful of early rules of international law were concerned regarding such matters as concluding treaties, respecting territorial integrity, and sending and receiving diplomatic envoys.[7]

Hans Morgenthau, a leading chunk theorist, once declared: "Today, no less than when it was first developed in the sixteenth century, sovereignty points to a political fact . . . the existence of . . . the supreme authority to enact and enforce legal rules within that territory."[8] Morgenthau further observed, "The actual inequality of states and their dependence upon each other has no relevance for the legal status called sovereignty. Panama is as sovereign a state as the United States, although in the choice of its policies and laws it is much more limited than the United States."[9]

6. Ibid., p. 31.
7. See also Hans Blix, *Sovereignty, Aggression, and Neutrality* (Stockholm: Almquist & Wiksell, 1970), p. 10.
8. Hans J. Morgenthau, *Politics Among Nations: The Struggle for Power and Peace* (New York: Alfred A. Knopf, 1948), p. 249. Morgenthau's view may be attributable in part to his grounding in Hobbesian philosophy. F. H. Hinsley summarized the views of Thomas Hobbes on sovereignty as follows: "In his scheme the sovereignty of the state was unlimited, illimitable, irresponsible and omnipotent, was necessarily concentrated in a single centre, and was armed with power." F. H. Hinsley, *Sovereignty* (New York: Basic Books, 1966), p. 143.
9. Morgenthau, *Politics Among Nations*, p. 248. In an attempt to buttress his rendition of the chunk theory, Morgenthau quoted Oliver Wendell Holmes: "[S]overeignty is pure fact." *American Banana Co. v United Fruit Co.*, 213 US 347, 358 (1909). However, since Justice Holmes was actually referring to sovereign jurisdiction—to whether a

In arguing that sovereignty should never be defined in terms of power, Alan James likewise contended that sovereignty is either present or absent. No state is 82 percent sovereign or 57 percent sovereign.[10] For such chunk theorists a political community either has sovereignty or lacks sovereignty. Joseph Frankel observed, "Irrespective of their power and size, in legal theory all states enjoy *sovereignty* in equal measure."[11] Communities that lack sovereignty must be some other type of political entity, perhaps a colony, a neutral zone, a mandate or trust or other nonself-governing territory, or a part of another sovereign state. Such entities neither enjoy the standard bundle of sovereign rights nor are encumbered by the standard bundle of sovereign duties.

Those who view the concept in terms of a monolithic chunk thus claim that sovereignty is indivisible. The French Constitution of 1791 proclaimed: "[S]overeignty is one and indivisible, inalienable and imprescriptible."[12] Philosopher Jacques Maritain likewise declared: "Sovereignty is a property which is absolute and indivisible, which cannot be participated in and admits of no degrees. . . ."[13] Hans Morgenthau went so far as to observe: "[P]erhaps the most important of the misunderstandings which have obscured the problem of sovereignty in the modern world [is] . . . the belief that sovereignty is divisible."[14] Morgenthau declared: "We have heard it said time and again that we must 'surrender part of our sovereignty' to an international organization for the sake of world peace, . . . that there are 'quasi-sovereign' and 'half-sovereign' states. . . . If

---

particular banana plantation lay in Panama or in Costa Rica—use of the quotation to support the chunk theory is questionable. Morgenthau's other citation to Holmes, "Sovereignty is a question of power, and no human power is unlimited," seems more in line with basket thinking. See *The Western Maid*, 257 US 419, 432 (1921).

10. Alan James, *Sovereign Statehood: The Basis of International Society* (London: Allen & Unwin, 1986), pp. 45–48.

11. Joseph Frankel, *International Politics: Conflict and Harmony* (Baltimore: Penguin Books, 1973), p. 38 (italics in the original). See also Robert H. Jackson, *Quasi-States: Sovereignty, International Relations, and the Third World* (New York: Cambridge University Press, 1990), p. 32.

12. K.W.B. Middleton, "Sovereignty in Theory and Practice," in *In Defense of Sovereignty*, ed. W. J. Stankiewicz (New York: Oxford University Press, 1969), p. 140.

13. Jacques Maritain, "The Concept of Sovereignty," in *In Defense of Sovereignty*, ed. W. J. Stankiewicz (New York: Oxford University Press, 1969), p. 51.

14. Morgenthau, *Politics Among Nations*, p. 258. See also Herbert A. Wilkinson, *The American Doctrine of State Succession* (Westport, Conn.: Greenwood Press, 1975), p. 119; James, *Sovereign Statehood*, p. 102.

sovereignty means supreme authority, it stands to reason that no two or more entities—persons, groups of persons, agencies—can be sovereign within the same time and space."[15]

The absolute qualities of sovereignty, its monolithic and indivisible nature, the deductive manner in which the concept may be analyzed—all these observations lead chunk theorists to posit that sovereignty is essentially a matter of reciprocity. Each sovereign state enjoys equal sovereign rights and duties by virtue of its sovereign status. No matter how large or small the state, each sovereign receives from the international community an identical gift upon attaining sovereign status—a package of rights and duties the same as those presented to every other entity gaining sovereignty in that same era.

However, since many rights and duties recognized under international law arise from treaties and conventions, chunk theorists do not claim that every state has the same sum total of rights and duties. Apart from the standard complement of rights and duties arising from its sovereignty, a state may well have taken on a range of other *nonsovereign* obligations and prerogatives. To consider one of many possible examples, although sovereignty is thought to enable a state to take the military measures it feels are necessary to ensure its national security, certain states have agreed under international conventions to accept significant parameters regarding the inspection of nuclear weapons, the use of poisonous gases, and various other such restrictions. The sum total of rights and duties enjoyed by such states will obviously differ from those that have not signed the same conventions. Nevertheless, chunk thinkers would counsel, the particular bundle of rights and duties arising from sovereign status remains constant for all sovereign states.[16]

---

15. Morgenthau, *Politics Among Nations*, pp. 258–59.

16. Note Robert Keohane's distinction between "formal sovereignty" and "operational sovereignty": "Formally sovereign states often limit their operational sovereignty by accepting constraints on their own actions, as they do when they enter into agreements establishing international regimes and organizations." Robert O. Keohane, *Sovereignty, Interdependence, and International Institutions*, Working Paper no. 1 (Cambridge, Mass.: Harvard University, Center for International Affairs, 1991), p. 1. Keohane goes on to argue that states often find it in their interests to limit their own operational sovereignty in order to enjoy the benefits of cooperative action with other states.

Chunk theory also nowhere implies that each state brings to bear equal influence in international affairs.[17] Kenneth Waltz observed:

> To say that a state is sovereign means that it decides for itself how it will cope with its internal and external problems, including whether or not to seek assistance from others and in doing so to limit its freedom by making commitments to them. States develop their own strategies, chart their own courses, make their own decisions about how to meet whatever needs they experience and whatever desires they develop. It is no more contradictory to say that sovereign states are always constrained and often tightly so than it is to say that free individuals often make decisions under the heavy pressure of events.[18]

Writing in the chunk tradition, K.W.B. Middleton observed: "To say that a state surrenders its sovereignty, or any particle of it, by the mere fact of entering into an obligation that imposes a limitation on the exercise of its sovereign rights, is like saying that a man necessarily becomes the servant of another by contracting with him."[19]

Just as unequal influence and varying objectives may cause states to act differently when confronted with the choice of retaining or circumscribing particular rights and duties, so sovereignty also offers no guarantee against inequitable results arising from an uneven distribution of power.[20] Indeed, the concept does not guarantee that sovereign rights and duties will necessarily be respected.[21] Instead, under the chunk theory sovereign status in

17. See Robert A. Klein, *Sovereign Equality Among States: The History of an Idea* (Toronto: University of Toronto Press, 1974), p. 7.

18. Kenneth N. Waltz, "Political Structures," in *Neorealism and Its Critics*, ed. Robert O. Keohane (New York: Columbia University Press, 1986), pp. 90–91.

19. Middleton, "Sovereignty in Theory and Practice," p. 153.

20. Robert Klein declared: "A great deal of confusion on the subject of legal equality arises because of muddled thinking over the rights which a state may assert in law and the degree of political influence it possesses." Klein, *Sovereign Equality Among States*, p. 7.

21. One example of a state whose sovereign rights have been regularly compromised both by civil war and by outside meddling is Lebanon. See Wade R. Goria, *Sovereignty and Leadership in Lebanon, 1943–1976* (London: Ithaca Press, 1985), and Sandra M.

international law is viewed simply as granting each state the same *sovereign* rights and duties.

As will be explained in the following chapter in more detail, those who adhere to the chunk theory of sovereignty have frequently applied their views to actual international issues. For instance, in 1936 the United States Supreme Court adopted a chunk approach to a case in which an American company had been accused of conspiring to sell weapons to Bolivia, an act that would have violated a joint resolution of Congress and a presidential proclamation of neutrality.[22] The Supreme Court considered whether the fact of the country's sovereignty granted the U.S. government the right to bar an American company from selling certain products abroad. Writing for the majority, Justice George Sutherland stated: "Rulers come and go; governments end and forms of government change; but sovereignty survives. A political society cannot endure without a supreme will somewhere. Sovereignty is never held in suspense. When, therefore, the external sovereignty of Great Britain in respect of the colonies ceased, it immediately passed to the Union."

In doctrinaire chunk fashion Justice Sutherland then spelled out certain rights and duties that sovereign status confers on every state. He wrote: "The powers to declare and wage war, to conclude peace, to make treaties, to maintain diplomatic relations with other sovereignties, if they had never been mentioned in the Constitution, would have been vested in the Federal government as necessary concomitants of nationality." And, he ultimately observed: "As a member of the family of nations, the right and power of the United States in that field [e.g., the conduct of foreign relations] are equal to the right and power of the other members of the international family."[23] Sutherland's opinion nicely illustrates the manner in which the absolute, chunk theory of sovereignty has been applied to resolve an international issue.

Saseen, "The Taif Accord and Lebanon's Struggle to Regain Its Sovereignty," *American University Journal of International Law and Policy* 6 (1990): 57–75.

22. *United States v Curtiss-Wright Export Corporation et al.*, 299 US 304, 316–17 (1936).

23. Ibid.

The Basket Approach to Sovereignty

United Nations Secretary-General Boutros Boutros-Ghali recently wrote: "A major intellectual requirement of our time is to rethink the question of sovereignty—not to weaken its essence, which is crucial to international security and cooperation, but to recognize that it may take more than one form and perform more than one function."[24] In fact, while the chunk perspective on sovereignty has had many adherents, it has never swept the field of opponents. Another notable group associates sovereignty not so much with formal, juridical equality as with degrees of practical, political inequality.

Professional students and practitioners of international relations who adhere to this second approach view sovereignty not in the absolute terms of a monolithic chunk but rather in variable terms, as a basket of attributes and corresponding rights and duties. While every state has a basket, the contents are by no means the same. A great power will have more sovereign attributes, and thus be more nearly de facto independent, than will a neutral or a satellite state.

The manner in which the concept of sovereignty is applied to international relations changes considerably when the concept is conceived of as a basket of rights and duties rather than as a monolithic chunk. Instead of proceeding by deductive reasoning, basket theorists empirically investigate the contents of each political community's basket of attributes to determine the extent of that actor's corresponding rights and obligations. To basket thinkers sovereignty is not something that must be possessed in full or not at all. Quite naturally, some states can be more sovereign than others. And sovereign status will mean something different to a state with substantial influence in international affairs than to a peer whose influence is of negligible account.

Within international relations scholarship one can find many references to sovereignty that illustrate basket thinking. One scholar wrote: "Sovereignty is a matter of authority and it may be relative."[25] Another noted: "[S]overeignty has traditionally been used

24. Boutros Boutros-Ghali, "Empowering the United Nations," Foreign Affairs 71 (1992/93): 99.

25. J. A. Andrews, "The Concept of Statehood and the Acquisition of Territory in the Nineteenth Century," The Law Quarterly Review 94 (1978): 424.

as a term to denote the collection of functions exercised by a state."[26] Yet another observed: "The rapid and extensive unraveling of the European colonial empires has given today's world an exceptional supply of states whose capacity to hang together and to stand alone, to achieve sovereignty in something more than a formal sense and to convert independence from theory into fact, is open to doubt."[27] A popular text on international relations declared: "Although all nation-states enjoy some of the legal privileges of sovereignty (for example, all member states in the United Nations General Assembly have equal voting rights), in practice some states are obviously more sovereign than others."[28]

These thinkers plainly are not conceiving of sovereignty in terms of a monolithic chunk of rights. In the basket tradition Hans Blix stated:

> As ownership is described as a bundle of rights, sovereignty may perhaps be described as a bundle of competences. There is no inherent reason against the voluntary acceptance of limitations upon the freedom of action in one field or in several fields, upon one or more of the competences in the bundle. Of course, such limitations do reduce the freedom of action of the state and thereby nibble at the sovereignty—as the concept is defined here. Most of that freedom will remain, however.[29]

Blix's approach thus treats sovereignty as a variable matter, dependent upon the relative competence of the state in carrying out the various functions of statehood.

In *The Exercise of Sovereignty* American diplomat Charles Burton Marshall likewise illustrated the basket approach to the term. Marshall first described what is meant by sovereignty by listing some of the principal components of a fully sovereign state, among

26. Ingrid DeLupis, *International Law and the Independent State* (New York: Crane, Russak and Co., 1974), p. 3.

27. Inis L. Claude, Jr., *States and the Global System: Politics, Law, and Organization* (New York: St. Martin's Press, 1988), p. 34.

28. Richard W. Mansbach, Yale H. Ferguson, and Donald E. Lampert, *The Web of World Politics: Nonstate Actors in the Global System* (Englewood Cliffs, N.J.: Prentice-Hall, 1976), p. 22.

29. Blix, *Sovereignty, Aggression, and Neutrality*, pp. 11–12.

them: "having a scheme of authority . . . capable of maintaining dependable social order," commanding "the allegiance of a determining portion of persons . . . encompassed in that area," creating and maintaining "a capacity and a will to command means and to devote them to give effect to common preferences," having "the capacity to enter into and to effectuate obligations," and having some agency "able to communicate authentically and conclusively on its behalf to others beyond the span of jurisdiction."[30]

Marshall went on to declare:

> These faculties and qualities listed are not easy to come by. Even under the most favorable circumstances, they require continuous cultivation. No society can afford to assume them to be an inherent endowment, a fixed reality. . . . The perils and perplexities in the world about us rise not so much from an excess of the constituent qualities of sovereignty in the entities passing as nation-states, as from an entirely opposite circumstance. A great many of them have not achieved those qualities. Reaching them may be beyond the ultimate capability of some.[31]

In reflecting on how certificates of statehood have been issued wholesale during the decolonization process, Marshall put his finger squarely on the chunk and basket distinction, writing: "Sovereignty as an expression of juristic status is in hand, but sovereignty as the sum of attributes of a successful modern society seems beyond reach of many."[32]

Basket theorists like Marshall plainly conceive of the concept in relative terms: for any state sovereignty can be, and often is, increased or decreased over time. Consequently, basket theory reflects a clear historical perspective. The basket theorist acknowledges that "the meanings that scholars and statesmen pack into the notion of sovereignty are different in different eras, just as society's

---

30. Charles Burton Marshall, *The Exercise of Sovereignty: Papers on Foreign Policy* (Baltimore: Johns Hopkins University Press, 1965), p. 5.

31. Ibid.

32. Ibid., p. 207. Toward the end of the book Marshall refers again to disparities between sovereignty as a status in world affairs and sovereignty as the sum of a state's attributes as a going concern (ibid., p. 209).

concept of suitable swimming attire is a variable over time."[33] Those applying sovereignty to international relations in the late twentieth century proceed in a decidedly different manner from those who applied the concept in the sixteenth century.

To illustrate how sovereign rights and duties are inherently variable, not static, the basket thinker might point out that in the 1890s the international community entitled a sovereign state to treat its citizens as it pleased. A century later, human rights campaigns have sharply challenged this historical entitlement.[34] A century ago sovereignty implied that a state could go to war whenever it pleased. Once again, states have renounced such a sovereign prerogative.[35] States also once claimed, and the international community acknowledged, the sovereign right to acquire and govern colonies. States today claim no such right.[36] Indeed, various imperial states voluntarily relinquished sovereignty over former colonies, as the British did in Belize, various Caribbean states, and Australia.[37]

33. Inis L. Claude, Jr., in a 25 September 1990 letter written to the authors. See also Djura Nincic, The Problem of Sovereignty in the Charter and in the Practice of the United Nations (The Hague: Martinus Nijhoff, 1970), pp. 9–12.

34. See W. Michael Reisman, "Sovereignty and Human Rights in Contemporary International Law," American Journal of International Law 84 (1990): 866–76. See also the interesting notion of "sphere sovereignty," as contrasted with "absolute sovereignty," in Johan D. Van der Vyver, "Sovereignty and Human Rights in Constitutional and International Law," Emory International Law Review 5 (1991): 321–443.

35. In his essay "Just Wars: Doctrines and Institutions" Inis Claude critically analyzed the development of what he characterized as the "legal fiction" of "war as a sovereign right." See Claude, States and the Global System, pp. 76–80.

36. Inis Claude wrote: "A major campaign has been waged in the United Nations to delegitimize colonialism, to invalidate the claim of colonial powers to legitimate possession of overseas territories—in short, to revoke their sovereignty over colonies. This movement culminated in the overwhelming adoption by the General Assembly of sweeping anticolonial declarations." Claude observed that India justified its invasion of Goa by arguing that "the process of collective legitimization had operated to deprive Portugal of any claim to sovereignty over Goa and thus of any right to protest the invasion." Ibid., p. 155. For a historical account of British sovereign rule over colonies in the nineteenth century, see W. Ross Johnston, Sovereignty and Protection: A Study of British Jurisdictional Imperialism in the Late Nineteenth Century (Durham: Duke University Press, 1973).

37. See Nii Lante Wallace-Bruce, "Two Hundred Years On: A Reexamination of the Acquisition of Australia," Georgia Journal of International Law and Comparative Law 19 (1989): 87–116. For commentary on the singular case of Gibraltar see Sir Joshua Hassan, "Gibraltar's Political and Constitutional Future: The Spanish Sovereignty Claim versus Gibraltar's Continuing Relationship with Britain and the Commonwealth," Parlia-

Over the past century the members of our system of states have moved to restrict the classical concept of sovereign immunity from an absolute theory in which a sovereign and its property could choose to be immune from all judicial processes of a foreign state,[38] to a markedly restricted theory in which such immunity is recognized only with respect to public acts, not to private or commercial acts.[39] Indeed, the United States has further peeled back the protective encasement of sovereign immunity in applying its criminal laws to the de facto leader of another sovereign state, General Manuel Antonio Noriega. Even though the general was commander-in-chief of the Panama Defense Force and was generally considered to be the leader of Panama,[40] the United States government indicted General Noriega twice,[41] and mounted an invasion of Panama largely aimed at his capture and forcible re-

---

mentarian 68 (1987): 58–61, and Howard S. Levie, *The Status of Gibraltar* (Boulder, Colo.: Westview Press, 1983).

38. In American jurisprudence Chief Justice John Marshall authored the classic statement of the absolute theory of sovereign immunity in *Schooner Exchange v M'Faddon & Others*, 11 US (7 Cranch) 116 (1812). However, other Americans recognized the concept much earlier. In *The Federalist* papers Alexander Hamilton observed: "It is inherent in the nature of sovereignty not to be amenable to the suit of an individual *without its consent*. This is the general sense and the general practice of mankind." Alexander Hamilton, John Jay, and James Madison, "The Federalist No. 81," *The Federalist: A Commentary on the Constitution of the United States* (New York: Random House, 1937), p. 529, cited in James Brown Scott, *Sovereign States and Suits Before Arbitral Tribunals and Courts of Justice* (New York: New York University Press, 1925), p. 115.

39. See Jack B. Tate, "The Tate Letter: Letter from the Acting Legal Adviser of the Department of State to the Department of Justice, May 19, 1952," *Department of State Bulletin* 26 (1952): 984–85. See also *Victory Transport, Inc., v Comisaría General de Abastecimientos y Transportes*, 336 F2d 354 (2d Cir. 1964). The restrictive theory has now been written into U.S. federal law. See *The Foreign Sovereign Immunities Act of 1976*, U.S. Code, vol. 28, sec. 1608 (1976). For an analysis of the act see *Letelier v Republic of Chile*, 488 FSupp. 665 (1980). (The authors are indebted to Brendan Behanna for suggesting that sovereign immunity illustrates how "the outer limits of sovereignty have been pulled back in certain areas.")

40. Formally, of course, the United States and many other countries refused to recognize the Noriega regime. The repercussions of the decision not to recognize General Noriega as the head of state in Panama is the subject of an interesting case involving the seizure by a Coast Guard cutter of 1,211 kilograms of cocaine from a Panamanian vessel in international waters. See *United States v Leuro-Rosas*, 952 F2d 616 (1st Cir. 1991).

41. See Mark Andrew Sherman, "An Inquiry Regarding the International and Domestic Legal Problems Presented in *United States v. Noriega*," *University of Miami Inter-American Law Review* 20 (1989): 393–428.

moval. Federal prosecutors eventually tried and convicted Manuel Noriega in U.S. federal court on racketeering and narcotics trafficking charges.[42]

Never before had the United States treated the head of a sovereign state in such a manner. Perhaps the most relevant precedent[43] occurred in March 1985 when U.S. officials arrested Norman Saunders, chief minister of the Turks and Caicos Islands, and charged him with conspiracy to traffic in cocaine. A federal court eventually convicted Saunders and sentenced him to eight years in prison. The cases of Norman Saunders and Manuel Noriega, however, can be readily distinguished from each other. First, American narcotics agents arrested Saunders in Miami; they did not remove him forcibly from his own country. Moreover, the Turks and Caicos was a self-governing dependency, not a sovereign state, and British authorities fully approved of the law enforcement actions.

Although many sovereign rights have eroded over time, changing circumstances have led the international community to permit states to adopt new sovereign rights as well. For example, classical international law barred acts of expropriation and nationalization of property owned by aliens as plainly unlawful. These days, as Eduardo Jiménez de Arechaga, former president of the International Court of Justice, declared: "[M]easures of nationalization or expropriation constitute the exercise of a sovereign right of the State and are consequently entirely lawful."[44]

Since World War II coastal states have successfully claimed various sovereign rights over offshore waters—from territorial seas to the continental shelf to the so-called exclusive economic zone. Indeed, the "Cod War," in which Great Britain sent warships off the coast of Iceland to protect British fishermen, demonstrates that

---

42. "Noriega Guilty on Eight of Ten Counts," *Washington Post*, 10 April 1992, p. 1.

43. See "Turks and Caicos Chief Minister Held for Drugs, Bribe," *The Reporter* (Belize), 10 March 1985, p. 5; "T & C Chief Minister Gets 8 Years for Drugs Plan," *The Reporter* (Belize), 15 September 1985, p. 4. See also Ethan A. Nadelmann, *Cops Across Borders: The Internationalization of U.S. Criminal Law Enforcement* (University Park: The Pennsylvania State University Press, 1993), p. 366.

44. Eduardo Jiménez de Arechaga, "State Responsibility for the Nationalization of Foreign-Owned Property," in *International Law: A Contemporary Perspective*, ed. Richard A. Falk, Friedrich V. Kratochwil, and Saul H. Mendlovitz (Boulder, Colo.: Westview Press, 1985), p. 547.

feelings can run as high concerning sovereign rights over water as over land.[45] This phenomenon of "creeping jurisdiction"[46] over coastal waters shows how states now enjoy certain sovereign rights that have been quite recently devised. It also illustrates how coastal states are accorded a different basket of sovereign rights and duties than that granted their landlocked peers.[47]

That the rights exercised by even the most powerful states in the name of sovereignty have changed rather dramatically over time suggests to the basket theorist that the concept is inherently variable, not absolute. As Quincy Wright concluded:

> Sovereignty in international law is thus a variable term. Each international person differs to some extent from every other in its capacity in law or in fact to establish normal legal relations with others. The line between a fully sovereign and a partly sovereign state is not precise and is continually changing with the development of international relations. Limitations which were yesterday considered impairments of sovereignty are today normal and vice versa.[48]

More recently, in coining the term "operational sovereignty" to denote "legal freedom of action," Robert Keohane observed, "Operational sovereignty does vary in the contemporary world,

45. For cardinal decisions involving disputed maritime boundaries, see *Delimitation of the Maritime Boundary Between Guinea and Guinea-Bissau* [Guinea v Guinea-Bissau], 19 *Reports of International Arbitral Awards* 148 (1985), and *Delimitation of the Maritime Boundary in the Gulf of Maine Area* [Can./US], 1984 *International Court of Justice Reports of Judgments, Advisory Opinions, and Orders* 246 (Judgment).

46. See Ken Booth, *Law, Force, and Diplomacy at Sea* (London: Allen & Unwin, 1985), especially pp. 37–45. Booth coined the phrase "creeping jurisdiction" to describe the steady expansion of sovereignty over the seas. See also Bernard H. Oxman, "Summary of the Law of the Sea Convention," in *International Law: A Contemporary Perspective*, ed. Richard A. Falk, Friedrich V. Kratochwil, and Saul H. Mendlovitz (Boulder, Colo.: Westview Press, 1985), p. 547.

47. Stephen Krasner wrote: "The exclusive economic zones agreed to in the Law of the Sea Treaty, and accepted even by those states that have rejected the Treaty itself, gives [sic] littoral states economic control over an area extending out at least 200 miles, but denies [sic] them the right to regulate shipping in this same area. Here is a form of territorial control that is not fully sovereign." Stephen D. Krasner, "Sovereignty: An Institutional Perspective," in *The Elusive State: International and Comparative Perspectives*, ed. James A. Caporaso (Newbury Park, Calif.: Sage Publications, 1989), p. 90.

48. Quincy Wright, *Mandates Under the League of Nations* (New York: Greenwood Press, 1968), p. 294.

from state to state and for the same states over time. Increasingly, states have limited their own operational sovereignty by entering into international agreements. . . ."[49] On the basis of such observations basket theory squarely holds that the connotations of sovereign status differ markedly for a Puerto Rican politician today than they did for a leader of sixteenth-century Austria. For the basket thinker the content of the concept of sovereignty has changed, is changing, and is bound to continue to change in the future.

Those adhering to the basket approach question the degree to which states actually apply the chunk theory of sovereignty in the world of action. They claim that, in reality, other political actors decide whether or not some entity is wholly sovereign and is entitled to a full complement of sovereign rights and duties after weighing such factors as geography, history, population, and economic and military strength. Such calculations can also be expected to change substantially over time. The influence of Japan today, calculated according to a modern power equation, would differ substantially from that of Japan in the years immediately following World War II. Consequently, if Japan were to choose to amend its constitution and increase its military power far beyond its current self-defense forces,[50] the international community would likely react to this assertion of a customary sovereign right quite differently than it would have in 1950.

Basket theorists are thus inclined to scoff at "nominally sovereign and juridically equal states."[51] They focus not on how states are theoretically supposed to act toward one another but on how states

49. Keohane, *Sovereignty, Interdependence, and International Institutions*, p. 1.

50. What seems to be restraining Japan from reasserting its military potential is not so much opposition from the international community as a deep-seated reluctance on the part of certain domestic constituencies that believe that Article 9 of the Japanese Constitution has kept their state from engaging in foreign adventures and has allowed their people to focus single-mindedly on developing economic potential. For an interesting article opposing deployment of Japanese troops, even for United Nations peacekeeping missions, see Tetsumi Takara, "Peacekeeping Without Force," *Japan Views* (August 1992), pp. 6–7.

51. The quoted phrase comes from British diplomat and international relations theorist Adam Watson. Adam Watson, *The Evolution of International Society* (London: Routledge, 1992), p. 1. Watson goes on to ask: "We are also aware that what actually happens on the international scene does not correspond very closely with what is supposed to happen: Why is there this discrepancy between the reality and the theory?" (ibid., p. 2).

actually do act. In this tradition the leaders of many less-developed countries have concluded that although their states might theoretically enjoy permanent sovereign rights over natural resources, the practical necessities of modern economic life demand concessions to foreigners, multinational companies, and international lending institutions like the International Monetary Fund. The desire to retain profits for national citizens must be balanced against the need for loans and foreign investment. And the desire to keep foreigners from dictating economic policy must be balanced against the need to attract investors to help provide jobs and develop infrastructure.[52] To leaders attempting to strike such delicate balances, while retaining the support of popular constituencies, the notion of a chunk of absolute rights has lost relevance from a practical standpoint. In 1989 Prime Minister Michael Manley of Jamaica observed:

> [T]he truth is . . . that it is an illusion to think that any country enjoys sovereignty in a . . . pure theoretical sense— the freedom to do whatever it likes. . . . [S]mall countries are much more constrained by economic dependence. They are fragile. . . . They have less capacity to influence the movement of economic trends in the world. And so people have to learn very early that there are severe limits in practice on this thing called sovereignty.[53]

The basket group argues that the independence of action traditionally expected of a sovereign may well be qualitatively different for an Iron Curtain satellite during the Cold War than for a small state closely interdependent with its neighbors, such as a Caribbean microstate. Similarly, a superpower will enjoy a sovereignty quite distinct from that accorded its allies. What sovereignty entails will differ substantially for the leadership of the United States and that of Fiji or Afghanistan or Papua New Guinea.

In contrast to the chunk theorists' emphasis on the indivisibility of sovereignty, those from the basket tradition believe sovereignty to be plainly divisible. Toward the end of the nineteenth century

52. See Blix, *Sovereignty, Aggression, and Neutrality*, p. 18.
53. Franklin W. Knight, "The State of Sovereignty and the Sovereignty of States," in *Americas: New Interpretive Essays*, ed. Alfred Stepan (New York: Oxford University Press, 1992), p. 24, citing interview, May 1991.

international lawyer Sir Henry Maine observed: "[T]his indivisibility of sovereignty . . . does not belong to International Law. The powers of sovereigns are a bundle or collection of powers, and they may be separated one from another."[54]

Pointing to the legal concept of a condominium arrangement in which two states act as joint tenants dividing sovereignty over a particular territory, Ian Brownlie likewise stated, "Sovereignty is divisible both as a matter of principle and as a matter of experience."[55] Raymond Aron wrote, "[I]ntermediate situations between independence and the total effacement of sovereignty have existed intermittently in the course of history, particularly during the last century."[56] Aron noted that the British Empire regulated colonial India through treaties that guaranteed internal independence.[57] However, Great Britain retained the rights to direct foreign affairs and to supervise internal administration, and it took on the duty of protecting the Indian states against aggression.[58]

---

54. Sir Henry Maine, *International Law* (London: J. Murray, 1890), p. 58, cited in F. A. Váli, *Servitudes of International Law: A Study of Rights in Foreign Territory*, 2d ed. rev. (New York: Frederick A. Praeger, 1958), p. 300. See also Hymen Ezra Cohen, *Recent Theories of Sovereignty* (Chicago: University of Chicago Press, 1937), p. 108 ("[T]he so-called antiquated conception of divided sovereignty . . . has reappeared as a useful tool in describing the nature of a political entity in the family of nations").

55. Ian Brownlie, *Principles of Public International Law* (Oxford: Clarendon Press, 1979), p. 118. An example of a long-standing condominium occurred between 1898 and 1956 when Great Britain and Egypt shared sovereign rule over the Sudan. For a chunk theorist's view of the condominium as an exception that proves the rule, see James, *Sovereign Statehood*, pp. 31–32. Compare Morgenthau, *Politics Among Nations*, p. 245 ("[O]n a given territory only one state can have sovereignty, that is, supreme authority, and . . . no other state has the right to perform governmental acts on its territory without its consent").

56. Raymond Aron, *Peace and War: A Theory of International Relations*, trans. Richard A. Howard and Annette Baker-Fox (New York: Frederick A. Praeger, 1967), pp. 741–42. In Aron's view, although sovereignty is at times divided, this is something of an unnatural state. "[T]he division [of sovereignty]," he wrote, "at least in our times, had a precarious and quasi-contradictory character so that in the long run external sovereignty is either achieved or effaced" (ibid., p. 742).

57. Aron argued: "Despite 'concessions' and the management of tariff duties by foreign officials, China, in the last century, had preserved most of her 'federative power.' She also continued to conduct her foreign relations through her own nationals." He also observed that, under the protectorate treaties with France, Tunisia and Morocco retained their internal autonomy even though they communicated with other states through the French resident alone: "[T]he authority responsible for legislating and enforcing respect for the laws, in the essentials, was Tunisian and Moroccan, not French." Ibid., p. 742.

58. Ingrid DeLupis likewise observed that the nineteenth-century capitulation treaties

In fact, the hierarchical, tributary relationships of many traditional Asian polities might be characterized as precursors to a basket way of thinking about sovereignty.[59] Various rulers in East and Southeast Asia—from Korea in the north to Siam in the south—gave tribute to the emperor of China, who in turn recognized them as legitimate sovereigns.[60] Those lesser sovereigns, in turn, often received tribute from less powerful states: the king of Cambodia granted tribute to the emperor of Vietnam and the king of Siam. Similarly, the king of the Ryukyu Islands[61] provided tribute both to China and to the Satsuma domain on Kyushu Island, which itself was a tributary of the Japanese emperor. In Southeast Asia small states such as Chiang Mai and Kengtung attached themselves to more powerful states such as Siam and Burma. Although generally independent in internal matters, these states enjoyed a basket of sovereign prerogatives quite different from those accorded the rulers of China and Japan.[62]

Conclusion

The implications and assumptions that underlie scholarship on how sovereignty is applied have not been subject to sufficiently

in China called for the consuls of various Western states to exercise certain judicial functions. DeLupis, *International Law and the Independent State*, pp. 21–22.

59. The authors are grateful to Professor Donald Seekins, director of the Asian Studies Program at Meio University in Nago, Okinawa, Japan, for his observations on the many traditional Asian polities that employed basket thinking. Donald Seekins in an 11 October 1993 letter written to the authors.

60. Until the late nineteenth century the kingdom of the Ryukyus sent tribute to the Manchu emperor in China twice every three years, and the Kingdom of Siam sent tribute once every three years. Korea sent tribute once every four years, and Sulu (in the southern Philippines) and Nepal once every five years. Laos and Burma sent tribute once each decade. See Quincy Wright, *The Existing Legal Situation as It Relates to the Conflict in the Far East* (New York: Institute of Pacific Relations, 1939), p. 32, citing Hosea B. Morse and Harley F. MacNair, *Far Eastern International Relations* (Boston: Houghton Mifflin, 1931), p. 345.

61. The Ryukyu kingdom encompassed present-day Okinawa and a number of smaller, neighboring islands, including Kume, Miyako, Taketomi, Ishigaki, and Iriomote.

62. Much the same story might be told of medieval Europe where, it has been observed, "powers and rights were . . . a patchwork of overlapping jurisdictions" forming a "heteronomous sovereignty." Friedrich V. Kratochwil, Paul Rohrlich, and Harpreet Mahajan, *Peace and Disputed Sovereignty: Reflections on Conflict over Territory* (Lan-

rigorous theoretical analysis. Although the chunk theorists may claim their approach to sovereignty to be the mainstream, doctrinaire view of the subject, a review of the scholarly literature reveals a continuing conflict between the chunk and the basket schools of thought. If one were to examine the actual behavior of states, as opposed to how political scientists claim that states do act or how international lawyers mandate that states should act, we would expect to find that both approaches to the concept have been applied to important international issues. To examine that hypothesis more carefully, we have devoted the following chapter to exploring circumstances in which the two theories appear at odds, including situations that might be termed "lesser sovereignty"[63] or, alternatively, "intermediate sovereignty."[64]

The basket thinkers claim that the widespread acceptance during the twentieth century of both forms of variable sovereignty—lesser and intermediate—suggests that their approach may be gaining the upper hand. The chunk approach is denigrated as unduly legalistic and formalistic: the focus on the abstract principles of sovereignty has led theorists to neglect the reality of how states interact.[65] Despite the numerous international relationships that impinge upon traditional notions of sovereign statehood, the chunk school disputes this conclusion. Chunk theorists see a clear historical

---

ham, Md.: University Press of America, 1985), p. 130. See also Joseph R. Strayer, *On the Medieval Origins of the Modern State* (Princeton: Princeton University Press, 1970), pp. 58–59. Strayer observed: "[I]n a sense . . . wars were necessary to complete the development of a system of sovereign states. . . . [I]n 1300 it was not clear who was independent and who was not, and it was difficult to draw definite boundaries in a Europe which had known only overlapping spheres of influence and fluctuating frontier zones."

63. Some who refer to variable sovereignty are focusing upon just what sovereignty implies for states that are generally acknowledged to be sovereign. These thinkers are concerned with variations in the contents of each sovereign state's basket of rights and duties. Henceforth we will refer to this form of variable sovereignty as "lesser sovereignty."

64. Another group that refers to variable sovereignty is speaking of political entities that have never been recognized as sovereign. These communities, a range of political entities emerging from colonialism more or less quickly, have attained varying degrees of independence. They are in an intermediate stage of life in the international community, encumbered by some substantial relationship to another power. Henceforth we will refer to this second form of variable sovereignty as "intermediate sovereignty."

65. For a similar criticism in a related context, see Robert H. Jackson and Carl G. Rosberg, "Why Africa's Weak States Persist: The Empirical and the Juridical in Statehood," *World Politics* 35 (1982): 4.

trend toward an international community made up of a multiplicity of full-fledged sovereign units.

We focus our attention next on how sovereignty has been applied in actual circumstances, and we analyze the rivalry that has long characterized the chunk and basket approaches. The evidence in Chapter 4 is thus directly relevant to one possible objection to our theoretical framework. Some readers might be inclined to argue that the chunk and basket theories do not conflict so much as they merely express two different aspects of sovereignty, with the status of sovereign statehood equated with the chunk approach and the bundle of recognized rights that are common to sovereign states equated with the basket approach. To determine whether that is the case, one must attend carefully to the manner in which sovereignty has been applied in practice to actual international disputes and assess whether adherents to each approach have not directly con-flicted with one another in the course of grappling with various international issues. In our view a fair reading of the evidence lays to rest the notion that the chunk and basket schools of thought may accurately be thought of as complementary rather than as in opposition.

4

How Is Sovereignty Applied in Practice?

A word is not a crystal, transparent and unchanged. [I]t is the skin of a living thought and may vary greatly in color and content according to the circumstances and the time in which it is used.

—Oliver Wendell Holmes, Jr.[1]

How scholars theorize about sovereignty should be grounded firmly in the ways in which international practitioners actually use the concept. Diplomats and politicians, jurists and arbiters, government officials and military leaders, and many others who are involved in international relations must often apply the concept of sovereignty to international issues. Yet, for all the frequency with which this term arises, those active in international relations remain deeply divided in the manner in which they make use of the idea.

The prior chapter argued that people today tend to view sovereignty either in absolute terms, as something that may be won or lost, or in variable terms, as something that may be increased or reduced. In metaphorical terms some conceive of sovereignty as a

---

1. *Towne v Eisner*, 245 US 372, 376 (1918), cited in W. Michael Reisman, "Sovereignty and Human Rights in Contemporary International Law," *American Journal of International Law* (hereafter *AJIL*) 84 (1990): 872–73.

chunk; others approach it in terms of a basket. The chunk thinkers assume that states, by virtue of their sovereign status, possess a set of identical rights and obligations. The basket thinkers are persuaded that sovereignty confers somewhat different rights and imposes somewhat different duties upon more and less powerful states.

Continuing discord between the chunk and basket theories of sovereignty marks the history of international sovereignty disputes. This conflict may be analyzed in court proceedings, in the lease of territory from one state to another, in the venerable concept of international servitudes, in foreign military occupation and dictated treaty terms, in external interference regarding national minorities, and in a range of political relationships among more and less powerful states.

International Legal Proceedings

Nationality Decrees in Tunis and Morocco

One contest between the chunk and basket approaches occurred in a 1923 proceeding before the Permanent Court of International Justice concerning nationality decrees in the kingdoms of Tunis and of Morocco, both then French protectorates.[2] France had enacted legislation that deemed certain categories of people in its protectorates to be French nationals.[3] French laws encumbered such individuals with certain duties such as military service. Some of these people, however, considered themselves British subjects under British law. On account of the conflicting laws Great Britain objected to the French legislation before the Council of the League of Nations. In response, France simply pointed to its sovereignty and denied that the council had jurisdiction to resolve the dispute.

2. *Nationality Decrees Issued in Tunis and Morocco* [Gr. Br./Fr.], *Permanent Court of International Justice Publications* (Ser. B.), No. 4, at 6 (1923) (Adv. Op.).

3. The first article of the decree issued by the president of the French Republic read: "Every person born in the Regency of Tunis of parents of whom one, justiciable as a foreigner in the French Courts of the Protectorate, was also born there, is French" (ibid., p. 6).

The PCIJ eventually issued an advisory opinion on the council's authority to consider the issue.

In *Nationality Decrees in Tunis and Morocco* the World Court's advisory opinion favored Great Britain. French sovereignty normally would allow France to enact whatever laws it pleased. Any questions arising under such laws would be matters of solely domestic jurisdiction. Hence, no international body would be clothed with authority to decide the case. In *Tunis and Morocco*, however, relevant international agreements restricted France's right to sovereign discretion in lawmaking. Consequently, the court upheld the British view that the Council of the League of Nations was indeed competent to hear the case. The PCIJ opinion read: "The question of whether a certain matter is or is not solely within the jurisdiction of a state is an essentially relative question; it depends upon the development of international relations."[4]

Basket thinkers would conclude that the *Tunis and Morocco* court viewed sovereignty as a shifting, rather than a fixed, quantity. The court reasoned that through signing treaties a state may be restricting its sovereign rights. Consequently, the contents of each state's basket of rights will differ depending upon that state's particular treaty obligations. Sovereignty is thus conceived theoretically in variable rather than absolute terms. From this perspective the World Court confirmed that the meaning of sovereignty will indeed differ from one sovereign state to another and for each sovereign state over time.

Those approaching sovereignty from the chunk perspective could respond by distinguishing between different types of legal obligations. Hans Morgenthau, for instance, once wrote: "A state can take upon itself any quantity of legal restraints and still remain sovereign, provided those legal restraints do not affect its quality as the supreme law-giving and law-enforcing authority. But one single legal stipulation affecting that authority is in itself sufficient to destroy the sovereignty of the state."[5]

In this tradition the chunk theorists reason that states receive basic international rights by virtue of their sovereign status. In

---

4. Manley O. Hudson, ed., *World Court Reports* (Washington, D.C.: Carnegie Endowment for International Peace, 1934), 1:156.

5. Hans J. Morgenthau, *Politics Among Nations: The Struggle for Power and Peace* (New York: Alfred A. Knopf, 1948), p. 247.

exercising their independent sovereign discretion, states are free to sign treaties that circumscribe those rights.[6] For example, a state signing a nuclear nonproliferation treaty restricts its right to build whatever weapons might be thought necessary to provide for its defense.[7] Thus, the chunk approach, focusing on sovereignty as a legal status that is either present or absent, does not dispute that different countries have different baskets of rights. The chunk school disputes only the notion that it is sovereignty that confers those different sets of sovereign rights. The chunk thinkers believe that, so long as its legal supremacy remains sacrosanct, sovereign status enables a state to circumscribe its rights as it pleases.[8]

Right of Passage over Indian Territory[9]

A similar tension between the chunk and basket approaches arose in a 1960 case before the International Court of Justice concerning a right of passage claimed by Portugal through the territory of India

6. Potentially, such treaties could go so far as to extinguish a state's sovereignty. Morgenthau argued that a state would no longer amount to the "supreme legal authority" if it granted to another state the right to veto its legislation or, more ambiguously perhaps, if it allowed the actual functions of government to be carried out by others. See ibid., p. 249. He wrote: "While . . . a state cannot lose its sovereignty by limiting its freedom of action through the conclusion of a great number of international treaties, it will have lost its sovereignty if its freedom of action no longer extends to those fundamental lawgiving and law-enforcing functions without which no government can under contemporary conditions maintain its authority within the national territory" (ibid., p. 252). Morgenthau may have had in mind Czechoslovakia's fate under the Munich agreement.

7. See United Nations, Treaty Series, "Treaty on the Non-Proliferation of Nuclear Weapons, signed at London, Moscow, and Washington," 1 July 1968, Treaties and International Agreements Registered or Filed and Recorded with the Secretariat of the United Nations (hereafter UNTS), vol. 729, no. 10485 (1968), pp. 161–75; United Nations, Treaty Series, "Treaty Banning Nuclear Weapons Tests in the Atmosphere, in Outer Space, and Under Water, signed at Moscow," 5 August 1963, UNTS, vol. 480, no. 6964 (1963), pp. 43–99.

8. These chunk theorists might well argue that they view sovereignty in terms of a chunk and a basket, not a chunk or a basket. Each state receives a chunk of rights and duties by virtue of its sovereign statehood. Thereafter, however, each state is free, in its sovereign discretion, to sign international agreements that chip away at particular rights. Consequently, the basket of one state will likely contain a slightly different chunk of rights and duties than the basket of another state.

9. Right of Passage over Indian Territory [Port. v. India], 1960 International Court of Justice Reports of Judgments, Advisory Opinions, and Orders (hereafter ICJ) 6 (Judgment).

to reach certain Portuguese enclaves. At that time Portugal had long possessed territories on the Indian subcontinent, which it had divided for administrative purposes into the districts of Goa, Diu, and Damão, each geographically separated from the others. While the district of Damão fronted on the Indian Ocean, it also included two enclaves, Dadrá and Nagar-Aveli, both of which were entirely surrounded by Indian territory.[10]

When Great Britain took sovereign control of the part of present-day India that surrounded these enclaves, the British chose not to challenge long-standing Portuguese assertions of sovereignty over these small communities. Rather than provoke a confrontation with Portugal, the British chose to countenance free passage both of Portuguese government officials and of private individuals and their goods from the port city of Damão to the enclaves. However, Portugal and Britain agreed that armed forces might not cross each other's territory unless the troops obtained permission or were engaged in a purpose enumerated in a treaty between the two states.[11]

In 1947 Great Britain transferred power to the Dominion of India, which became a sovereign republic; however, the traditionally Portuguese territories remained under the control of Portugal. Then, in 1954 rebels in Dadrá overthrew Portuguese authorities. Thereupon India refused Portugal's request for its officials to cross Indian territory in order to enter Dadrá and Nagar-Aveli. India justified its actions by citing the evident tension in the surrounding Indian communities and concluded: "The passage of those officials across Indian territory might also lead to other undesireable consequences in view of the strong feelings which have been aroused by the repressive actions of the Portuguese authorities."[12] With India's acquiescence Portugal took the dispute to the International Court of Justice for resolution.

When the World Court heard the case, lawyers for India argued—in the chunk tradition—that Indian sovereignty permitted the government to refuse passage across India's sovereign territory.

10. See F. A. Váli, *Servitudes of International Law: A Study of Rights in Foreign Territory*, 2d ed. rev. (New York: Frederick A. Praeger, 1958), p. 123.

11. "Treaty of Commerce and Extradition between Great Britain and Portugal, signed at Lisbon, 26 December 1878," *The Consolidated Treaty Series* (hereafter CTS), ed. Clive Parry, vol. 154, 1878–79 (Dobbs Ferry, N.Y.: Oceana Publications, 1980), p. 86.

12. *Right of Passage over Indian Territory*, at 43.

Control of territory, after all, is thought to be inherent in sovereignty. Portuguese lawyers conceded that India was sovereign in the territory to which Portugal claimed the right of passage. However, they declared that the right of passage had been absolutely necessary for Portugal to exercise *its* sovereignty in the enclaves. Further, India had customarily permitted passage and had honored the terms of the treaties that had delineated the right of passage. On account of that behavior, the Portuguese lawyers concluded, India's basket no longer included the right to refuse passage across its territory. In essence Portugal argued that while sovereignty customarily implies control by a state over matters within its sovereign territory, that state's behavior, coupled with treaties that it has signed, can circumscribe that control.

The ICJ proved receptive to the basket approach to sovereignty. Since passage into the enclave had been accepted as law by India and Portugal, the World Court reasoned that Portugal did have a right of passage across the sovereign territory of India with regard to private persons and their goods and to civil officials, subject to regulation by India. However, Portugal's traditional right had never extended to the passage of its armed forces or police and their ammunition. For those matters Portugal had always been obligated to obtain India's permission to cross its territory, permission that India could freely withhold. The ICJ thus ruled that, even though a right of passage did exist, under the particular circumstances of this case India had not acted contrary to its obligations.

In sum, although Portugal did persuade the court that the basket theory of sovereignty was to be preferred to the chunk theory advanced by India, India persuaded the court that its basket of sovereign rights still included the right to refuse passage to Portuguese armed authorities. Once again, the chunk and basket theories had conflicted, forcing an international court to choose one over the other in settling a serious dispute.

The Lease of Territory

Since at least the Treaty of Poona in 1779,[13] governments have decided, from time to time, to lease some portion of their territory

13. In the Treaty of Poona of 1779 the Maratha ruler in present-day India granted to the Portuguese a "revenue tenure" over several villages (ibid., pp. 37–38).

to another state. The lessor-lessee relationship can turn traditional notions of sovereign statehood on their head. First, a powerful state can sometimes compel a weaker country to sign a lease and thereby relinquish its exclusive control over all the territory within its boundaries. In addition, a powerful lessee state may be entirely unwilling, or at least exceedingly reluctant, to allow a weaker lessor state to exercise the power of eminent domain.[14] Both instances serve to highlight how chunk and basket thinking is often at odds.

Under the Hay-Varilla Treaty of 1903 Panama granted to the United States "in perpetuity the use, occupation and control of a zone of land and . . . water for the construction, maintenance, operation, sanitation and protection" of the Panama Canal.[15] The ten-mile-wide Canal Zone extended across the isthmus and three marine miles both into the Caribbean Sea to the east and into the Pacific Ocean to the west.[16] Within the Canal Zone Panama granted to the United States all the rights, power, and authority "which the United States would possess if it were the sovereign of the territory . . . to the entire exclusion of the exercise by the Republic of Panama of any such sovereign rights, power or authority."[17]

However, determining just what Panama's ultimate sovereignty over the Canal Zone has implied for the contents of Panama's basket of sovereign rights and duties has proved to be an elusive task for jurists of both countries. On several occasions American courts ruled that the lease of territory did not extinguish, or even diminish, Panamanian sovereignty over the Canal Zone.[18] However, after

14. According to one authority, "the right of eminent domain is the right of the state . . . to reassert, either temporarily or permanently, its dominion over any portion of the soil of the state on account of public exigency and for the public good. . . . Eminent domain is the highest and most exact idea of property remaining in the government, or in the aggregate body of the people in their sovereign capacity." *Black's Law Dictionary: Definitions of Terms and Phrases of American and English Jurisprudence, Ancient and Modern*, 5th ed. rev. (St. Paul, Minn.: West Publishing Co., 1979), p. 470.

15. See Váli, *Servitudes of International Law*, p. 254.

16. The General Treaty of Friendship and Co-operation signed by Panama and the United States in 1936 slightly altered the geographical extent of the Canal Zone. More important, the United States renounced the idea of perpetual control of the Zone. See ibid., p. 255.

17. Ibid., p. 254. Váli observed: "The rights of the United States in the Panama Canal Zone offer an example of the most complete transfer of jurisdiction over a territory without its being a cession in the technical international law sense. . . . Outwardly, the United States acts and appears as the sovereign of the Canal Zone. It has all the rights except one: the right of disposition over territory." Ibid., pp. 254–55.

18. See *Canal Zone v Coulson*, 1 *Canal Zone Supreme Court Reports* 50 (1907), in

several cases raised the issue of whether alleged criminals might appropriately be extradited to or from the Zone, the Supreme Court of Panama held that the country's extradition treaty with the United States failed to apply since the Canal Zone "does not form part of the territory of the United States of America."[19] Shortly thereafter the same court ruled that the marriage of two Panamanians in the Canal Zone is "deemed to have taken place abroad."[20] Nevertheless, later that same decade the Panamanian Supreme Court decided that the air space above the Zone was subject to Panama's jurisdiction. On the basis of this record one authority concluded: "[I]n some respects the Canal Zone is considered foreign territory, and in other respects not foreign territory, from the Panamanian point of view."[21]

The legal and political issues regarding the effect of the Canal Zone on the territorial sovereignty of Panama may be clarified through the chunk and basket approaches to the concept. Does the existence of the Canal Zone in any way diminish Panamanian sovereignty? A member of the chunk school of thought would conclude that it does not: Panama remains sovereign despite having opted to lease a large portion of territory to a stronger power. Indeed, a chunk theorist might argue that the Panamanian government, exercising its sovereign discretion, freely chose to assume the lessor-lessee relationship with the United States. With the passage of time Panama attempted merely to alter, not to repudiate, the treaties establishing that relationship.

Cases and Other Materials on International Law, ed. Manley O. Hudson (St. Paul, Minn.: West Publishing Co., 1929), pp. 397–400, cited in Váli, Servitudes of International Law, 255 n. 6. The Supreme Court of the Canal Zone observed: "It is apparent from an examination of the treaty that the United States is not the owner in fee of the Canal Zone, but has the use, occupation and control of the same in perpetuity as long as they comply with the terms of the treaty and pay the $250,000 in gold coin, per annum, of the United States to the Republic of Panama." Hudson, ed., Cases and Other Materials on International Law, p. 399. See also Ingrid DeLupis, International Law and the Independent State (New York: Crane, Russak and Co., 1974), pp. 214–15, and Ian Brownlie, Principles of Public International Law (Oxford: Clarendon Press, 1979), pp. 116–17.

19. See Re Burriel, Case No. 53, The Annual Digest of Public International Law Cases (hereafter cited ADPILC), 1931–32 (Supreme Court of Panama, 20 June 1931), and Re Bartlett, Case No. 51, ADPILC, 1929–30 (Supreme Court of Panama, 17 February 1930). Both cases were cited in Váli, Servitudes of International Law, p. 261.

20. Lowe v Lee, Case No. 44, ADPILC, 1933–34 (Supreme Court of Panama, 2 January 1934), cited in Váli, Servitudes of International Law, p. 261.

21. Váli, Servitudes of International Law, p. 262.

Such a formalistic interpretation of Panamanian history is likely to disturb many who hail from the basket way of thinking. Focusing not on theoretical, juridical equality but on the actual power differences of each party, a basket theorist might argue that shortly after Panama depended upon American military protection to break away from Colombia the newly sovereign state accepted a basket of sovereign attributes that lacked a critical component: the exclusive control of all of its land surface. The Canal Zone has always derogated from Panamanian sovereignty since a more powerful state compelled a weaker country to relinquish its sovereign control over territory. Through the years the international community has repeatedly endorsed Panamanian sovereignty, yet the country's basket of rights will have differed from those of its neighbors for nearly one hundred years.[22] To the basket theorist the Panama Canal Zone illustrates how the meaning of sovereignty has long differed for a great power and a fledgling republic dependent on outside assistance for its very survival.

After the initial government of the new sovereign state of Cuba leased land to the United States, the chunk and basket approaches to sovereignty collided somewhat differently. In 1903 the Cuban government agreed by a treaty, ratified in 1939, to lease territory around Guantánamo Bay for an American coaling station and naval base.[23] In return, the United States was to pay the Cuban govern-

22. During the Panama Canal negotiations in 1978 Senator Dennis DeConcini attempted to revive the Platt amendment philosophy by demanding that the Neutrality Treaty include an amendment specifically authorizing the United States to intervene in Panama with whatever measures might be deemed necessary to keep the canal open and operating in the face of external or internal threats. See Cyrus Vance, *Hard Choices: Critical Years in America's Foreign Policy* (New York: Simon & Schuster, 1983), pp. 153–54.

23. "Agreement for the Lease to the United States of Lands in Cuba for Coaling and Naval Stations, 23 February 1903," *Treaties, Conventions, International Acts, Protocols, and Agreements between the United States of America and Other Powers, 1776–1909* (hereafter *TCIAUS*), ed. W. M. Malloy, vol. 1 of 2 (Washington, D.C.: U.S. Government Printing Office, 1910), pp. 358–59. The agreement stated: "The Republic of Cuba hereby leases to the United States, for the time required for the purposes of coaling and naval stations, the following described areas of land and water situated in the Island of Cuba. . . ." Article III further specified: "While on the one hand the United States recognizes the continuance of the ultimate sovereignty of the Republic of Cuba over the above described areas of land and water, on the other hand the Republic of Cuba consents that during the period of occupation by the United States of said areas under the terms of this agreement the United States shall exercise complete jurisdiction and control over and within said areas with the right to acquire (under certain conditions to

ment two thousand dollars annually.[24] Although both parties seemed content with this arrangement for some years, the 1959 communist revolution on the island dramatically changed the Cuban government's perspective.

For the Fidel Castro regime the American base took on a hostile and menacing aspect. Since Castro came to power on January 1, 1959, the United States has continued to send Cuba the annual lease payment. However, the Cuban leader has repeatedly denounced the presence of more than six thousand American military personnel on his island. He has reportedly cashed only the first check and has demanded that the United States withdraw its troops.[25] Yet despite the protests of the Castro government, and despite the vindication of the sovereign right to eminent domain in other circumstances,[26] the United States has refused to surrender control of the military base. A basket thinker might conclude that a lessor state in the position of Cuba in fact enjoys a basket containing fewer sovereign rights than does the basket of a great power that is unlikely to have foreign military bases on its territory in the first place and that could forcibly eject foreign soldiers if necessary.

---

be hereafter agreed by the two Governments) for the public purposes of the United States any land or other property therein by purchase or by exercise of eminent domain with full compensation to the owners thereof." See also discussion in Váli, *Servitudes of International Law*, pp. 226–28.

24. See "Lease to the United States by Cuba of Land and Water for Naval or Coaling Stations in Guantánamo and Bahia Honda, 2 July 1903," *TCIAUS*, ed. W. M. Malloy, vol. 1 of 2 (Washington, D.C.: U.S. Government Printing Office, 1910), pp. 360–61.

25. See "E.U. permanecerá en Guantánamo, a pesar de demandas de Fidel Castro," *La Prensa* (Panama), 24 September 1991, p. 3A.

26. The Suez Canal crisis affirmed the sovereign right of eminent domain. In July 1956 President Gamel Abdel Nasser announced that Egypt would nationalize the Suez Canal Company and compensate its shareholders. Great Britain, France, and the United States—whose ships frequently used the Canal and whose citizens comprised many of the shareholders—protested. Egypt had recognized that the Suez Canal formed an international waterway and, more arguably, had agreed not to alter the existing arrangement until 1968. In response, President Nasser noted that the nationalization decree concerned an Egyptian company, organized under Egyptian law, operating on Egyptian soil. After several months of negotiations and brief hostilities involving Anglo-French and Israeli forces, the foreign powers withdrew and Egypt's nationalization of the Canal Company stood. See Louis Henkin, *How Nations Behave: Law and Foreign Policy*, 2d ed. rev. (New York: Columbia University Press, 1979), p. 253 ("By nullifying all efforts to establish some permanent international control for the Canal, the Suez-Sinai affair helped confirm the right of a nation to exercise eminent domain within its territory, even as to property which had some international character, and even in the face of an undertaking not to do so").

Whereas the Panama Canal treaties, signed and ratified under the administrations of President Jimmy Carter and General Omar Torrijos of Panama, are likely to restore the Canal Zone and canal operations to unquestioned Panamanian control,[27] the hostility between Washington and Havana has prevented any similar negotiations aimed at restoring the Guantánamo area to Cuban hands. According to chunk theory sovereign status affirms the right to exclusive control of national territory. However, through its actions the United States government seems to have advanced a basket approach to the Guantánamo base issue. By refusing to allow Cuba to exercise eminent domain, the American government has underscored the idea that Cuba's basket of sovereign rights differs from those of other sovereign states. Thus, although the island's sovereign status is indisputable, Cuba's communist government has long lacked exclusive control over its national territory.

Similarly, one might argue that a basket approach to sovereignty long governed the relationships between China and various Western powers.[28] In the Sino-British Treaty of Nanking in 1842, after Britain's victory in the First Opium War, China ceded Hong Kong Island to Great Britain "in perpetuity."[29] Then, in the Convention of Beijing of 1860 after the Second Opium War the British acquired the tip of Kowloon Peninsula and Stonecutters Island in Hong Kong harbor.[30] In 1898, after yet another defeat—this time in the Sino-Japanese War of 1894 to 1895—the Chinese leased territory for naval bases to Germany (Kiaochow in Shandong Province), France

27. See generally William L. Furlong and Margaret E. Scranton, *The Dynamics of Foreign Policymaking: The President, the Congress, and the Panama Canal Treaties* (Boulder, Colo.: Westview Press, 1984); Howard Raiffa, *The Art and Science of Negotiation* (Cambridge, Mass.: The Belknap Press of Harvard University Press, 1985), pp. 166–86; Vance, *Hard Choices*, pp. 140–57; and Zbigniew Brzezinski, *Power and Principle: Memoirs of the National Security Adviser, 1977–1981* (New York: Farrar, Straus & Giroux, 1983), pp. 134–39.

28. For a succinct historical sketch of these territorial transactions see Kevin P. Lane, *Sovereignty and the Status Quo: The Historical Roots of China's Hong Kong Policy* (Boulder, Colo.: Westview Press, 1990), especially pp. 3–4. See also Peter Wesley-Smith, *Unequal Treaty 1898–1997: China, Great Britain, and Hong Kong's New Territories* (Hong Kong: Oxford University Press, 1980).

29. "Treaty between China and Great Britain, signed at Nanking, 29 August 1842," *CTS*, ed. Clive Parry, vol. 93, 1842 (Dobbs Ferry, N.Y.: Oceana Publications, 1980), p. 467.

30. "Convention of Friendship between China and Great Britain Signed at Peking, 24 October 1860," *CTS*, ed. Clive Parry, vol. 123, 1860–61 (Dobbs Ferry, N.Y.: Oceana Publications, 1980), p. 73.

(Kwangchouwan opposite Hainan Island), Russia (Port Arthur and Dalny on the Laiodong Peninsula), and Great Britain (Weihaiwei across the Chihli Gulf from Port Arthur).[31] Finally, in the Convention of Beijing in 1898 China agreed to lease to Britain more than 370 square miles of land, including a much larger portion of Kowloon Peninsula, 235 islands, and 2 bays.[32]

Western states also compelled China to set aside residential areas in Chinese ports for foreigners. The Chinese eventually granted to nine foreign powers thirty-six "concessions": territories that were leased to the foreign state in perpetuity to be sublet to its residents.[33] In those areas foreigners were responsible for their own local administration regarding such matters as roads, sanitation, taxation, police protection, and building regulations.[34] Indeed, the Western diplomatic corps provided for its own exclusive use of an area "in which Chinese shall not have the right to reside and which may be made defensible."[35]

Throughout China citizens of Western powers enjoyed an expansive interpretation of the principle of extraterritoriality that allowed their national courts to exercise jurisdiction over any offense their nationals might be alleged to have committed in China.[36] This essentially exempted foreigners from Chinese criminal law. Equally significant, in the leased territories the Western powers razed Chinese forts, stationed their own military and police contingents,

---

31. Lane, *Sovereignty and the Status Quo*, pp. 3–4. See also Quincy Wright, *The Existing Legal Situation as it Relates to the Conflict in the Far East* (New York: Institute of Pacific Relations, 1939), pp. 36, 68–69.

32. "Convention between China and Great Britain respecting an Extension of Hong Kong Territory, signed at Peking, 9 June 1898," CTS, ed. Clive Parry, vol. 186, 1897–98 (Dobbs Ferry, N.Y.: Oceana Publications, 1980), p. 310.

33. Wright, *Existing Legal Situation*, p. 71.

34. Ibid., p. 70, citing Westel W. Willoughby, *Foreign Rights and Interests in China*, 2 vols. (Baltimore: Johns Hopkins University Press, 1927), 1:500–503.

35. See Article VII of the Boxer Protocol of 1901, cited in Wright, *Existing Legal Situation*, p. 72.

36. See Article XXI of the Sino-American Extraterritorial Treaties in the compilation of decisions of the United States Court for China, called *Extraterritorial Cases*, edited by Charles Sumner Lobingier, 2 vols. (Manila: Bureau of Printing, 1920), 1:1 ("[C]itizens of the United States who may commit any crime in China shall be subject to be tried and punished only by the Consul, or other public functionary of the United States, . . . according to the laws of the United States"). See also John V. A. MacMurray, *Treaties and Agreements with and Concerning China, 1894–1919* (New York: Oxford University Press, 1921), p. xiii, cited in Wright, *Existing Legal Situation*, p. 22.

and compelled the withdrawal of Chinese troops.[37] In 1915, as a culminating insult, Japan forced China to accede to the Twenty-One Demands: an effort that put much of Manchuria, eastern Inner Mongolia, and the Shandong Province under Japanese control.

At the time the unequal treaties were negotiated and put into effect, the international community had already recognized China's sovereign statehood. Western states had long signed treaties with Chinese emperors and had sent numerous diplomatic missions to be received in Beijing. The country had been invited to participate in various international conferences, including the Hague conferences of 1899 and 1907. Even the treaties establishing the concessions recognized China's ultimate sovereignty.[38] Consequently, the nationality of Chinese citizens living in the leased areas was not to be affected by the presence of the foreign power.[39] Nonetheless, the Western powers, intent on opening China to commerce, repeatedly failed to accord the Chinese government a monolithic chunk of sovereign rights the same as those enjoyed by other sovereign states.

Restrictions on the contents of their basket of sovereign rights long chafed Chinese officials and the Chinese people. Shortly after bowing to a Japanese ultimatum in May 1915, Yuan Shih-k'ai, president of the Chinese Republic after the abdication of Sun Yat-sen, declared: "Hereafter, no port, bay or island along the coast of China will be ceded or leased to any foreign country. The Ministries of War and Marine and the officials on the seacoast are hereby made responsible for defence of the same so that the sovereignty of the nation may be consolidated."[40]

During the Paris Peace Conference at the conclusion of World War I, China bid for a monolithic chunk of sovereign rights the same as those accorded other sovereign states.[41] In particular, China

37. Wright, *Existing Legal Situation*, pp. 74–75.

38. In 1921 the Chinese delegation at the Washington Conference declared: "Though the exercise of administrative rights over the territories leased was relinquished by China to the lessee power during the period of the lease, the sovereignty of China over them had been reserved in all cases. The leases were all creatures of compact, different from cessions both in fact and in law." Váli, *Servitudes of International Law*, p. 278.

39. Ibid., p. 277.

40. Lane, *Sovereignty and the Status Quo*, p. 18, citing MacMurray, *Treaties and Agreements*, p. 1,215.

41. Before the conference the Chinese government submitted a position paper stating: "[T]he Chinese Government hope that the interested Powers will, out of their sincere regard for the sovereign rights of China and the common interests of all nations having

attempted to exercise its right to eminent domain over the territories leased to other states, a right that had actually been written into certain of the treaties.[42] The Chinese delegation stated:

> As prolongation of the foreign control over leased territories constitutes a continual lordship, whose injurious effects tend from day to day to increase, the Chinese government feel in duty bound to ask for restitution of these territories, with the assurance that, in making their proposal, they are conscious of, and prepared to undertake, such obligations as the relinquishment of control may equitably entail on them as regards the protection of rights or property-owners therein and administration of the territories thus restored to the complete control of China.[43]

The Western powers declined to act on China's requests,[44] and China refused to sign the Treaty of Versailles.

In 1921 at the Washington Conference the Chinese delegation again requested other states to "respect and observe the territorial integrity and political and administrative independence of the Chinese Republic."[45] The Chinese delegation announced: "All special rights, privileges, immunities or commitments, whatever their

---

trade relations with her, make a declaration . . . to the effect that they have not any sphere of influence or interest in the Republic of China, nor intend to claim any; and that they are prepared to undertake a revision of such treaties, agreements, notes, or contracts previously concluded with her as . . . may be constructed to have conferred on them, . . . reserved territorial advantages or preferential rights or privileges to create spheres of influence or interest impairing the sovereign rights of China." See "Questions for Readjustment, Submitted by China to the Peace Conference," *The Chinese Social and Political Science Review* 5A (1920): 116. See also Lane, *Sovereignty and the Status Quo*, pp. 21–22.

42. See, for instance, Quincy Wright's discussion of the Sino-American Treaty of 1858, Article I of which stated: "[I]n making concessions to the citizens or subjects of foreign powers of the privilege of residing on certain tracts of land, or resorting to certain waters of that empire for purposes of trade, [the Chinese Emperor] . . . has by no means relinquished his right of eminent domain or dominion over said land and waters." Wright, *Existing Legal Situation*, p. 12.

43. Lane, *Sovereignty and the Status Quo*, p. 22, citing "Questions for Readjustment, Submitted by China to the Peace Conference," pp. 144–45.

44. France and Britain had secretly agreed to support Japan's policies in China. Lane, *Sovereignty and the Status Quo*, p. 22, citing Wesley R. Fishel, *The End of Extraterritoriality in China* (New York: Octagon Books, 1974), p. 38.

45. Lane, *Sovereignty and the Status Quo*, pp. 23–24.

character or contractual basis, claimed by any of the Powers in or relating to China are to be declared, and all such or future claims not so made known, are to be deemed null and void. . . . Immediately, or as soon as circumstances will permit, existing limitations upon China's political, jurisdictional and administrative freedom of action are to be removed."[46]

Despite the Chinese pleas and pronouncements the other powers at the Washington Conference refused to alter the existing arrangements in China. Rather, they stalled and attempted to placate the Chinese delegation by calling for a commission to investigate China's complaints. Four years later, when the commission finally convened, its representatives refused even to consider the issue of the territories leased to other states. Only after a series of bilateral discussions, starting with the Anglo-Chinese Treaty of 1930, did China begin to recover the leased territories.[47] Once begun, the slow process of recovering sovereignty would continue throughout the remainder of the century, with the Kowloon Peninsula and Hong Kong returning to China in 1997 and Macao in 1999.

While chunk theorists might remind us that sovereignty entails the power to make commitments—even commitments that circumscribe sovereign rights[48]—the basket school of thought might conclude that as a lessor state China's basket of sovereign rights differed markedly from that of the lessee states. Without incurring any comparable obligations the lessees used their superior military power to compel the Chinese government to accept the leased arrangements in order to further Western objectives of increasing commercial intercourse with China. Thereafter, the lessee states were long unwilling to allow the lessor to exercise the power of eminent domain. To the basket theorist the lack of any real reciprocity in the unequal treaties reveals the flaw in the chunk thinkers'

---

46. Ibid., p. 24.

47. Wright, *Existing Legal Situation*, p. 69.

48. One political scientist wrote: "[S]overeignty cannot be impaired by an international contract; the very making of the treaty is sufficient evidence of the possession of sovereignty by the contracting parties." See Helen Dwight Reid, *International Servitudes in Law and Practice* (Chicago: University of Chicago Press, 1932), p. 32. Similarly, in the *North Atlantic Coast Fisheries Arbitration* before the Permanent Court of Arbitration in 1910 Sir William Robson argued that international law allows a state "to limit the exercise of its own sovereign rights in certain particulars, without any detriment to its other sovereign rights or its general national sovereignty" (ibid., p. 31).

argument that China simply opted to circumscribe its sovereign rights.

Whether such treaty obligations do or do not imply limitations on a state's sovereignty depends upon whether one approaches the concept from the deductive, absolute view favored by the chunk school of thought or the inductive, variable view preferred by the basket thinkers. A chunk theorist would deny that treaties infringe on state sovereignty since "treaties are normally terminable and . . . the state, therefore, is in a position to resume its plenary power and cast off the treaty obligations. . . . [T]he voluntary assumption of treaty obligations should not be regarded as a limitation upon but rather as an expression of the state's sovereignty."[49]

Basket thinkers, however, not only question the voluntariness of such treaties but focus upon the notably unequal terms of many such agreements. Certain rights seem to be taken from the basket of one state and placed within the basket of another. Moreover, as one basket thinker concluded, "[T]he fact remains that, while they are in force, treaty obligations . . . frequently limit the freedom of action of states."[50] They conclude that when the chunk and basket approaches to sovereignty clash in a lessee-lessor relationship, the basket theory seems to describe more accurately how international relations is actually conducted.

The manner in which states have applied the concept of sovereignty to issues regarding the lease of territory thus nicely illustrates the clash of chunk and basket thinking. One scholar noted: "There are a number of international treaties whose object is to give to one State the right of administration, i.e., more or less complete exercise of jurisdiction, over a part of the territory of another State. . . . [W]hatever their name, they have one common feature: the sovereignty of the territorial State is expressly preserved while the exercise of sovereign rights is handed over to another State."[51] In such circumstances the two approaches to sovereignty contend with one another, and tangible consequences flow from the result of the engagement.

---

49. Hans Blix, *Sovereignty, Aggression, and Neutrality* (Stockholm: Amquist & Wiksell, 1970), p. 11. The reader should note that Blix, as a basket theorist, was merely characterizing a view that he questions.

50. Ibid.

51. Váli, *Servitudes of International Law*, p. 273.

International Servitudes

An international servitude has been defined as a "particular and localised restriction"[52] on territorial sovereignty. The term refers to a right held by one sovereign state to exercise some authority within the territory or the territorial seas of another sovereign state for a substantial period of time.[53] Sometimes the foreign state is entitled to carry out some action within the jurisdiction of another sovereign; at other times a sovereign state is obliged not to exercise some of its customary rights and duties within its own boundaries. While the beneficiaries of an international servitude may be the citizens of a state, the right belongs to one sovereign state (or, in rare cases, to an international organization) at the expense of another sovereign state.[54] Finally, to adopt the terminology of domestic property law in common law systems, an international servitude is said to "run with the land": that is, a state that succeeds to the territory burdened by the servitude is also obligated by it.[55]

Treaties between or among states abound with examples of international servitudes. For instance, states have often signed agreements permitting the fishermen of other states to fish within their territorial waters. Less frequently, states have allowed foreign fishermen to come ashore to dry and cure fish.[56] Similarly, states have often agreed to create rights of transit over their land or water for citizens of other states, as in the case between India and Portugal previously discussed.[57] Especially when steamships required coal-

---

52. Ibid., p. 20.

53. International lawyers differ on precisely how long the commitment must be designed to last in order to qualify as an international servitude. Some deny that a commitment for a period of years properly qualifies as a servitude. Others deny that the commitment must be "in perpetuity" but claim that it must nonetheless be "permanent": that is, while the treaty need not state that the commitment lasts forever, it must at least be open-ended and thus contemplate a perpetual undertaking. See discussion in Reid, *International Servitudes in Law and Practice*, pp. 19–21.

54. Ibid., p. 15.

55. Váli, *Servitudes of International Law*, p. 320.

56. See, for instance, "Definitive Treaty of Peace between Great Britain and the United States signed at Paris, 3 September 1789," *CTS*, ed. Clive Parry, vol. 48, 1781–83 (Dobbs Ferry, N.Y.: Oceana Publications, 1980), p. 492. See also Váli, *Servitudes of International Law*, pp. 72–73, and Reid, *International Servitudes in Law and Practice*, pp. 62–98.

57. See generally Váli, *Servitudes of International Law*, pp. 107–52, and Reid, *International Servitudes in Law and Practice*, pp. 167–76. The British-Belgian Conven-

ing stations, various governments have allowed foreign states to maintain coal deposits for naval and merchant fleets.[58] Indeed, states have occasionally granted to some other country rights over natural resources within their territories, whether pasture, timber, or minerals.[59] Even the seat of the United Nations amounts to an international servitude since the headquarters district in New York and the premises in Geneva are under the control and authority of the UN rather than of Switzerland or the United States.[60]

When confronted by issues relating to international servitudes, scholars and practitioners have once again split on how to apply the concept of sovereignty. In the chunk tradition one scholar asserted: "[S]ervitudes do not derogate from [a state's] . . . sovereignty, and, indeed, cannot do so. The very existence of the grant is conclusive evidence of their possession of the power to make it."[61] She continued: "The term . . . seems to the lay mind to connote a servile relationship, thereby creating a false impression at the

tion of 1921 contained a particularly broad example of such rights. Article 2 provided: "Great Britain undertakes to grant freedom of transit across East Africa by the routes which are or will be most adapted for transit, either by railway, lake, navigable watercourse, or canal, to all persons, to mails, to all goods, ships, railway carriages and trucks, coming from or proceeding to, the Belgian Congo, and for the purpose, passage through territorial waters will be permitted. . . ." League of Nations, Treaty Series, "Convention between Great Britain and Belgium with a View to Facilitating Belgian Traffic Through the Territories of East Africa, signed at London," 15 March 1921, Société des Nations 5, no. 138 (1921), pp. 319–27.

58. For an example see "Treaty between Germany and Spain confirming the Cession of the Carolines etc., signed at Madrid, 30 June 1899," CTS, ed. Clive Parry, vol. 187, 1898–99 (Dobbs Ferry, N.Y.: Oceana Publications, 1980), p. 375. Article III stated: "Spain will be allowed to establish and to keep, even in time of war, deposits of coal for her war and merchant fleets: one in the archipelago of the Carolines, another in the archipelago of the Pellew Islands, and a third in the archipelago of the Mariana Islands."

59. See Váli, Servitudes of International Law, pp. 182–92.

60. Section 9 of the Headquarters Agreement provided: "The headquarters district shall be inviolable. Federal, state or local . . . officials of the United States, whether administrative, judicial, military, or police, shall not enter the headquarters district to perform any official duties therein except with the consent of and under any conditions agreed to by the Secretary-General." United Nations, Treaty Series, "Agreement between the United Nations and the United States of America Regarding the Headquarters of the United Nations, signed at Lake Success," 26 June 1947, UNTS, vol. 11, no. 147 (1947), pp. 11–41. See also United Nations, Treaty Series, "Interim Arrangement on Privileges and Immunities of the United Nations concluded between the Secretary-General of the United Nations and the Swiss Federal Council," 11 June 1946 (Berne) and 1 July 1946 (New York), UNTS, vol. 1, no. 8 (1947), pp. 163–80.

61. Reid, International Servitudes in Law and Practice, p. xxi.

outset, for the servitude actually involves neither active service, nor subjection, but merely a grant of permission to make use of a state's resources; or an agreement to refrain from using its own territory to the disadvantage of another state."[62]

Other authorities, however, view international servitudes rather differently. In 1914 the Supreme Court of Cologne seemed to adopt a basket approach to a curious dispute involving an international servitude. The Prusso-Netherlands boundary treaty of 1816 transferred sovereignty over certain districts on the German-Dutch frontier to Prussia. However, Article 19 acknowledged that a coal mine in one of the districts had long belonged to the Abbey of Rolduc. Consequently, the treaty specified that the Dutch government retained the authority to continue mining coal. The treaty further declared: "Neither under the pretext of instructions issued to its engineers, nor by imposts or other burdens, may the Government of Prussia interfere with or restrict the mining of coal or the bringing of coal mined to the surface, nor may it place any hindrance in the way of its being marketed."[63]

In 1914 a legal dispute arose when a homeowner, living in German territory, claimed that the Dutch government mine had damaged his houses and that its operator, the Aix-la-Chapelle–Maastricht Railway Company, owed him compensation. Eventually the Supreme Court of Cologne ruled: "[U]nder the boundary treaty between Prussia and the Netherlands . . . by which the territorial sovereignty of the two neighboring states was mutually defined, . . . [p]arts of the districts of Kerkrade and Rolduc go to Prussia, but the Dutch Government retains the right to carry on mining in the ceded parts."[64] The majority opinion continued:

> This means . . . the exclusion of certain sovereign rights resulting from territorial sovereignty in the ceded parts. In so far as the right to mine coal and other minerals contained in

62. Ibid., p. 20.

63. "Boundary Treaty between the Netherlands and Prussia, signed at Aix-la-Chapelle, 26 June 1816," CTS, ed. Clive Parry, vol. 66, 1816–17 (Dobbs Ferry, N.Y.: Oceana Publications, 1980), pp. 194–95. See also Váli, Servitudes of International Law, p. 182.

64. Aix-la-Chapelle–Maastricht R.R. Co. v Thewis, 8 Zeitschrift für Völkerrecht (1914, Heft 4/5), reprinted in AJIL 8 (1914): 907–13 (Supreme Court of Cologne, VII Civil Div., 21 April 1914). (The Royal Dutch Government was a third-party intervenor in the case.)

this coal-field comes into question, part of this territorial sovereignty remains in Holland. . . . [A] sort of international servitude has arisen by which Holland is as a State entitled . . . in the matter of this mine, to exercise its own legislative authority and police supervision; that is, it has real sovereign rights with respect to the object situated within the territory of the foreign state.[65]

A basket theorist would conclude that the German court held, in effect, that Prussia's basket of sovereign rights did not include police supervision and other government authority over the Dutch mine. The treaty of 1816 had dictated that those sovereign rights belonged in the Dutch basket, not the Prussian basket.

As these examples illustrate, the field of international servitudes amounts to yet another area in which relations between states demonstrate how the chunk and basket approaches to sovereignty contend with one another. An adherent to the chunk theory would maintain that states possess a set of identical rights and obligations by the fact of their sovereignty, however they may decide to alienate certain of those rights over time. A proponent of the basket theory would argue that international servitudes, once again, reveal the variable nature of the concept: a state can be more sovereign or less sovereign depending upon the contents of its particular basket.

Foreign Military Occupation and Dictated Treaty Terms

When military forces occupy a foreign country and dictate treaty terms to a surrendered foe, the notion of sovereignty as a monolithic chunk, typically claimed by the losers, is often subverted by a basket approach more in keeping with the victor's objectives. Once again proponents of the two views clash on theoretical grounds.

In describing the essence of sovereignty, chunk thinker Hans Morgenthau observed: "The individual state has the right to give itself any constitution it pleases, to enact whatever laws it wishes

---

65. Váli, *Servitudes of International Law*, pp. 183–84.

regardless of their effect upon its own citizens, and to choose any form of administration."[66] In the twentieth century, however, victorious powers have repeatedly chosen not to subjugate and annex defeated states but to extract a favorable agreement and install a puppet government or, at least, a friendly regime. The basket thinker would conclude that the terms of these agreements often result in a type of lesser sovereignty. In such postwar agreements a state forfeits what has long been considered a fundamental sovereign right by restricting its weapons, fortifications, and armed forces, or by accepting a particular political ideology, imposed by outsiders.[67]

Given these relatively common encroachments on sovereign rule, one might ask, does a defeated state lacking in certain fundamental sovereign rights retain its sovereignty at all? Consider the case of Germany under Allied occupation. For administrative purposes the Allied Powers partitioned the German state into four zones: American, British, French, and Soviet. During the immediate postwar period Germany plainly did not possess a monolithic chunk of rights equal to those asserted by a powerful sovereign. The German state, however, continued to exist as a sovereign legal personality. During the occupation the international community attributed German territory to the German state and not to the Allied states that occupied it for the time being.[68]

A chunk thinker might propose that the international community tends to impute to defeated countries under foreign occupation a legal fiction of sovereignty. The belief seems to be that sovereign attributes comparable to those existing before the war will ultimately be recovered by the vanquished state. The basket thinker might advance a simpler explanation. If one examines how the concept of sovereignty was actually put into practice, the international community treated Germany in the immediate postwar period as a defeated sovereign state: one whose lack of influence resulted in a basket absent certain common sovereign rights. In this

---

66. Morgenthau, *Politics among Nations*, pp. 245–46.

67. Ibid., p. 248.

68. Brownlie, *Principles of Public International Law*, p. 111. For a discussion of French sovereignty during the Allied occupation of France in 1815 see Georg Schwarzenberger, "The Forms of Sovereignty," in *In Defense of Sovereignty*, ed. W. J. Stankiewicz (New York: Oxford University Press, 1969), p. 170.

view the postwar international community penalized occupied Germany and Japan by according those states a substantially diminished basket of sovereign rights, one markedly different from those enjoyed by the victors in the war.

Examples of such dictated peace treaty provisions abound. The cease-fire terms drawn up by the United Nations Security Council after the Persian Gulf War prohibited Iraq from taking various steps often thought to be the prerogative of a sovereign state, including acting to advance ballistic, biological, chemical, or nuclear weapons programs.[69] The Security Council not only ordered the Iraqi government to live up to its obligations under the Nuclear Non-Proliferation Treaty and the 1972 Convention on Biological and Toxin Weapons,[70] but it also forced Iraq to destroy all chemical weapons and all ballistic missiles with a range greater than 150 kilometers.[71] Although no convention or treaty bans the mere possession of such missiles or chemical weapons, the United Nations dictated those terms to Iraq without any evident concern for the monolithic chunk of rights to which some presume all sovereign states are entitled.[72] Moreover, the Security Council soon announced a "no-fly zone" over large portions of Iraqi territory that gravely restricted the military's ability to repress civilian opponents to the Saddam Hussein regime. And the international community applauded such

69. See "The Cease-Fire Resolution" in U.S. Congress, House, Committee on Foreign Affairs, *U.N. Security Council Resolutions on Iraq: Compliance and Implementation*, 101st Cong., 2d sess., 1992, p. 31, especially paragraphs 7–13. For an account of the origins and mechanisms of the sanctions against Iraq see Christopher C. Joyner, "Sanctions, Compliance, and International Law: Reflections on the United Nations' Experience Against Iraq," *Virginia Journal of International Law* 32 (1991): 1–46.

70. United Nations, Treaty Series, "Convention on the Prohibition of the Development, Production, and Stockpiling of Bacteriological (Biological) and Toxin Weapons and on Their Destruction," 10 April 1972, *UNTS*, vol. 1015, no. 14860 (1972), p. 163.

71. Security Council Resolution 687 reads: "Iraq shall unconditionally accept the destruction, removal, or rendering harmless, under international supervision, of: (a) All chemical and biological weapons and all stocks of agents and all related subsystems and components and all research, development, support and manufacturing facilities; (b) All ballistic missiles with a range greater than 150 kilometers and related major parts, and repair and production facilities." See U.S. Congress, House, Committee on Foreign Affairs, *U.N. Security Council Resolutions on Iraq*, p. 31.

72. Anthony Clark Arend, "The United Nations and the New World Order," *The Georgetown Law Journal* 81 (1993): 498. After pointing out that the 1925 Geneva Gas Protocol prohibits only the wartime *use* of gas, Arend observed that many signatories to the Protocol have reserved the right to retaliate with gas against a first use of gas by an adversary (ibid.).

dictated treaty terms with virtual unanimity. Basket theorists, of course, would take the UN treatment of Iraq as evidence that a defeated country often lacks the complement of sovereign rights enjoyed by the victors.

Once troops are withdrawn, treaty terms dictated by occupying forces may continue to cast doubt on the defeated country's exercise of full sovereign rights. During the American occupation of Japan, for instance, U.S. officials consciously constructed a liberal democratic political system and incorporated that system into the new Japanese Constitution of 1946.[73] Although the Japanese, if left to their own devices, might have created a comparable political regime, American pressure in the immediate postwar period wholly subverted Japan's freedom to choose its own form of government. While a sovereign state is supposed to be free to select whatever laws, constitution, and administrative system it pleases,[74] the United States withheld this sovereign right from Japan for a considerable period of time. And if Americans did impose the Japanese constitution on a defeated country, then Article 9 could be interpreted as a further derogation of sovereignty, since it denies to Japan the sovereign right to maintain an armed force to provide for the country's defense.

Analogous situations occasionally have arisen when a stronger power has dictated the contents of a constitution to a less powerful state just emerging from colonialism. The 1901 Platt amendment to the Cuban Constitution, inserted after the Spanish-American War, restricted the Cuban government's freedom of action by barring Cuba from relinquishing territorial control to any foreign power and from entering into any international treaty that would "tend to impair" its independence.[75] The amendment even granted the

73. See Takeshi Ishida and Ellis S. Krauss, "Democracy in Japan: Issues and Questions," in Democracy in Japan, ed. Takeshi Ishida and Ellis S. Krauss (Pittsburgh: University of Pittsburgh Press, 1989), pp. 9–10.

74. Morgenthau wrote, "The individual [sovereign] state has the right to give itself any constitution it pleases, to enact whatever laws it wishes regardless of their effects upon its own citizens, and to choose any system of administration." Morgenthau, Politics among Nations, pp. 245–46.

75. See Article I in "Agreement for the Lease to the United States of Lands in Cuba for Coaling and Naval Stations, 23 February 1903," TCIAUS, ed. W. M. Malloy, vol. 1 of 2 (Washington, D.C.: U.S. Government Printing Office, 1910), p. 362. Though the agreement does not directly confront this issue, the proscription against territorial

United States the right to intervene to preserve Cuban independence or to maintain a government adequate to protect life, property, and individual liberty.[76] Rather than acknowledging or affirming Cuban sovereignty, the provisions of the Platt amendment hearkened to the terms frequently imposed on commonwealth states or colonies.[77]

During the three decades in which the Platt amendment was in force the United States exercised its right to intervene from 1906 to 1909 when American troops actually occupied the island. The status of Cuban sovereignty during the occupation focuses attention on many of the same issues as those raised by the experiences of postwar Germany and Japan. But did Cuba properly qualify as a sovereign state during the remaining years between 1901 and 1934, years when Cuba was not occupied by American troops but was acting under the threat of intervention should the terms of the constitution be violated?

Some would say that during those years the Platt amendment cast into doubt Cuba's de jure independence. Others might hold that Cuba was indeed de facto independent regardless of the terms of the amendment. Yet, despite the fact that Cuba lacked certain fundamental rights commonly associated with sovereignty—most notably, the right to nonintervention in its affairs—Cuba's peers in the international community treated the government as a sovereign equal throughout the period the Platt amendment was in force.[78]

---

relinquishment by Cuba presumably did not apply to U.S. coaling and naval stations on the island.

76. Ibid. The amendment also stipulated that Cuba could not contract any public debts in sums beyond its ordinary revenue and that Cuba would sell territory to the United States for naval stations. The United States even compelled the Cuban government to provide urban sanitation to prevent recurring epidemics and diseases. See also "Treaty with Cuba Embodying the Platt Amendment, signed at Havana, 22 May 1903," *Documents of American History*, ed. Henry Steele Commager (Englewood Cliffs, N.J.: Prentice-Hall, 1973), 2:28.

77. For instance, the Tydings-McDuffie Act of 1934, which provided for Philippine independence after an interim commonwealth period, stated that the United States "would supervise foreign affairs and exercise supreme military control, that decisions by Philippine courts would be subject to review by the U.S. Supreme Court, and that the United States might intervene to preserve the Philippine government, protect life, property, and individual liberty and to discharge the governmental obligations as provided in the Constitution." Wright, *Existing Legal Situation*, p. 42 n. 21.

78. Hans Morgenthau pointed out that foreign interference and foreign influence are difficult to distinguish. Had the U.S. government chosen to establish permanent and

To the basket theorists this again suggests that the international community simply regarded Cuba as possessing a basket containing fewer sovereign rights than that enjoyed by a fully sovereign state. As in the case of the American occupation of Japan, the other members of the international community saw Cuba as having the sovereign status that brings with it a basket of rights and duties but accepted the reality that the Cuban basket lacked some of the constituent contents often associated with such a basket.

External Interference Regarding National Minorities

Efforts by a state or group of states to dictate how a country resolves issues regarding national minorities[79] also underscore the differences between chunk and basket thinking on sovereignty. One example occurred after World War I at the Paris Peace Conference discussions concerning the sovereignty of Poland. The virtuoso Polish pianist, Ignacy Jan Paderewski, then serving as his country's minister of foreign affairs, insisted that Polish sovereignty be conceived of as a monolithic chunk of rights and duties the same in content as the sovereignty of other states.

Under the prevailing circumstances, however, the Allies preferred to apply the basket theory of sovereignty. Allied leaders declared that since Poland lacked the attributes of a great power, certain rights accorded to other sovereign states would be excluded

---

complete control over the Cuban government, "Cuba would have been no more a sovereign state than were the Indian states under British domination." But when the United States subjected Cuban territory to military occupation from 1906 to 1909, "authority within the Cuban territory was exercised by the armed forces of the United States and not by the government of Cuba. The government of Cuba, therefore, was no longer sovereign." With debatable logic Morgenthau next argued that since the Cuban government was the supreme law-giving and law-enforcing authority in its territory after evacuation of American troops in 1909, Cuba had regained its sovereignty unless the United States intended to intervene. Morgenthau, *Politics among Nations*, p. 251.

79. We join Hurst Hannum in defining a "national minority" as "a numerically smaller, non-dominant group distinguished by shared ethnic, racial, religious, or linguistic" attributes. See Hurst Hannum, *Autonomy, Sovereignty, and Self-Determination: The Accommodation of Conflicting Rights* (Philadelphia: University of Pennsylvania Press, 1990), p. 50.

from the Poles' basket. On this basis the Allies imposed detailed regulations regarding how Poland should manage its minorities.[80] To a basket thinker the conclusion is plain that Poland accepted a basket containing fewer sovereign rights than those enjoyed by more powerful international counterparts.[81]

Similarly, when attempts to exercise a full complement of sovereign rights are likely to cause continuing trouble abroad, leaders sometimes search for a solution derived from basket theory. Consider the dispute between Austria and Italy regarding the inhabitants of the "Alto Adige": South Tyrol.[82] After World War I Italy took over this German-speaking region, once an integral part of the Hapsburg Empire. Various efforts to force the inhabitants to discard their German culture had the contrary effect of increasing local German nationalism. The German population in South Tyrol eventually appealed to Austria to intercede on its behalf with Italy.

Shortly after World War II Austria and Italy attempted to settle the matter through an agreement in which Italy pledged to safeguard the rights of ethnic Austrians and allow South Tyrol a degree of special autonomy.[83] After uneven implementation of this agreement and investigations by Italy and a mixed commission, the Council of Europe recommended that the issue be submitted to the International Court of Justice. However, perhaps because of fears that the ICJ would impose a chunk solution on a dispute that might be handled more flexibly through basket theory, Austria argued that the dispute concerned a political issue that ought to be resolved through negotiations.[84] In the South Tyrol Package of 1969 the two

80. The Austrian State Treaty, which redefined the borders of Austria after World War II, also included provisions protective of Slovene and Croat minorities (ibid., pp. 57–58).

81. Inis L. Claude, Jr., *National Minorities: An International Problem* (Cambridge, Mass.: Harvard University Press, 1955), p. 31.

82. The facts of the dispute are drawn primarily from the accounts found in Hannum, *Autonomy, Sovereignty, and Self-Determination*, pp. 432–40; Friedrich V. Kratochwil, Paul Rohrlich, and Harpreet Mahajan, *Peace and Disputed Sovereignty: Reflections on Conflict over Territory* (Lanham, Md.: University Press of America, 1985), pp. 130–31; and Philip C. Jessup, *The Price of International Justice* (New York: Columbia University Press, 1971), pp. 40–41. See also Antony E. Alcock, *The History of the South Tyrol Question* (London: Michael Joseph, 1970).

83. The Italian Constitution also offers special protection to linguistic and cultural minorities in the Valle d'Aosta, Friuli-Venezia Giulia, and Trentino-Alto Adige. See Hannum, *Autonomy, Sovereignty, and Self-Determination*, p. 68.

84. See Jessup, *The Price of International Justice*, pp. 40–41.

states ultimately agreed to more specific guarantees of autonomy, including permitting the use of the German language in schools, the media, and the local government, and access to official positions by South Tyroleans.[85]

Italy thus bound itself to govern in accordance with minority-rights provisions imposed after negotiations with a neighboring state. The chunk school would contend that Italy had indeed taken on a legal restriction, but not one that affected the country's supreme law-giving and law-enforcing capacity. A chunk thinker might find it perfectly natural that Italy thus exercised its sovereign decision-making capacity to resolve troublesome issues concerning the South Tyroleans. The basket school, however, would focus on how the Italian government responded to outside pressure by submitting to a diminution of the fundamental sovereign right to enact whatever laws it pleased. A basket thinker might argue that the result of the negotiations amounted to the Italians accepting a basket with fewer sovereign rights and more sovereign duties than many other states.

Such minority-rights provisions, inserted into agreements or treaties[86] or constitutions[87] after international negotiations, illustrate how the chunk and basket approaches to sovereignty can conflict in the practice of international affairs. Perhaps the most well known example occurred after World War I, when the League of Nations supervised a series of treaties focusing on the rights of national minorities in certain of the defeated powers and in various newly emerging states and territories. Many commentators criticized the treaties for applying only to the weak and defeated.[88] To basket thinkers such observations simply confirm their view that sovereignty is not applied uniformly to the powerful and the powerless.

85. In *Peace and Disputed Sovereignty* the authors conclude: "What is particularly significant . . . is that Italy acknowledged Austria's right to negotiate for a minority group situated in the polity of another state. Through bilateral agreements and multilateral resolutions jurisdictional matters traditionally regarded as under the purview of domestic affairs were recognized as a legitimate international concern. Kratochwil et al., p. 131.

86. For instance, the Treaty of Berlin of 1876 protected "the traditional rights and liberties" of the religious community located on Mount Athos in Greece. Hannum, *Autonomy, Sovereignty, and Self-Determination*, p. 51.

87. For example, Hannum points to the guarantees for Greek and Turkish minorities written into the Bulgarian Constitution of 1878 (ibid.).

88. Ibid., p. 54.

Restrictions on a state's ability to govern its people as it pleases are imposed on certain states but not on others.

A more recent example, parallel in certain respects, is the agreement by Great Britain to allow Hong Kong to revert to the People's Republic of China as a Special Administrative Region (SAR) enjoying rights and privileges different from those that apply to the remainder of the mainland. Since the people of Hong Kong are 98 percent Chinese, they will not constitute an ethnic minority after the planned return of the colony to China in 1997. However, Hong Kong's inhabitants will form a cultural minority, one that the terms of the reversion agreement attempt to protect.[89]

The secret negotiations between the United Kingdom and China concerning the future of Hong Kong, that resulted in what both sides have acknowledged is a binding international agreement, can be readily analyzed in terms of basket theory. While the British recognized that Chinese leaders were prepared to use force, if necessary, to reassert their sovereignty, and while the British were clearly in no position to defend Hong Kong for any extended period of time, the Chinese government proved receptive to compromising on just what rights the People's Republic might gain over Hong Kong's inhabitants.

Initially, British negotiators seem to have hoped that the People's Republic would accept continued British administration in exchange for the United Kingdom's formal recognition of China's sovereignty. The Chinese, however, proved unwilling to countenance any British presence after 1997. Nevertheless, China did agree to create a territorial zone that would cover Hong Kong and would guarantee its inhabitants certain special rights. The People's Republic agreed that for at least fifty years the Special Administrative Region would "enjoy a high degree of autonomy, except in foreign and defence affairs. . . ."[90]

---

89. We define culture as "the fundamental beliefs, opinions, and values of a given society, all of which are products of that society's specific historical experience." Julie Marie Bunck, *Fidel Castro and the Quest for a Revolutionary Culture in Cuba* (University Park: The Pennsylvania State University Press, 1994), p. xi. See also Hannum, *Autonomy, Sovereignty, and Self-Determination*, p. 124.

90. "Joint Declaration of the Government of the United Kingdom of Great Britain and Northern Ireland and the Government of the People's Republic of China on the Question of Hong Kong, initialed at Peking, 26 September 1984," *International Legal Materials* 23 (1984): 1371.

The Joint Declaration goes on to state that the SAR government will be composed of local inhabitants, including a democratically elected chief executive, and will be vested with executive, legislative, and independent judicial power, including that of final adjudication.[91] The Chinese even agreed that the social and economic systems now in place in Hong Kong would remain unchanged, as would the laws currently in force. Under the terms of the agreement the Hong Kong dollar will continue to circulate and remain freely convertible, and the PRC government will not levy taxes. In foreign affairs the SAR will be authorized to issue its own exit and entry travel documents. It will even be permitted to conclude its own agreements with states and international organizations.

The future of Hong Kong's Special Administrative Region is exceedingly difficult to forecast. As 1997 approaches, to what extent can the city's business community continue to thrive, even as the flight of nervous capitalists increases? After Hong Kong reverts to the PRC, will the communist regime attempt to subvert the protective provisions in the Joint Declaration? Will China eventually move to repress the inhabitants of Hong Kong, as Chinese authorities suppressed demonstrations in Tiananmen Square and in Tibet? Or will the economic attractions of a stable, prosperous Hong Kong provide the necessary incentive for the "one country, two systems" formula to succeed? Alternatively, how much longer can the People's Republic of China outlive the many communist regimes that have already expired? While answers to all of these questions are quite speculative, the sovereignty issues evident in the manner in which Britain and China decided to resolve the Hong Kong question remain instructive.

A chunk thinker might be inclined to focus upon how Hong Kong was not permitted independence. Indeed, Great Britain never seriously pressed on the Chinese the possible solution of granting Hong Kong's inhabitants a right to self-determination. Rather, even after a lengthy lease, China ultimately regained the sovereign control over Hong Kong that it had once voluntarily handed to Britain. To the chunk school the reversion of Hong Kong vindicates their view of leased territories as examples of the exercise of a state's sovereign will in creating a temporary state of affairs that casts

91. Ibid.

no doubt on the underlying sovereignty of the lessor state. The experience of Hong Kong thus foreshadows what the chunk school might expect to happen in Panama and Guantánamo as well.

A basket thinker might respond that the negotiations between Britain and China never developed into a discussion of how a monolithic chunk of rights and duties over Hong Kong was to be transferred from one power to another. Instead, the debate centered on the issue of which particular, typical sovereign rights would be excluded from China's basket. The Joint Declaration, then, represented the fruits of Great Britain's efforts to resolve a dispute over territorial sovereignty by influencing how the People's Republic will deal with political, social, and economic issues regarding its cultural minority—the Chinese people of Hong Kong. The proposed resolution envisions China enjoying a basket of rights in Hong Kong markedly different from that enjoyed by most great powers over a portion of their sovereign territory. The basket school would conclude that, once again, persons actively involved in grappling with a difficult international problem opted for a variable, rather than an absolute, approach to the concept.

State-To-State Political Relationships

The tension between the chunk and basket perspectives may also be examined both when a state exists within a larger power's sphere of influence and when a state opts for neutral status.[92] The arrangements of satellite, protectorate, association, condominium, colony, and perhaps even close ally may deprive a sovereign state in practice of certain attributes commonly associated with sovereign rule. For instance, a sovereign state is thought to have the right to make its own decisions about relationships with other states. As

92. In a lecture series delivered shortly after he served as viceroy to India, Britain's Lord Curzon stated that a "sphere of influence" implied "no exterior power but one may reassert itself in the territory so described." See ibid., p. 15, citing George Nathaniel (Lord) Curzon, Frontiers (Oxford: Clarendon Press, 1907), p. 42. The prospect of the Great Power reasserting itself within its sphere seems to suggest the basket thinking that characterized Great Britain's relations with the Raj during the colonial period. Compare Lord Curzon's formulation with that of Quincy Wright who distinguishes a "sphere of interest" from a "sphere of influence" in Wright, Existing Legal Situation, p. 78.

Morgenthau put it, "[The sovereign state] is free to have whatever kind of military establishment it deems necessary for the purpose of its foreign policy which, in turn, it is free to determine as it sees fit."[93] Yet to what extent did superpower satellites during the Cold War actually enjoy this sovereign right?[94]

In the Brezhnev Doctrine,[95] the Soviet Union claimed that Eastern bloc states retained the "sovereignty of restraint" of a satellite. The Soviets thus tried to modernize the concept of sovereignty to justify intervention in Hungary and Czechoslovakia and the exercise of substantial control over other satellites.[96] Similarly, some would conclude that during the invasion of Grenada both the Organization of Eastern Caribbean States and the United States acted on the assumption that Grenada lacked the sovereign right to determine its own form of government, a right enjoyed by more powerful and independent states.[97]

93. Morgenthau, *Politics among Nations*, p. 246.

94. See Thomas M. Franck and Edward Weisband, *Word Politics: Verbal Strategy Among the Superpowers* (New York: Oxford University Press, 1971), pp. 48–69. The authors noted: "In the Guatemalan and Cuban crises, two small nations of the Western [H]emisphere sought to exert a sovereign will that was perceived by the United States as inimical to its essential self-interest and to the collective policy of the Americas. In both instances, the small state pursued military policies that introduced Communist weapons into Latin America. In both cases, the United States, and with lesser enthusiasm, the Organization of American States, demanded an end to these policies and as a last resort used or facilitated the use of force to compel a change. Ibid., p. 48.

95. See ibid., pp. 33–47 ("[A]ccording to these concepts, any socialist country's sovereignty is invariably subject to the norms of the socialist community," p. 34).

96. Franck and Weisband argued: "By the . . . invasion [of Czechoslovakia], a set of principles, later known as the Brezhnev Doctrine, had been devised by Soviet strategists to justify their initiative. . . . In substance, they asserted that Czechoslovakia, being a 'Communist' state in the Eastern European 'commonwealth,' was subject to the norms and discipline of the regional grouping. The United States had previously established the very same principles, particularly in the Johnson Doctrine, as the basis for our relations with the states of our 'commonwealth'—the Western [H]emisphere. The Brezhnev Doctrine faithfully echoes official U.S. pronouncements made during the covert overthrow of the government of Guatemala, the Cuban missile crisis, and the invasion of the Dominican Republic." The authors concluded: "Thus the Soviets were able to claim, credibly, that the principles upon which they were acting were those we ourselves had devised to justify our conduct in the Americas, and that by our rhetoric we had implicitly signaled our consent to their application in the case of Czechoslovakia." Ibid., pp. 5–6.

97. It is interesting to compare the normative propositions drawn by Franck and Weisband from the Czechoslovakia invasion with the justifications advanced by Professor John Norton Moore of the University of Virginia School of Law for the American invasion of Grenada. Compare ibid., pp. 39–40, and John Norton Moore, *Law and the*

Repeated American interventions in Caribbean and Central American states, starting with the Big Stick policy of President Teddy Roosevelt, might also be taken as evidence of a basket approach to sovereignty. Franklin Knight wrote: "By the end of World War I the United States seemed to have a double standard for sovereignty, one applied to the European states and another to the neighboring states in the hemisphere. The Latin American response to the North American attitude was an insistence on state sovereignty as an absolute right."[98] Again, basket theory would counsel that Latin Americans failed to influence the United States toward a chunk approach to sovereignty and away from the basket conception that long prevailed among American policymakers. Indeed, U.S. intervention in Guatemala, the Dominican Republic, Chile, Nicaragua,[99] Grenada, Panama, and Haiti illustrates how policymakers across the mainstream American political spectrum adopted a basket approach to the sovereignty of America's southern neighbors, at least with regard to the principle of nonintervention in the internal matters of another sovereign state.

Other interesting sovereignty considerations arise when a state is neutralized.[100] Neutralization typically occurs after one or more powers have guaranteed continued independence and territorial

---

Grenada Mission (Charlottesville: University of Virginia, Center for Law and National Security, 1984).

98. Franklin W. Knight, "The State of Sovereignty and the Sovereignty of States," in *Americas: New Interpretive Essays*, ed. Alfred Stepan (New York: Oxford University Press, 1992), p. 20. In comparing the deference that American police officials showed toward the sovereignty of other countries in which they were operating, Ethan Nadelmann likewise observed: "Respect for foreign sovereignty has climbed noticeably in the domain of international law enforcement, albeit not so much that the Bahamas' sovereignty is given the same deference as Canada's." Ethan A. Nadelmann, *Cops across Borders: The Internationalization of U.S. Criminal Law Enforcement* (University Park: The Pennsylvania State University Press, 1993), p. 188.

99. Indeed, the Reagan administration's substantive legal arguments concerning the military and paramilitary activities the United States undertook against Nicaragua during its civil war amounted to a novel application of the notion of collective self-defense. See Louis B. Sohn, "The International Court of Justice and the Scope of the Right of Self-Defense and the Duty of Non-Intervention," in *International Law at a Time of Perplexity*, ed. Yoram Dinstein and Mala Tabory (Boston: Martinus Nijhoff, 1989), pp. 869–78. See also *Military and Paramilitary Activities in and against Nicaragua* [*Nicar. v US*], 1986 *ICJ* 6 (Judgment).

100. A comprehensive general work is Cyril E. Black, Richard A. Falk, Klaus Knorr, and Oran R. Young, *Neutralization and World Politics* (Princeton: Princeton University Press, 1968).

integrity to a state, subject to that state's pledge not to compromise its neutral status by such acts as taking up arms or joining alliances. Among the states that have been neutralized at some interval during their history are Switzerland (since 1815), the Vatican (since 1929), Austria (since 1955), Laos (1962–75),[101] Belgium (1839–1919), Luxembourg (1867–1940), and Honduras (1907–23).[102]

In certain cases the decision to take on neutral status highlights the tension between the chunk and basket approaches. For instance, European states led by Great Britain prevailed upon Belgium to accept neutralization in order to thwart French territorial expansion into the Low Countries. Belgium, however, "always tended to regard neutralization as an unjustified limitation on its sovereignty imposed as a condition of its independence."[103] A group of more powerful states compelled a weaker peer to accept neutralization by threatening to withhold recognition of sovereign status. This suggests that some neutralized sovereign states may have been deprived of the right to look after their national security[104] as their leaders saw fit. While a chunk theorist might dismiss such pressure tactics as simply the daily fare of international politics, a basket thinker might conclude that Belgium's basket of sovereign rights differed notably from those of its peers in the Concert of Europe.

Rather than accepting neutralization, some weak political entities have come under the formal protection of a greater power through

101. Laos accepted neutral status after a fourteen-state United Nations conference in 1961 to 1962. However, the rapid disintegration of coalition government in the country was followed by the war in neighboring Vietnam. Not only was Laotian air space repeatedly violated by the belligerents, but the United States dropped large quantities of bombs on suspected communist strongholds in the country.

102. See ibid., especially pp. 21–32. Over the years various nonstate actors have also been neutralized, including islands such as Malta, the Samoas, the Aalands, and the Ionians, and free cities and territories such as Cracow, Danzig, Trieste, Tangier, and the Rhineland. See ibid., pp. 31 and 33, and the discussions in Váli, *Servitudes of International Law*, pp. 263–72, and Hannum, *Autonomy, Sovereignty, and Self-Determination*, pp. 370–75 (Alands), 375–79 (Danzig), 400–406 (Cracow), and 400–406 (Trieste).

103. Black et al., *Neutralization and World Politics*, p. 25.

104. We join Inis Claude in defining national security as "the safety of a state—the ability of a state to survive, to maintain its territorial integrity and political independence, and to sustain the values to which its people are dedicated in the face of actual or potential external interference." Inis L. Claude, Jr., "Theoretical Approaches to National Security and World Order," in *National Security Law*, ed. John Norton Moore, Frederick S. Tipson, and Robert F. Turner (Durham, N.C.: Carolina Academic Press, 1990), p. 31.

a protectorate treaty. Others have accepted an association relationship in which an associated power takes sole responsibility for conducting the entire spectrum of the weaker state's foreign relations[105] and in which the greater power itself has the discretion to determine whether a particular issue is related to defense or external affairs.[106]

States with widely varying military physiques have participated in such relationships. In the heyday of colonialism Great Britain protected Tonga and Zanzibar, Japan protected Korea,[107] and France protected Tunisia and Morocco. Today, small powers like New Zealand, the Netherlands, and Switzerland have engaged in associations or protectorates with the Cook Islands, the Netherlands Antilles,[108] and Liechtenstein, respectively. And, of course, larger powers have also sustained such relationships, as the examples of France and Monaco, Great Britain and St. Kitts and Nevis,[109] and the United

105. See Hurst Hannum, "The Foreign Affairs Powers of Autonomous Regions," Nordic Journal of International Law 57 (1988): 273–88. Note that the government of the territory still retains control over internal affairs. See Alan James, Sovereign Statehood: The Basis of International Society (London: Allen & Unwin, 1986), p. 104.

106. See Thomas M. Franck, Control of Sea Resources by Semi-Autonomous States: Prevailing Legal Relationships between Metropolitan Governments and Their Overseas Commonwealths, Associated States, and Self-Governing Dependencies (Washington, D.C.: Carnegie Endowment for International Peace, 1978), pp. 7–8. Franck observed: "[Under the] West Indies Act . . . determination of whether a matter relates to defense and external affairs or is within the 'Peace, Order and Good Government' power of the government of the associated state is itself a matter reserved to the United Kingdom government." He further observed: "Section 7 (2) also gives the British government power to amend the laws of an associated state where that appears to it necessary 'in the interests of . . . defence and external affairs. . . .' A certification by the British secretary of state that a matter relates to defense or external affairs 'shall in any proceedings be conclusive evidence of the facts so certified.' " See also West Indies Act of 1967, 4 Halsbury's Statutes of England, 3d ed. rev., p. 611, especially chap. 4, sec. 1 (2).

107. Although Japan formally annexed Korea in 1910, for the preceding five years the Japanese had instituted a protectorate relationship over the country. During that period the Japanese succeeded in barring a Korean mission from attending the Hague Conference of 1907, presumably on the grounds that Korea was no longer a sovereign state. See Wright, Existing Legal Situation, 22 n. 8.

108. The Netherlands Antilles are composed of Aruba, Bonaire, Curaçao, and the Windward Islands.

109. Thomas Franck has compared the relative powers of Britain in its association relationships with Antigua, Dominica, St. Lucia, St. Kitts and Nevis, St. Vincent, and (originally) Grenada with the powers of New Zealand in Niue and the Cook Islands and has concluded that New Zealand restricted the powers of its associated states to a substantially lesser extent than did Britain. See Franck, Control of Sea Resources by Semi-Autonomous States, pp. 7–11.

States and Guam, Puerto Rico, and American Samoa attest.[110] In each case, in exchange for controlling the foreign policy of the weaker state, the greater power pledged to defend its weaker partner from foreign aggression.

Depending upon the character of the agreement chunk theorists typically approach protected or associated states by arguing either that they have simply not attained or maintained sovereign status or, less frequently, that they are fully sovereign and have merely employed the protecting state as their agent.[111] To the basket theorists, who are less concerned with trying to find "the line" that distinguishes sovereign from nonsovereign entities, such relationships merely underscore how frequently states in fact conceive of sovereignty in degrees. That a protectorate has certain sovereign attributes, but not others, reflects the fact that life in the international arena is decidedly inegalitarian in many critical respects.

The same tensions evident in the association or protectorate relationship can surface after a small, weak state is granted its formal independence and assumes sovereign status in the eyes of the international community. Consider, for instance, the fact that for many years Great Britain stationed considerable military forces in Belize. Not only did Britain retain exclusive jurisdiction over its own forces in Belize, but for a number of years it loaned to the host government a British officer to lead the Belizean Defence Force (BDF). Since the Guatemalan government claimed all Belizean territory until the fall of 1991, Belizean officials welcomed British protection and fully consented to the military arrangement.

A chunk theorist might point out that, if so requested by Belizean authorities, the British would almost certainly have respected Belizean sovereignty, vacated the country, and withdrawn their commanding officer from control of the BDF.[112] A basket theorist might

110. In the fall of 1991 two other similar relationships ended with the smaller entity achieving sovereign status. The Marshall Islands and the Federated States of Micronesia, each once under foreign protection as trust territories, were accorded sovereign status and accepted into membership in the United Nations.

111. Quincy Wright, *Mandates Under the League of Nations* (New York: Greenwood Press, 1968), p. 301.

112. In fact, in the spring of 1993 the British decided to withdraw from their defense commitment in Belize, turning responsibility for defense over to local authorities while maintaining only a small training base. See "British Presence in Belize Will Continue for Training of UK Troops," *The Belize Times* 16 May 1993, p. 1; "British Forces Winding Down! Training Facility But No Defence Role," *The Reporter* (Belize), 16 May 1993, p. 1.

respond by pointing to the respective power differences between Belize and other sovereign states. From this perspective the relatively weak Belizean state enjoyed a lesser sovereignty than more powerful states, a fact that led to a period in which foreigners led the Belizean armed forces. Basket theory would suggest that the harsh realities of international life—in particular, the fact that Belize long feared a stronger and hostile neighbor—directly affected the scope of its sovereign rule.[113] In short, circumstances in the international society of states conspired against Belize enjoying that nominal juridical equality touted by the chunk thinkers. The basket theorists would thus conclude that leaders of Great Britain and Belize experience quite different baskets of sovereign attributes and thus exercise somewhat different sets of sovereign rights and duties.

Considerably more rare than either a colony, an association, a protectorate, or a neutralized state is a condominium. When used as a term of international law, "condominium" denotes an arrangement in which two or more states act as joint tenants and share governing power over a single territory. For example, since 1278 the state of Andorra in the Pyrenees Mountains has been jointly governed by the French state and the bishop of Urgel in Spain. During the late nineteenth century, Germany, Great Britain, and the United States instituted a tripartite condominium over the Samoan Islands. From 1898 to 1956 Great Britain and Egypt[114] jointly governed the Sudan.[115] More recently, in November 1971 Iran and

---

113. Surprisingly, perhaps, such a practice is not unique. In other cases, such as Glubb Pasha in Jordan, a foreign officer has assumed a leading position in another sovereign state's army. Indeed, the practice of having foreigners assume leading government positions is not confined to military matters. In 1990 the chief justice of the Belizean Supreme Court was Lebanese, the director of the Office of Public Prosecutions hailed from Ghana, and the solicitor general came from India. Thus, seven years after Belizean independence, British Loan Service officers held many of the highest posts in the country's judicial system.

114. Instead of correctly identifying Great Britain and Egypt as the states jointly governing the Sudan, certain authorities mistakenly assert that Great Britain and France shared the condominium. Such an error confuses the eastern Anglo-Egyptian Sudan with the western French Sudan, one of the territories of French West Africa, lying between the Sahara and the Ivory Coast.

115. See "Agreement between Egypt and Great Britain relative to the future Administration of the Sudan, signed at Cairo, 19 January 1899," CTS, ed. Clive Parry, vol. 187, 1898–99 (Dobbs Ferry, N.Y.: Oceana Publications, 1980), pp. 155–57. For an interesting, though now quite dated, work see Vernon A. O'Rourke, The Juristic Status of Egypt and

the state of Sharjah, shortly to become a founding member of the United Arab Emirates, agreed to set aside their respective sovereignty claims and jointly govern the islands of Abu Musa and the Greater and Lesser Tunb, near the Strait of Hormuz.

During the summer of 1992 leading government officials in Japan and Russia proposed that the Northern Territories dispute—an issue that had festered ever since Soviet forces occupied the islands at the close of World War II—be resolved by one of several proposed schemes of joint government.[116] Since a formal condominium might prove unwieldy, some outside observers counseled the parties to "disaggregate" sovereign rights: that is, to divide the military task of supervising the neutral military status of the islands from the legal and administrative tasks regarding the islanders' social and cultural life.[117]

Although such divisions of responsibility might be taken as evidence of a basket approach to sovereignty, chunk theorists might observe that the chief problem with virtually all such arrangements has been that both outside powers tend in practice to vie for control.[118] In the late nineteenth and early twentieth centuries Great Britain and France attempted to govern the South Pacific islands then known as the New Hebrides in a joint naval commission that

---

the *Sudan* (Baltimore: Johns Hopkins University Press, 1935). See also Abdallah Ali al-Iryan, *Condominium and Related Situations in International Law with Special Reference to the Dual Administration of the Sudan and the Legal Problems Arising Out of It* (Cairo: Fouad University Press, 1952). A recent memoir is Hussein Zulfaker Sabry, *Sovereignty for Sudan* (London: Ithaca Press, 1982). The ongoing civil strife in the Sudan and the possible autonomy for southern Sudan is analyzed in Hannum, *Autonomy, Sovereignty, and Self-Determination*, pp. 308–27.

116. Japanese Foreign Minister Michio Watanabe proposed that Russia recognize Japanese sovereignty paired with continued Russian administrative control of two of the major islands. Several months later, Oleg Rumyantsev, president of Russia's influential Constitutional Committee, proposed that Russia return sovereign control of Kunashiri and Etorofu Islands while sharing a "joint sovereignty" over Habomai and Shikotan Islands. See *Daily Yomiuri* (Japan), 21 April 1992, p. 1, and *Daily Yomiuri* (Japan), 26 July 1992, p. 1.

117. Kratochwil et al., *Peace and Disputed Sovereignty*, p. 131. Theoretically, their counsel echoes the general principles advanced by Professor Emeritus Roger Fisher, longtime director of the Negotiation Program at Harvard Law School. See generally Roger Fisher, "Fractionating Conflict," in *International Conflict and Behavioral Science*, ed. Roger Fisher (New York: Basic Books, 1964), pp. 91–109.

118. See *Daily Yomiuri* (Japan), 4 December 1992, p. 10A.

eventually came to be called the Franco-British Condominium of 1906.[119] The bureaucratic confusion that ensued in law, education, and politics soon led many of those dealing with the governments to refer to them not as "The Condominium" but as "The Pandemonium"! To date, fears of similar confusion have barred agreement on such a resolution to the Northern Territories controversy.

Disputes over colonial relationships have also given rise to chunk and basket conflict. For instance, in 1885 Germany took possession of Yap Island in the South Pacific. Though the German government recognized that Spain had original title to the islands, the Germans justified their actions on the grounds that Spain had withdrawn its sovereignty by leaving the islands unoccupied. The parties eventually took the dispute to the pope for resolution.

Rather than handing a monolithic chunk of rights over Yap Island to either side, the pope settled the controversy by requiring Spain to establish a regular administration for the islands and allowing Germany full liberty of commerce, navigation, and fishing. He also granted Germans the right to establish a naval station and coaling depot, and allowed German citizens to establish plantations on the same footing as Spanish subjects.[120]

Basket theory is also readily applied to the developing position of England in three major cities in seventeenth- and eighteenth-century India.[121] For many years the English exercised a generous

119. See generally "Protocol between France and Great Britain concerning the New Hebrides signed at London, 27 February 1906," CTS, ed. Clive Perry, vol. 200, 1905–6 (Dobbs Ferry, N.Y.: Oceana Publications, 1980), pp. 328–51. Article I, paragraph 1 of the protocol read: "The Group of the New Hebrides, including the Banks and Torres Islands, shall form a region of joint influence, in which the subjects and citizens of the two Signatory Powers shall enjoy equal rights of residence, personal protection, and trade, each of the two Powers retaining jurisdiction over its subjects or citizens, and neither exercising a separate control over the Group."

120. See James Brown Scott, Sovereign States and Suits before Arbitral Tribunals and Courts of Justice (New York: New York University Press, 1925), pp. 95–97. Yap Island eventually became a League of Nations mandate, administered by Japan, "subject to rights of the United States with respect to entry and residence of its nationals and electrical communications under the treaty of 1921." See Wright, Existing Legal Situation, pp. 40, 73.

121. The following facts are drawn from H. H. Dodwell, "The Development of Sovereignty in British India," in The Cambridge History of India, ed. H. H. Dodwell, 6 vols. (New York: Macmillan Co., 1929), 6:589–92. More generally see "Sovereignty and the British Empire," in Hymen Ezra Cohen, Recent Theories of Sovereignty (Chicago: University of Chicago Press, 1937), pp. 93–108.

complement of sovereign rights over Bombay, which the Portuguese had ceded to them. In Bombay the English levied taxes, coined money, administered justice, and maintained troops for defense of the island. All inhabitants were considered English subjects.

In contrast, England long held Madras under a series of arrangements with local Hindu and Muslim rulers that explicitly restricted English rights. For instance, while the English could fortify Madras for a period of years, they owed as much as half of the customs duties as rent. Moreover, coins were to be inscribed with figures of Hindu deities rather than English symbols. Thus, the colonial rulers of Madras plainly exercised different sovereign rights and duties than did their colleagues in Bombay.

During the same era English authorities in Calcutta were permitted to try all Europeans for alleged criminal offenses; however, native inhabitants were tried in courts administered by the local ruler. Writing of Bengal, one authority concluded that even as English power increased, the colonial authorities hesitated "to assume formal sovereignty over the territories which in fact they controlled. Neither the Crown nor the [East India] Company was prepared . . . to lay claim to territorial sovereignty in India."[122] Basket theory would conclude that once again the demands of international life called for sovereignty to be divided in accordance with the variable qualities of the term, not to be treated as an indivisible monolith.

In summary, in thinking about this spectrum of state-to-state political relationships, chunk theorists firmly maintain that no political entity can be 67 percent sovereign. Hence, they focus on demarcating the boundary between sovereign and nonsovereign entities and justifying why a Cold War satellite retained its sovereignty but a turn-of-the-century protectorate was denied the same status.

For their part, the basket thinkers take terms like condominium, commonwealth, and colony, protectorate, association, and ally, even such pejorative terms as "satellite," "Finlandization," and "banana republic," to stand for the proposition that states have

---

122. Dodwell, "The Development of Sovereignty in British India," 6:592. Dodwell argued that British assertion of sovereignty in India was "spasmodic and incomplete" until 1813 when it became "definite and full" (ibid., 6:605).

differing degrees of independence, sovereign status, and sovereign rights and duties. Political relationships between states underscore the variable nature of the concept. Writing before the downfall of the Soviet bloc, Barry Buzan asked: "Can Czechoslovakia and Poland really be said to be equally sovereign to Britain and West Germany in terms of deciding for themselves how they will cope with their internal and external problems? If they cannot, then it has to be conceded that sovereignty, like power and independence, also varies in degree among states, since all four countries enjoy recognition as states by virtually every standard criteria."[123] Quincy Wright similarly concluded: "Although abhorrent to absolutist political theorists and to modern international law, unquestionable instances have existed which can only be described as divided or suspended sovereignty, though it is also true that they have usually proved temporary or transitional. Confederacies, federations, protectorates, spheres of influence, suzerainties, self-governing dominions, all suggest such a situation."[124]

Conclusion

The cardinal task confronting the scholar of international politics is to describe accurately how international relations are conducted. Hence, a fruitful area of inquiry is to compare the various theories of sovereignty with the actual behavior of states. As the twentieth century draws to a close, we might ask which school of thought is perceiving the reality of sovereignty more accurately? Does the international community actually rely to some degree on both theories? Finally, is one or the other of the approaches likely to prevail in the years ahead?

Both the chunk and the basket schools of thought on sovereignty claim that the actual behavior of states supports their vision of how the concept is applied in international relations. From the basket perspective the absolute view of sovereignty as a monolithic chunk, or as indivisible, is increasingly disfavored both in practice and in

123. Barry Buzan, *People, States, and Fear: The National Security Problem in International Relations* (Chapel Hill: University of North Carolina Press, 1983), p. 43.
124. Quincy Wright, "Sovereignty of the Mandates," *AJIL* 17 (1923): 694.

theory. These observers see international relations played on a larger chessboard than ever before. At each moment many more chess pieces cooperate and compete. Such a system is marked by pawns as well as knights and rooks, kings and queens. Many political communities have been deprived of certain attributes commonly associated with sovereign rule. The basket theorists argue that sovereignty is regularly being applied in a variable and divisible manner.

The chunk theorists contend that this spectrum of modern relationships simply raises the issue of precisely where the division lies between sovereign states and nonsovereign entities.[125] The chunk thinkers point out that states in such relationships are regularly considered either to be sovereign or to be well on the road to eventual, and perhaps inevitable,[126] sovereign statehood. These observers view many of the instances cited by the basket school as temporary regimes that illustrate the ingenuity of politicians, diplomats, and international lawyers but that were never designed to permanently resolve particular political problems. Essentially, they dismiss the examples raised by the basket theorists as the exceptions that prove the rule.[127] The natural rejoinder for the basket thinkers is that exceptions cannot prove a rule: they can prove only a rule's limitations. They would take the exceptions to the chunk theory as evidence of the superiority of their own perspective on sovereignty.

The basket theorists seem to us to be persuasive in claiming that the spectrum of modern relationships between states buttresses the

125. Morgenthau, *Politics among Nations*, p. 249.

126. Robert Klein observed: "Today, the principle of self-determination . . . has resulted in a striking phenomenon: the indiscriminate creation of a multiplicity of sovereign states. . . . The national boundaries of some of the recent participants in world affairs are a caprice. Rarely are they pertinent to natural geography. Rarely do they encompass all persons with a common culture, religion, race, or even, in the case of Africa, tribal affiliation." Robert A. Klein, *Sovereign Equality Among States: The History of an Idea* (Toronto: University of Toronto Press, 1974), p. 144.

127. See James, *Sovereign Statehood*, pp. 31–32. After setting forth his chunk perspective, Morgenthau noted frankly: "Great difficulties . . . beset the application of these abstract standards to actual situations and concrete issues. At the root of the perplexities which attend the problem of the loss of sovereignty there is the divorce, in contemporary legal and political theory, of the concept of sovereignty from the political reality to which the concept of sovereignty is supposed to give legal expression." Morgenthau, *Politics among Nations*, p. 249.

notion that certain states, in practice, have more sovereign attributes and responsibilities than others. Such diverse historical examples as the Canal Zone in Panama, the Guantánamo Bay base in
Cuba, the occupations of Germany and Japan, the Platt amendment
in Cuba, the Soviet Union's Cold War satellites, and the British
leadership of the Belizean armed forces coexist uneasily with the
chunk theory of how sovereignty is actually being applied to international life.

We conclude that, since the international community seems in
practice to have adopted a variable approach to sovereignty on
numerous occasions, the meaning of the term can indeed differ
markedly for a satellite, a superpower, a defeated state, a newly
independent nation, and a large and populous superpower. Though
wholly unable to sweep the field of opponents, the variable approach to sovereignty that envisions a basket of sovereign rights
and duties may be gaining the upper hand among scholars and
statespersons.

That so many states with such markedly different abilities to
exert influence in international society have attained sovereign
status in the post–World War II era is a fact of profound theoretical
significance. We think that the proliferation of sovereigns helps to
explain the increasing reliance on basket thinking.

If the standards for attaining sovereignty were more challenging
to achieve and if the community of sovereign states were more
homogeneous, states might find the notion of according sovereigns
an identical chunk of rights and duties to be more palatable. In fact,
however, recent decades have seen the advent of microstates in the
Pacific, the Caribbean, and elsewhere and the development of
suprastates, as in the European Union. This may suggest that
leaders tend to rely on a basket approach to sovereignty precisely
because the current international system of states is so heteroge-
neous. When according rights and duties on the basis of corresponding sovereign attributes, one might distinguish between the
sovereignty of Malta, of France, and of Europe. Each has its basket,
but the contents of those baskets naturally differ.

Indeed, basket theory could be hailed for its flexibility: a substantial advantage in managing conflicts[128] and organizing international

---

128. One recent source observed: "[T]he state system has developed in ways that have

life. Perhaps the chunk thinkers are trying to force a circular peg into a square hole by attempting to impose an equalitarian legal theory on a decidedly inequalitarian world. While there must always be some gap between the dictates of legal theory and actual behavior—whether that of states in international relations or people in domestic life—the chunk theory appears to basket thinkers like ourselves to stretch that gap to unsatisfactory proportions.

---

tended to leave all rights bundled together and linked to the concept of sovereignty. . . . While this arrangement makes for clear definitions of jurisdictions, . . . it hinders resolution of interstate problems of a shared environment. One possible solution is to untie the knots in this indivisible bundle of state rights. These rights were not always so indivisibly bound. . . . Allowing for shared jurisdiction within the same geographical area can lend flexibility to negotiating situations." Kratochwil et al., *Peace and Disputed Sovereignty,* pp. 129–30.

5

Why Is Sovereignty Useful?

Having learned that sovereignty is not the sole concept that states need in their relations with each other—a sign of sophistication and progress—we long for the sovereign state to be superseded altogether. And forgetting that sovereignty is only a concept, we seek to supersede the sovereignty of the individual state by superseding the individual state itself.

—F. H. Hinsley[1]

That so many have employed the concept of sovereignty with such frequency should not be taken to imply that sovereignty is uniformly regarded as a laudable feature of international life. Scholars often speak sternly of sovereignty, disapproving of it as immoral, dismissing it as outmoded, or imploring that it be fundamentally altered in short order.[2] Just as certain observers disagree on how sovereign status is attained and what sovereignty implies, so do many people differ on the extent to which sovereignty is useful. Is sovereignty a central pillar of international relations? Is it alterna-

1. F. H. Hinsley, "The Concept of Sovereignty and the Relations between States," in *Theory and Reality in International Relations*, ed. John C. Farrell and Asa P. Smith (New York: Columbia University Press, 1967), p. 66. Hans Morgenthau once noted that the term has been subjected to more denunciations than serious studies. Hans J. Morgenthau, *Politics Among Nations: The Struggle for Power and Peace* (New York: Alfred A. Knopf, 1948), p. 243.

2. F. H. Hinsley, *Sovereignty* (New York: Basic Books, 1966), p. 215.

tively—or perhaps additionally—an unfortunate constraint imped-
ing the development of a better system?

In recent years debates on the value of sovereignty have brought
forth ardent defenders and acerbic critics. Both of these groups
often appear to have in mind a particular agenda that is apparently
aided or hindered by the concept. Indeed, the camps of critics and
defenders alike have attracted most unlikely bedfellows from both
the mainstream and the fringes of political philosophy. Marxists,
world federalists, human rights advocates, and supranationalists of
various stripes have found common ground in criticizing sovereignty. Conservatives supporting the status quo in international
affairs have joined to uphold the concept with Third World leaders
and others who wish to protect less powerful states. Each of these
perspectives on the value of sovereignty merits critical examination.

The Critics of Sovereignty

The Marxist Critique

Marxist-Leninist theory squarely criticizes the concept of state
sovereignty. The state itself is viewed as a product of class, an
instrument of oppression, and the essence of dictatorship.[3] According to Vladimir Ilyich Lenin, the state "is the product and the
manifestation of the irreconcilability of class antagonisms."[4] The
ultimate hope of Marxist-Leninists is to see the state wither away altogether.

Given their ideological roots in Marxist-Leninist doctrine, one
might have expected Soviet leaders to have been uncompromising
critics of the concept of sovereign statehood.[5] In fact, however,
a series of purportedly doctrinaire Marxist-Leninists adamantly
supported the philosophical notion of sovereignty, even while

3. Charles T. Baroch, The Soviet Doctrine of Sovereignty (New York: American Bar
Association, 1970), p. 8.
4. Ibid., p. 7 (quoting Vladimir Lenin, State and Revolution).
5. For a thorough explication of Soviet views on sovereignty, see Viktor Sergeevich
Shevtsov, National Sovereignty and the Soviet State, trans. Nick Bobrov (Moscow:
Progress Publishers, 1974).

strictly circumscribing the meaning of sovereignty for states within their spheres of influence.[6] In part, perhaps, the Soviets viewed sovereign statehood as the lesser of two evils. Since the Soviet leadership abhorred the idea of world government on anything other than communist principles, policymakers resisted any international organization that might evolve toward governing control over communist states.

On a more practical plane the Soviets seem to have understood the rhetorical value of sovereignty in the postcolonial developing world. Curiously, despite a markedly aggressive Cold War foreign policy, the Soviet Union for many years largely succeeded in avoiding the labels of imperialist, colonialist, or interventionist power. Indeed, as one authority recently noted: "[W]hen independent republics proliferated in the wake of a Soviet state unwilling or unable to enforce its claims to sovereignty, the achievement of independence by these new states was almost always termed 'secession,' not 'decolonization.'"[7] That the Soviets studiously avoided outright claims of sovereignty over the states they in fact controlled must account for a large part of the explanation.[8] In contrast, since the Third World tends to associate the United States with the imperialism and colonialism exercised primarily by Western European powers, the American government was roundly denounced for a series of lesser assaults on sovereignty that typically, although not exclusively, included a measure of support for the very principles of liberty, democracy, and human rights championed in the United Nations Charter.

In any event, far from wholly repudiating the concept, the Soviet government—by its rhetoric—enthusiastically took up the banner of sovereign statehood. The Soviet Constitution of 1936 accorded all eleven republics "equal rights" and "sovereign rights," including the right to secede from the Union.[9] During the Cold War Soviet

6. The best work on Soviet attitudes toward sovereignty within the Soviet bloc is Robert A. Jones, *The Soviet Concept of "Limited Sovereignty" from Lenin to Gorbachev: The Brezhnev Doctrine* (New York: St. Martin's Press, 1990).

7. Ian S. Lustick, *Unsettled States, Disputed Lands: Britain and Ireland, France and Algeria, Israel and the West Bank–Gaza* (Ithaca: Cornell University Press, 1993), p. 22.

8. Indeed, Vietnam followed suit in installing a puppet regime in Cambodia rather than trying to absorb a recognized sovereign state.

9. Quincy Wright, *The Existing Legal Situation as it Relates to the Conflict in the Far East* (New York: Institute of Pacific Relations, 1939), 46 n. 2.

leaders constantly invoked sovereignty as a defensive device for states threatened by "imperialist" intrusions. They also jealously guarded the domestic jurisdiction of communist states against interference by the United Nations. Thus, in a strange theoretical somersault the Soviet government appeared to some critics of the concept of sovereignty to be more reactionary than revolutionary.

Only in the Brezhnev Doctrine, which attributed a qualified sovereignty to the Iron Curtain countries, did the Soviet leaders flirt with Marxist reservations concerning the concept.[10] Even here, Moscow chose not to disclaim sovereignty but merely to redefine it. According to Soviet doctrine sovereignty was to be considered a "political-legal quality of state power, reflecting its independence of any other power within and without the boundaries of the country; and consisting in the right of the state to run its affairs independently and freely."[11] The essence of this definition lies in the Soviet concept of state power, that is, the power of the official party.

The Communist Party justified state control by claiming that it alone represented the interests of the working class. In order to support "the international solidarity of the Communist Parties in their global task of building socialism,"[12] the Brezhnev Doctrine dictated that the Communist Party must subordinate traditional nation-state interests to supranational party-state interests. The concept of sovereignty, then, took on a different international meaning that directly contradicted the notion of sovereignty as independence from higher authority. As one author explained, "[T]he sovereignty of each socialist country cannot be opposed to the world of socialism . . . [which] is indivisible and its defense is the common cause of all communists."[13]

10. See Geoffrey L. Goodwin, "The Erosion of External Sovereignty?" in *Between Sovereignty and Integration*, ed. Ghita Ionescu (New York: John Wiley and Sons, 1974), p. 105. See generally Boris Meissner, *The Brezhnev Doctrine* (Kansas City, Mo.: Park College, Governmental Research Bureau, 1970). For a view of the Marxist approach to sovereignty and colonialism see Christos Theodoropoulous, *Colonialism and General International Law: The Contemporary Theory of National Sovereignty and Self-Determination* (Lagos, Nigeria: New Horizon Publishing House, 1988).

11. Baroch, *The Soviet Doctrine of Sovereignty*, p. 8.

12. Ibid., p. 20. The quotation refers to the doctrine of limited sovereignty as applied to Czechoslovakia in 1968.

13. Ibid., quoting from "Sovereignty and International Duties of Socialist Countries," *Pravda* (Soviet Union), 25 September 1968.

The International Organization Critique

Those concerned with the development of international organization[14] in the twentieth century have regularly been attracted by one of two broad visions of the proper role for such organizations. Some expect international organizations merely to reflect the state system; others emphasize the prospects that international organization will reform the international community.[15] The latter group have often united to criticize the concept of sovereignty.

The camp that views international organizations as reflectors of the state system focuses upon the conservative blueprints drawn up by the founders of the League of Nations and United Nations. Rather than eliminating or even eroding the concept of sovereignty, the founders aimed to respect and sustain it. They were content to assume that sovereignty would continue to be the primary organizing factor in international life. As Israeli diplomat Abba Eban observed: "[The founders] were trying to globalize the idea of a concert of sovereign states, not to discard it."[16] Consequently, both the League of Nations and the United Nations carefully preserved the ability of sovereign states to veto various actions with which they did not agree.[17] Mindful of their sovereign prerogatives, states

14. By "international organization" we mean the process through which people come together in cooperative undertakings to pursue international objectives. "International organizations" are particular groupings that assume different forms in different stages of the process of international organization. See generally Inis L. Claude, Jr., *Swords into Plowshares: The Problems and Progress of International Organization*, 4th ed. rev. (New York: Random House, 1971), p. 4.

15. See Inis L. Claude, Jr., *The Record of International Organizations in the Twentieth Century* (Taipei, Taiwan: Tamkang University Press, 1986), especially pp. 36–46. See also Charles Pentland, "International Organizations and Their Roles," in *Perspectives on World Politics*, ed. Richard Little and Michael Smith, 2d ed. rev. (New York: Routledge, 1981), pp. 241–49.

16. Abba Eban, *The New Diplomacy: International Affairs in the Modern Age* (New York: Random House, 1983), p. 246.

17. Eban noted: "[T]he League of Nations was so respectful of sovereignty that it gave a veto power to every member, large and small. Under Article 5 of the Covenant, any member could frustrate a resolution, simply by voting against it either in the Council or in the Assembly" (ibid.). The classic analysis of the Security Council veto is found in Claude, *Swords into Plowshares*, pp. 141–62. For the vetoes that different UN members have concerning committing peacekeeping forces and participating in them see Alan James, "Unit Veto Dominance in United Nations Peace-Keeping," in *Politics in the United Nations System*, ed. Lawrence S. Finkelstein (Durham, N.C.: Duke University Press, 1988), pp. 75–105.

have also been exceedingly reluctant to take steps toward creating a standing military force under the control of the UN secretary-general.

This first group emphasizes that international organizations have not been conceived as revolutionary experiments designed to transform the nature of the international system. Rather, they have been creatures of states, formed by states, aimed at helping states to cooperate more efficiently and effectively to bring about additional prosperity and fewer bloody disputes. Consequently, the record of international organizations tends to reflect both the collaboration and the conflict found within international society.

The competing vision expects that international organizations will play a critical role in reforming, or even revolutionizing the current system. It views the sovereign state as under considerable stress and postulates that the international community may undergo radical change. Rather than envisioning international organization as a means to help states maintain order and stability, the reformist model seeks to control states: to improve the conduct of international affairs by cutting down to size the unruly and irresponsible states that flourish in international politics. In this vein the standard conception of twentieth-century international organization might be viewed as a mission *against* states: "We must crack their monoliths, integrate and subordinate them, cut their claws, keep them away from one another's throats and off one another's backs, subject them to coercive restraint, tame them by cutting into their sovereignty and then rope them together."[18]

While the particular schemes for reforming the state system through international organization vary widely, perhaps the most comprehensive postwar blueprint may be found in the theory of functionalism. Functionalism promoted the "evolution of a network of international organizations of varying size and shape, each of them tailored to the requirements for effective cooperative action to deal with a particular type of problem."[19] States, according

18. Inis L. Claude, Jr., "The Peace-Keeping Role of the United Nations," in *The United Nations in Perspective,* ed. E. Berkeley Tompkins (Stanford, Calif.: Hoover Institution Press, 1972), pp. 56–57. We should emphasize that Claude does not present this as his view, merely as the view of many advocates of international organization.

19. Inis L. Claude, Jr., "Theoretical Approaches to National Security and World Order," in *National Security Law,* ed. John Norton Moore, Frederick S. Tipson, and Robert F. Turner (Durham, N.C.: Carolina Academic Press, 1990), pp. 31–45. More

to this view, should create and operate specialized agencies. By interacting in each technical forum, the international community should try to overcome the competitiveness, political differences, and inadequacies inherent in the state system. Functionalists hoped that collaboration to advance human welfare would ultimately take precedence over selfish sovereign concerns.

In concluding that a system of independent sovereign states is intrinsically irrational and dangerous, the functionalists posited that the steady growth of cooperation among agencies would eventually eliminate the barriers that separate states. Functionalist theory advanced from the premise that sovereignty is a variable concept. These theorists expected that through international regulatory activity the sovereignty of states would gradually be reduced.[20] The functionalists predicted that as people in different societies became accustomed to interacting horizontally, such vertical divisions as the boundaries of states would diminish in importance.[21] Consequently, as functionalism progresses, territorial sovereignty disputes would wane. All eventually will see the sense in merging states together and eliminating the pernicious notion of sovereign statehood.

Whether hailing from the functionalist school or not, the reformists speculate that the organization of human communities into sovereign states is becoming anachronistic. Alongside the increasing relevance of transnational contacts, the development of international organizations promises a new and improved international system. Essential to such reform is the repudiation of state sovereignty. Thus, this latter group of international organization scholars often join together to denigrate the concept of sovereignty.

The Supranationalist Critique

Related to the idea of international organization is the notion of supranationalism: that is, the transfer of some degree of sovereignty

---

generally, see David Mitrany, *A Working Peace System* (Chicago: Quadrangle Books, 1966).

20. See Inis L. Claude, Jr., *States and the Global System: Politics, Law, and Organization* (New York: St. Martin's Press, 1988), p. 50.

21. See Friedrich V. Kratochwil, Paul Rohrlich, and Harpreet Mahajan, *Peace and Disputed Sovereignty: Reflections on Conflict over Territory* (Lanham, Md.: University Press of America, 1985), pp. 25–26.

from the member states to a policymaking or executive body standing over them.[22] Since World War II both visionary and practical
efforts to integrate states into larger groupings have flourished.
These campaigns, favoring regional unification or even world government, have often been marked by critiques that the concept of
sovereignty is outmoded or counterproductive. Supranationalists
have regularly lamented that sovereign states stubbornly interfere
with their plans to create a transformed and improved international
system. In the course of creating new political communities, they
propose either pooling[23] or scrapping sovereignty.

The more extreme group of supranationalists, advocates of world
government of one stripe or another, long rejected the notion of a
multistate system composed of sovereign units. To world federalists
state sovereignty was the root of all evil in international politics. It
undermined the transcendent goal of establishing world law, world
government, and thereby world peace.[24] This group advocated
initially reducing the modern state's stature and ultimately replac-
ing it altogether. The world federalist school saw sovereignty as an
immoral and anachronistic concept that automatically brought war
in its train.[25] To achieve their objectives, world federalists proposed
a suprastate authority serving as the instrument of order with

22. For a more detailed comparison of the terms "international organization" and
"supranationalism" see Claude, Swords into Plowshares, p. 109.
23. Shirley Williams defines "pooled sovereignty" as sovereignty "that is . . . collec-
tively held by an association of states that reaches decisions on specified matters by a
qualified majority." Shirley Williams, "Sovereignty and Accountability in the European
Community," in The New European Community: Decisionmaking and Institutional
Change, ed. Robert O. Keohane and Stanley Hoffmann (Boulder, Colo.: Westview Press,
1991), p. 156.
24. Grenville Clark and Louis B. Sohn, World Peace Through World Law: Two
Alternative Plans (Cambridge, Mass.: Harvard University Press, 1966). See also Mary
Catherine Bateson, "Beyond Sovereignty: An Emerging Global Civilization," in Contending Sovereignties: Redefining Political Community, ed. R.B.J. Walker and Saul H. Mendlovitz (Boulder, Colo.: Lynne Reinner Publishers, 1990), pp. 145–58.
25. Inis Claude wrote: "[The world federalist group] sees war as a necessary, natural,
and inescapable product of the multistate system; consequently, it proposes to abolish
and replace the system, rather than to tinker with it. The problem of modern man is not
to correct minor flaws in the operation of the international system, or to equip the system
with improved apparatus, or to remove wicked and foolish men from its managerial
board, or to prevent troublesome states from disrupting it, but to recognize its inherent
defectiveness and take the drastic step of dismantling 'the absurd architecture of the
present world.'" Inis L. Claude, Jr., Power and International Relations (New York:
Random House, 1962), p. 498. See also Frederick H. Hartmann, The Relations of Nations
(New York: Macmillan, 1966), p. 305.

substate entities constituting the governed community. Accordingly, they argued that international institutions are not granted sufficient sovereignty and that states are granted too much sovereignty.

Most thoughtful observers have found the arguments of supranationalists intent on regional integration to be substantially more compelling than grandiose schemes for world government. While proposals aimed at economic, judicial, or political integration and regional organizations of varying stripes have occurred around the globe, the efforts to unify Europe stand as the leading example of supranationalism in practice.[26] And the extent to which the sovereignty of the constituent states should be subordinated to the effort to unite Europe has divided national citizens perhaps even more sharply than it has political leaders.

Some European Union advocates have portrayed the unification campaign in terms of a debate between narrow-minded and short-sighted disciples of sovereign statehood and farseeing leaders who are looking beyond the petty quarrels of national leaders toward the broader regional benefits of economic prosperity. Others believe that as the unification effort has moved forward, decisionmaking has been splintered.[27] Since European leaders must now consider both national interests and regional interests, that is, the interests of that body of states that makes up the European Union, one might imagine a meshing of individual sovereignties to have occurred. Whether the result will be as flexible and sound as a coat of mail or as flimsy and readily penetrable as a window screen remains to be seen.[28]

26. To trace the progression of the sovereignty debate see Robert O. Keohane and Stanley Hoffmann, eds., *The New European Community: Decision-Making and Institutional Change* (Boulder, Colo.: Westview Press, 1991); William Wallace, "What Price Independence? Sovereignty and Interdependence in British Politics," *International Affairs* 62 (1986): 367–89; and Luxemburgensis, "The Emergence of a European Sovereignty," in *Between Sovereignty and Integration*, ed. Ghita Ionescu (New York: John Wiley and Sons, 1974), pp. 118–34.

27. As Robert Keohane wrote: "[H]igh levels of political integration make it difficult to identify the source of 'will' that is the essence of the classical idea of sovereignty. Europe is increasingly governed by a complex decision-making process, in which authority is not concentrated in a single body but conferred on different entities at different times by rules." Robert O. Keohane, *Sovereignty, Interdependence, and International Institutions*, Working Paper no. 1 (Cambridge, Mass.: Harvard University, Center for International Affairs, 1991), pp. 2–3.

28. For the coat-of-mail metaphor we are indebted to our students at George Washington University, who attributed the notion to our then-colleague, Abba Eban.

The process by which European states, by fits and starts, have pooled authority has resulted in various not wholly consistent developments for sovereignty. To date, the constituent states in the European Union have retained their formal sovereignty within the international community. For instance, each continues to cast votes in the United Nations and to send its own diplomatic corps abroad. However, European law now takes precedence over national law on certain issues,[29] and the citizens of states in the European Union can take certain cases to European courts rather than to their national tribunals.[30]

However, those unifying developments have been tempered by the notion of subsidiarity—that is, the principle that European executive jurisdiction should be limited to "appropriate levels" where states cannot act alone.[31] Moreover, many of the civil servants staffing the institutions of the European Union remain closely linked to their national governments, not only through continued nationalist sentiments but through their desire for professional advancement.[32] In the European Union, as in other international bodies, bureaucrats remain answerable to national constituencies on many different levels. Thus, while theoretical arguments over just where sovereignty lies may have been subordinated to the more pressing and practical problems inherent in unifying a continent, it seems fair to conclude that sovereignty issues continue to dog the path of European supranationalism.

Whether the sovereign status of the individual European states will ever be wholly replaced remains open to doubt. So, too, does the question of whether the effort to unify Europe is singular or one that will be replicated elsewhere. And the various consequences of splintering decision-making authority among national and supranational institutions continue to be quite difficult to foretell. In any event, those engaged in pressing forward supranationalism, of both regionalist and globalist varieties, have rarely rushed to defend the

29. Ibid., p. 15.

30. It is interesting to recall that medieval European states typically expressed internal sovereignty by exercising "the right to give final judgment in a high court." Joseph R. Strayer, On the Medieval Origins of the Modern State (Princeton: Princeton University Press, 1970), p. 61.

31. Walter Goldstein, "Europe after Maastricht," Foreign Affairs 71 (1992): 128.

32. See Williams, The New European Community, pp. 155, 161–62.

venerable concept of sovereignty; rather, they have typically viewed it as an unfortunate, outdated vestige of a simpler era in international affairs.

The Human Rights Critique

Human rights advocates have questioned whether the development of political morality has not been slowed by the concept of sovereignty. To what extent should a government be entitled to deflect criticism of human rights abuses by pointing to its sovereign right to act as it pleases in domestic matters? To what extent can sovereignty, or the phrase "domestic jurisdiction," still be used as a shield by governments abusive of their citizens? Would not an international system shorn of the notion of sovereignty be a place more respectful of human rights?

According to classical international law the principle of state sovereignty barred outside intervention that might have offered support to the internal victims of tyrannical rulers.[33] Early views of sovereignty thus emphasized authority: the notion of absolute domestic supremacy implied that sovereign rulers could act at their pleasure within the boundaries of their states. After noting that being forced to tolerate law passed by legislatures is "the last calamity which can befall a man of our rank," Louis XIV in his Mémoires observed: "It belongs exclusively to the head to deliberate and to decide, and all the functions of the other members only consist in the execution of the commands which have been given to them."[34]

Even after World War I many states refused to allow the League of Nations to safeguard rights of minorities through international

33. Martin S. Soroos, Beyond Sovereignty: The Challenge of Global Policy (Columbia: University of South Carolina Press, 1986), p. 230. As recently as the late nineteenth century, scholar John Burgess could write: "Sovereignty [is] . . . original, absolute, unlimited, universal power over the individual subject and over all associations of subjects." John W. Burgess, Political Science and Comparative Constitutional Law, 2 vols. (Boston: Ginn and Co., 1893), 1:52, cited in Vernon A. O'Rourke, The Juristic Status of Egypt and the Sudan (Baltimore: Johns Hopkins University Press, 1935), pp. 10–11.

34. James Brown Scott, Sovereign States and Suits before Arbitral Tribunals and Courts of Justice (New York: New York University Press, 1925), 6 n. 1, citing Charles Dreyss, Etude sur les Mémoires de Louis XIV pour l'instruction du Dauphin (Paris: Didier, 1860), pp. 6, 405.

supervision. A sovereign leader often could abuse citizens without enduring outside attention, much less intervention, because "despite the premises and implications of the League Covenant, the states of the world continued in general to act as if the principle of sovereignty were the fundamental precept of the international order."[35]

In much the same way the phrase "a man's house is his castle" expressed the traditional idea that the head of a household was a virtually absolute authority concerning the matters within the walls of the home. However, during the twentieth century the notion that cardinal responsibilities also inhere in authority challenged these absolute views in international as well as domestic societies. These days a superior domestic authority is entitled to intervene in matters once considered the exclusive province of the head of the family, such as cruelty or neglect shown toward spouse or children. Similarly, these days the international community seems to consider that cruelty or neglect of a people justifies outside intervention, though the permissible scope and appropriate instruments of that intervention are not yet clearly defined.[36]

To assist in their campaign to extend civil, political, and social rights across the globe, human rights advocates have thus attacked traditional interpretations of state sovereignty.[37] People increasingly believe that they possess rights, not merely as citizens of a state, but by virtue of their status as human beings.[38] And human rights campaigns have persuaded many leaders in the international community that sovereignty no longer implies that a state is entitled

35. Inis L. Claude, Jr., *National Minorities: An International Problem* (Cambridge, Mass.: Harvard University Press, 1955), p. 42.

36. Professor Donald Seekins suggested that sovereignty-as-authority might be characterized as "shepherd sovereignty": in the words of Thrasymachus in Plato's *Republic*, the shepherd can do as he likes with his sheep because he owns them. Seekins contrasted "shepherd sovereignty" with "householder sovereignty," spelled out above, and concluded that a regime like the military government in Burma might lack sovereignty precisely because it fails to protect and promote human rights. Professor Donald M. Seekins, director of the Asian Studies Program, Meio University, Nago, Okinawa, Japan, in an 11 October 1993 letter written to the authors.

37. See, for instance, Myres McDougal and Lung-Chu Chen, "Introduction: Human Rights and Jurisprudence," *Hofstra Law Review* 9 (1981): 337–46.

38. Michael Ross Fowler, *Thinking about Human Rights: Contending Approaches to Human Rights in U.S. Foreign Policy* (Lanham, Md.: University Press of America, 1987), p. 217.

to treat its citizens as it pleases. That entitlement, once indisputable, now seems to have vanished from the sovereignty basket. Consequently, employing traditional views of sovereignty to defend against claims of human rights violations has lost some measure of its effectiveness.

In the 1990s the international community has moved, with varying degrees of forcefulness, to intervene in the internal affairs of various sovereign states that have been unable or unwilling to halt egregious human suffering within their borders.[39] In Cambodia, Somalia,[40] Bosnia, and Rwanda the United Nations has used humanitarian concerns to justify multilateral intervention.[41]

In a philosophical development that reflects the flexibility of the term, certain scholars have attempted to take sovereignty, long a shield for tyrants, and turn it into a sword to be used against human rights abusers. In using sovereignty in the sense of de facto internal independence, Michael Reisman wrote: "International law is still concerned with the protection of sovereignty, but, in its modern sense, the object of protection is not the power base of the tyrant who rules directly by naked power or through the apparatus of a totalitarian political order, but the continuing capacity of a population freely, to express and effect choices about the identities and policies of its governors." Reisman continued: "The Chinese Government's massacre in Tiananmen Square to maintain an oligarchy against the wishes of the people was a violation of Chinese sovereignty. The [Nicolai] Ceaucescu dictatorship was a violation of Romanian sovereignty. President [Ferdinand] Marcos violated Phil-

---

39. See generally David Forsythe and Kelly Kate Pease, "Human Rights, Humanitarian Intervention, and World Politics," *Human Rights Quarterly* 15 (1993): 290–314.

40. See Jonathan Stevenson, "Hope Restored in Somalia?" *Foreign Policy* 91 (1993): 138–54. For a historical account of an earlier attempt at humanitarian intervention see Stephen Schott, "United States Relief to Civilian Victims of the Biafra-Nigeria Civil War," in *The United Nations: A Reassessment; Sanctions, Peacekeeping, and Humanitarian Assistance*, ed. John M. Paxman and George T. Boggs (Charlottesville: University Press of Virginia, 1973), pp. 105–13.

41. For an interesting exchange of conflicting views on humanitarian intervention see Ian Brownlie, "Thoughts on Kind-Hearted Gunmen," in *Humanitarian Intervention and the United Nations*, ed. Richard B. Lillich (Charlottesville: University Press of Virginia, 1973), pp. 139–48, and Tom J. Farer, "Humanitarian Intervention: The View from Charlottesville," in *Humanitarian Intervention and the United Nations*, ed. Richard B. Lillich (Charlottesville: University Press of Virginia, 1973), pp. 149–64. See also Richard B. Lillich, "A United States Policy of Humanitarian Intervention and Intercession," in

ippine sovereignty, General [Manuel] Noriega violated Panamanian sovereignty, and the Soviet blockade of Lithuania violated its sovereignty."[42]

Human rights champions have also suggested that abuses might be better countered in regional, than in national, court systems. Hence, the members of the European Community were persuaded to permit individual citizens, under the European Convention on Human Rights, to appeal over the jurisdiction of their national court systems to the European Court of Human Rights. Yet, whether such a solution to the tension between human rights and state sovereignty may be exported to other regions is open to question. Certainly, the Inter-American Court of Human Rights has been unsuccessful in attaining comparable powers. The fact that, for all their successes, human rights campaigns continue to encounter difficulties in persuading governments to curtail abuses suggests that the implications of the classical view of sovereignty remain a formidable hurdle to be overcome by those concerned with promoting respect for human rights.

The Defenders of Sovereignty

Although many groups criticize sovereignty as outmoded or troublesome, others staunchly defend the concept as a vital component of the modern state system. Economists, international relations theorists, and international legal scholars have at different times and for varying reasons voiced support for the concept.

The International Order Defense

Sovereignty's defenders have often argued that the concept helps to bring order to the international system. We have already noted

---

Human Rights and American Foreign Policy, ed. Donald P. Kommers and Gilburt D. Loescher (Notre Dame, Ind.: University of Notre Dame Press, 1979), pp. 278–98.

42. W. Michael Reisman, "Sovereignty and Human Rights in Contemporary International Law," *American Journal of International Law* 84 (1990): 872. Reisman continued: "In each case, the violators often brazenly characterized the condemnation as itself a violation of their sovereignty. Sadly, some organizations and some scholars, falling victim to anachronism, have given them comfort. In modern international law, sovereignty can be violated as effectively and ruthlessly by an indigenous as by an outside force." Ibid.

that the concept of sovereignty determines status by effectively identifying a group of important actors with special rights and duties. Sovereignty's function of providing a recognized legal and political hierarchy can help contribute stability to international relations by creating expectations of how political entities are to behave.

Since some political actors are endowed with sovereign status, while a range of others are not, certain issues are taken up by the international community and given special attention, while others are set aside. The demands, dilemmas, and petitions of the sovereign states command notice in a manner that can be the envy of nonsovereign actors. Consequently, sovereignty can narrow the matters to be dealt with to those involving the most powerful and influential category of political actors. While nonsovereign entities might view it as unjust, the narrowing function of sovereignty helps to ensure that important international issues receive the attention necessary to resolve them.

In addition, modern states have taken advantage of sovereign prerogatives to regulate the flow across state borders of people, goods, weapons, plants, even diseases and ideas. Years ago gypsies routinely wandered across European borders, as Native Americans and tribal Africans did across borders on their continents. Travelers and tourists visited foreign states without having to concern themselves with such trappings of sovereignty as passports and visas. And if the movement of people across boundaries lacked order, the regulation of potentially harmful goods was also much less comprehensive than is the case today.

As government has developed toward a more paternalistic outlook, customs officials and other state authorities have attempted to protect consumers, farmers, manufacturers, and many other groups of citizens by regulating a considerable spectrum of human activities that cross boundary lines. This enormous endeavor, which has gained extraordinary momentum during the twentieth century, has been the exclusive province of the governments of sovereign states. It has been undertaken by one government after another as one of the chief prerogatives of sovereignty. Sovereignty's advocates claim that in this regard, too, the concept brings order to the international realm.

From the perspective of the defenders of international order the concept of sovereignty can also serve to protect the weak from more powerful aggressors. After invading Austria, Adolf Hitler reportedly asked, "What can words like . . . 'sovereignty' mean for a state of only six million?"[43] In invading Kuwait in 1990 the Iraqi regime of Saddam Hussein posed the same question to the international community. The international order defender might answer such aggressors by pointing out that sovereign status in the postwar period has proved to be virtually indestructible. With the exception of states created through a wartime division, such as South Vietnam or East Germany, or states later divided into their constituent parts, such as the Soviet Union or Yugoslavia, no sovereign country has been extinguished from the map since the Soviet Union took over the Baltic states in 1940. Since the international community has now accepted the reassertion of Latvian, Lithuanian, and Estonian sovereignty, the disappearance of the once sovereign Baltic states proved to be a temporary, albeit lengthy, state of affairs. One might observe that, although states resembling aggressive boa constrictors have existed, they have found squeezing their prey into submission to be far easier than swallowing it whole.

Thus, by assisting in delineating independent territorial entities, the concept of sovereignty contributes to international order by creating a class of political entities that are expected, in the ordinary course of events, to be permanent fixtures on the international scene.[44] Notwithstanding the acts of Iraq against Kuwait or the rhetoric of Guatemala concerning Belize, for many years sovereign

43. Alan James, *Sovereign Statehood: The Basis of International Society* (London: Allen & Unwin, 1986), p. 2.

44. Although sovereignty is often referred to as a stabilizing concept of order, a political entity can, of course, gain or lose sovereignty over a particular territory. The ranks of sovereign states are not immutable. A country's sovereign territory today may well fall under the rule of a different country in the future. See generally Raymond Aron, *Peace and War: A Theory of International Relations*, trans. Richard A. Howard and Annette Baker-Fox (New York: Frederick A. Praeger, 1967), p. 742. Classical international law recognizes four principal methods for a government to establish sovereignty over a particular territory: through conquest, that is, by a victorious state completely subjugating and declaring its intent to annex a territory; through cession, that is, by the ceding state agreeing with the acquiring state to transfer sovereign rights; through prescription, that is, by possessing the territory over a long and peaceful period; and by contiguity, that is, by occupying territories that form a natural geographic unit. For a slightly different approach see J. A. Andrews, "The Concept of Statehood and the Acquisition of Territory in the Nineteenth Century," *The Law Quarterly Review* 94 (1978): 408–27.

states have refrained from absorbing other sovereign states into their territory. The defenders of sovereignty are prepared to give the concept some credit for this state of affairs.

Since shades of gray, rather than stark black-and-white tones, usually characterize international politics, one might expect to find certain drawbacks alongside the benefits that sovereignty provides in helping to order the international community. In fact, the concept of sovereignty can also lead to irresponsible behavior, as states proudly flaunt their independence, churlishly shun cooperative ventures, or childishly resist following another's initiatives. Inis Claude recently noted: "The notion of sovereignty is, among other things, a rationale for setting an autonomous course, for going one's way. Sovereignty tends to lead to independicitis, an inflamed sense of autonomy. The temptation for states is always not so much to follow the leader as to dump upon the leader as much as possible of the burden of carrying out the more onerous and risky tasks that the world requires."[45]

The critics argue forcefully that in no area of international life are the drawbacks of sovereignty for international order more evident than in the manner in which states have practically rejected collective security,[46] even as some have rhetorically adopted it. While the problems in moving a collective-security scheme from the drawing board to the battlefield are legion,[47] chief among them is a notion rife with implications for the student of sovereignty. Collective security assumes that states will be willing to cast aside independent decision making that takes into account particular circumstances and particular interests in favor of adherence to a single principle—opposition to aggression.

45. Inis L. Claude, Jr., *The United States in a Changing World* (Jerusalem: Academon Press, The Hebrew University, 1993), p. 34.

46. By "collective security" we mean a defensive scheme in which each member of a group of states guarantees that aggression—an attack on any country anywhere—will be met by the combined resistance of the entire group of states. The commitment to resist all aggression, whether directed against friend or foe, distinguishes collective security from a mutual defense alliance.

47. See Arnold Wolfers, *Discord and Collaboration: Essays on International Politics* (Baltimore: Johns Hopkins University Press, 1962), especially pp. 167–204; Eban, *The New Diplomacy*, pp. 259–65; Inis L. Claude, Jr., *American Approaches to World Affairs* (Lanham, Md.: University Press of America, 1986), pp. 51–67; and Claude, "Theoretical Approaches to National Security and World Order," pp. 31–45.

The skeptics rightly question whether either the Korean War[48] or the Persian Gulf War[49] ought properly to be considered a collective-security venture, as opposed to a selective response against a particular instance of aggression. And a principal reason that collective-security schemes have not enjoyed much success—beyond a bland, and easily shattered, rhetorical consensus—is the fact that states often greatly value autonomous, sovereign decision making and instinctively distrust sweeping, cooperative, global initiatives in the field of national security.

Nevertheless, on balance, sovereignty's defenders insist, the concept contributes much of value to the international order. It establishes a legal and political hierarchy and helps to create expectations of behavior. It assists in focusing the attention of key actors on critical issues. It provides a legitimate framework for regulating harmful human activities. And it can serve to protect the weak from more powerful, aggressive states. To eliminate sovereignty, its supporters fear, would be akin to removing the keystone from the arch of modern international life.

The Sovereign Equality Defense

Others view sovereignty as a great leveler. These defenders applaud sovereign statehood for according the same measure of sovereign rights to each state no matter how powerful or weak, rich or poor, large or small. Theoretically, of course, the roots of sovereign equality are intertwined with those of a chunk theory of sovereignty. As Inis Claude observed, "[I]f sovereignty is a monolithic chunk of rights which must be possessed in full or not at all, then it follows that every political entity possessing that attribute must be considered the equal of every other such entity."[50] Sovereignty thus might stand for mutual respect between states and acknowledgment of reciprocal rights and duties.

From this perspective sovereignty also seems to express confidence in the ability of all states to govern themselves and to

---

48. See Wolfers, *Discord and Collaboration*, pp. 167–80.

49. See Inis L. Claude, Jr., "The Gulf War and Prospects for World Order by Collective Security," in *The Persian Gulf Crisis: Power in the Post–Cold War World*, ed. Robert F. Helms II and Robert H. Dorff (Westport, Conn.: Praeger Publishers, 1993), pp. 23–38.

50. Claude, *National Minorities*, p. 32.

participate on an equal basis in international society. In an encyclical letter that attests to the popularity of this view, Pope John XXIII once stated: "All men are equal in their natural dignity. Consequently there are no political communities which are superior by nature and none which are inferior . . . since they are bodies whose membership is made up of these same human beings. Because all states are by nature equal in dignity, each has the right to exist and to be primarily responsible for its own future."[51] Thus, sovereignty might be said to promote the self-determination of political communities, particularly since people intent on exercising self-determination are almost invariably aiming to create a sovereign state.

In the functioning of international organizations the principle of sovereignty has led to the corollary of formal sovereign equality in voting matters. From the Hague conferences at the turn of the twentieth century through the United Nations Charter down to the present day, the international community has hailed the sovereign equality of each of its members by advancing the principle of one state, one vote. In many international organizations the idea of sovereign equality in voting has been justified as a necessary measure to defend weak states from their more aggressive or powerful peers.

The Economic Development Defense

Other defenders endorse the concept on the grounds that a system of sovereign states promotes economic development. Stephen Krasner, for one, argued that "a single, absolutist empire . . . would have stultified private initiative."[52] An international system of sovereign states "facilitated economic development by providing

51. Pope John XXIII, Encyclical Letter (12 April 1963), quoted in Robert A. Klein, *Sovereign Equality Among States: The History of an Idea* (Toronto: University of Toronto Press, 1974), pp. 143–44. Compare this theoretical statement with the largely fruitless and unhappy consequences of efforts by aborigines to attain self-determination. See Guntram F. A. Werther, *Self-Determination in Western Democracies: Aboriginal Politics in a Comparative Perspective* (Westport, Conn.: Greenwood Press, 1992).

52. Stephen D. Krasner, "Sovereignty: An Institutional Perspective," in *The Elusive State: International and Comparative Perspectives*, ed. James A. Caporaso (Newbury Park, Calif.: Sage Publications, 1989), p. 69. Krasner goes on to suggest that a system of sovereign states may no longer be the optimal way to organize political life.

an environment sufficiently orderly to permit rational economic calculations." He concluded: "Over the last five hundred years, the sovereign state has been a powerful instrument of human progress."

Others have viewed the concept as granting to less powerful states a potent weapon to use against economic aggression and foreign exploitation of natural resources. Third World leaders demanded that the development of natural resources be considered a matter of sovereign right. They effectively challenged the legitimacy of concessions made to multinational corporations at a time when Third World states were weak and international resource markets unfavorable.[53] Consequently, the protective mantle of sovereignty might be viewed as ameliorating the harsh winds of international capitalism.

In fact, during the course of decolonization international law developed to authorize sovereign states to expropriate natural resources and industry owned by foreigners.[54] States ranging in size and ideology from Cuba to Mexico, from Iran to Brazil, effectively expropriated foreign properties in order to take advantage of significant economic, human, and natural resources. The economic imperialism defense cites these cases of expropriation as praiseworthy attempts by leaders to exert their sovereign authority in a world dominated by hostile economic interests.

The Usefulness of Sovereignty

What does the debate between the critics and defenders reveal about the usefulness of sovereignty? To what degree is sovereignty a beneficial concept in modern international relations? Is sovereignty a curse, a blessing, or perhaps a mixed blessing for the international community?

53. See Soroos, *Beyond Sovereignty*, p. 55. For a view of the other side of this coin, that is, the efforts by countries to attract foreign investment and compete for the favors of attractive investors, see Dennis J. Encarnation and Louis T. Wells, Jr., "Sovereignty En Garde: Negotiating with Foreign Investors," *International Organization* 39 (1985): 47–78.

54. See, for instance, Eduardo Jiménez de Arechaga, "State Responsibility for the Nationalization of Foreign-Owned Property," in *International Law: A Contemporary Perspective*, ed. Richard A. Falk, Friedrich V. Kratochwil, and Saul H. Mendlovitz (Boulder, Colo.: Westview Press, 1985), pp. 546–57.

We find some merit in the economic imperialism defense, particularly in the notion that sovereignty helps to protect the weak in economic as well as military competition. Certainly, through business laws and regulations sovereign states have served to influence, if not always to discipline, multinational companies operating within their borders. The ability of the state—indeed, the responsibility of the state—to regulate such corporations causes them to tailor their activities, to some extent, to suit foreign ways of life.

However, a substantial multinational corporation can often flex considerable economic muscle in the face of the sovereign state through its technological capabilities, its employment of local citizens, and its financial resources. The powerful current of state influence on the multinational is thus paralleled by a substantial countercurrent of corporate influence on the state. And many examples attest to the ability of particular multinationals to influence politics quite dramatically, both by aboveboard means such as campaign contributions, and, occasionally, by underhanded tactics such as bribes or intimidation.

Thus, while the order imposed by the sovereign state on corporations acting within its borders is real, it is tempered by the practical fact that multinational companies are often able to exercise influence, particularly on Third World states, such that the government adopts certain of its laws and the people adapt certain of their ways of life to suit corporate management. We believe that in such a contest sovereignty lends a critical arrow to the quiver of a weak state by permitting the expropriation of foreign property.

However, we are not entirely persuaded that the principle of sovereign equality is as praiseworthy as certain of the defenders of sovereignty would have it. Proclaiming states to be equal when in so many important respects they are manifestly unequal lends an air of unreality to the enterprise of conducting international relations. In terms of power, capability, and influence, states differ dramatically, as they do in population, territory, natural resources, and industrial capacity. Thus, sovereign equality does not so much describe reality as it purports to change it.[55] While supporters of the concept hope that the fiction of equality may elevate weak states

---

55. Inis L. Claude, Jr., "The Tension Between Principle and Pragmatism in International Relations," *Review of International Studies* 19 (1993): 226.

to the status of their more powerful brethren, the emphasis of equality over hierarchy could result in responsibilities being shirked and institutions functioning less effectively.

Certainly, the value of sovereign equality in international organizations is not self-evident. Should the 8,400 people on Nauru, the smallest sovereign state in the South Pacific, be granted a vote equal to that enjoyed by the hundreds of millions of Chinese or Indians or Americans or Indonesians? On what reasoning should a tiny, sparsely populated, state such as the Vatican, comprising 1.4 square kilometers of territory, automatically be granted the same vote as a large and populous Great Power?[56] Indeed, could one not question the voting procedures of the Organization of American States where seven Central American and thirteen Caribbean republics could combine to outvote all the states of South America, despite the fact that the population of Central America and the Caribbean amounts to fewer than the number of Colombian citizens alone?[57]

Should the decisions of international organizations take on even greater importance in the years ahead, the notion that tiny or weak states must naturally stand on an equal footing in international organizations with large, powerful states is likely to cause continuing tension. The more compelling conclusion is that states should at times decide issues on a sovereign equality basis and at times find a more appropriate voting formula, depending on the nature of the forum or, even more precisely, on the nature of the issue being put to vote. For instance, altering the voting principles of the International Monetary Fund to a sovereign-equality basis would court disaster by divorcing financial decision making from the donor states. Yet, changing the principle of sovereign equality in the UN General Assembly would detract from that forum's desirable role as a prominent weathervane indicating the views of the international community of states.[58] In short, sovereignty's supporters fail

56. James Crawford, "Islands as Sovereign Nations," *International and Comparative Law Quarterly* 38 (1989): 277–98. See generally Richard A. Herr, "Microstate Sovereignty in the South Pacific: Is Small Practical?" *Contemporary Southeast Asia* 10 (1988): 182–96.

57. See "Election Has OAS Nations Sizing Each Other Up: Contest Between Big Colombia and Small Costa Rica Epitomizes Hemispheric Rivalry," *Washington Post*, 23 March 1994, p. A8.

58. For a provocative essay entitled "Collective Legitimization as a Political Function of the United Nations," see Claude, *States and the Global System*, pp. 145–59. Claude

to persuade us that the sovereign equality voting formula proves the usefulness of sovereignty. As basket thinkers we fear that undue adherence to the corollary of sovereign equality may well become a shortcoming of sovereignty instead of one of its benefits.[59]

In the debate between the supporters of state sovereignty, who view international organizations as reflecting the international community, and the critics, who see them as reforming the system, we adopt a middle position. In our view international organizations are designed both to help states to cooperate and to encourage them to move toward progressive goals. Sometimes the representatives of states will carry out an undertaking at the bidding of their government through some particular organization. At other times the international organization itself takes an initiative, relying upon and occasionally molding the support of states.

While that brand of reform is by no means incompatible with state sovereignty, a tension certainly can exist, particularly in such ambitious endeavors as the state-building enterprises the United Nations has undertaken in Somalia and Mozambique.[60] When an international organization turns from the task of providing humanitarian relief[61] to the even more thorny project of building, or rebuilding, a modern state, the organization has moved into an extremely sensitive area both for potential sovereign authorities within that state and for neighbors and other states strategically interested in that state-building process.

However, while state building is likely to prove controversial and

argued: "While the voice of the United Nations may not be the authentic voice of mankind, it is clearly the best available facsimile thereof, and statesmen have by general consent treated the United Nations as the most impressive and authoritative instrument for the expression of a global version of the general will" (p. 150).

59. Political thinkers from various perspectives have likewise criticized sovereign equality. See George F. Kennan, *The Cloud of Danger: Current Realities of American Foreign Policy* (Boston: Little, Brown & Co., 1977), pp. 29–30. For similar views voiced by Louis Halle and Robert Klein see Klein, *Sovereign Equality Among States*, pp. xv, 144. See also David Mitrany, *The Progress of International Government* (New Haven, Conn.: Yale University Press, 1933), especially pp. 53–96. For a general treatment of sovereign equality see Bernard Gilson, *The Conceptual System of Sovereign Equality* (Leuven: Peeters, 1984).

60. See "Building a Nation in Mozambique," *Washington Post*, 31 October 1993, p. A27.

61. For articles spelling out certain administrative and philosophical difficulties encountered in early humanitarian relief projects see Schott, "United States Relief to Civilian Victims," pp. 105–13, and Farer, "Humanitarian Intervention," pp. 149–64.

while its record is likely to be dotted with failures, there does not seem to be much evidence that the international community would prefer to have interested powers rather than an international organization meddling in state building. Thus, it seems likely that in this "state-spawning era"[62] the international community is prepared to tolerate the tension between state sovereignty and ambitious state-building enterprises by international organizations.

We do not find the critique of sovereignty offered by more radical advocates of reform through international organization to be especially forceful. Despite grand hopes for functionalist cooperation, political conflict has regularly spilled over into nonpolitical agencies and significantly reduced their effectiveness.[63] Thus, the functionalist critique of sovereignty appears overdrawn. The more radical proponents of sweeping change through international organization, such as the world federalists, often seem to assume that peace and justice will inevitably be served by centralizing power.[64] The opposite conclusion, that centralized power threatens peace more comprehensively and insidiously, appears to us to be more plausible.

As for the human rights critique, we are neither convinced that the concept of sovereignty causes human rights abuses nor that eliminating the concept would bring about substantial improvement in human rights conditions. As F. H. Hinsley observed:

> In the past one hundred years, both within and between communities, men have often indulged in the excessive or the dubious use of political power. This use or misuse of power would have occurred if the concept of sovereignty had never been formulated, as it did before the concept was formulated. But because it was now condoned or justified in some quarters by reference to that concept, the concept itself was . . . brought into disrepute.[65]

62. The phrase is drawn from Claude, "The Peace-Keeping Role of the United Nations," p. 58.

63. Eban, *The New Diplomacy*, p. 278.

64. See Claude, *Swords into Plowshares*. See also Roger Fisher, *Points of Choice: International Crises and the Role of Law* (Oxford: Oxford University Press, 1978), pp. 23–24.

65. Hinsley, *Sovereignty*, p. 218.

Attention to human rights has resulted in an increasing number of international treaties signed both by sovereign states that typically respect human rights and by some that at present do not. Equally important, the revolution in communications has exposed the realities of human rights abuses to far-flung public attention. Since sovereign states usually find a positive national image to be beneficial for purposes ranging from international finance and trade to ideological propaganda, human rights organizations and concerned states have succeeded in focusing increased attention on abuses and in aiding certain victims of human rights violations.[66]

Indeed, one might argue that a key benefit of the basket approach to sovereignty gaining ascendance over the chunk view is that the traditional entitlement of nonintervention in internal affairs is in the process of being overturned, particularly in less powerful states. The walls of state sovereignty—once thought impregnable in regard to human rights violations—now often appear riddled with peepholes and surrounded by a noisy and hostile crowd. Under such circumstances proponents of human rights might best be advised to continue to clarify just what constitute human rights violations and just when humanitarian intervention is called for and to redouble efforts to exact a full price in adverse publicity when internationally recognized standards are flouted.[67] Such a practical course of action seems to us preferable to an attempt to subvert the system of sovereign states itself.

Conclusion

As we initially observed, the concept of sovereignty has seemed to some to be on the decline. Among other important pieces of evidence, the passionate debate between critics and defenders helps to lay to rest the view that sovereignty is a concept whose time

---

66. For suggestions as to how a state might negotiate with a human rights offender to influence the abusive government to treat its own citizens decently see Fowler, *Thinking about Human Rights*, pp. 225–34.

67. For an analogous argument see Roger Fisher, "Intervention: Three Problems of Policy and Law," in *Essays on Intervention*, ed. Roland J. Stanger (Columbus: Ohio State University Press, 1964), pp. 13–17.

has now passed. References to sovereignty are multiplying today precisely because the concept is on the whole a useful and largely positive feature of modern international life. Although terms such as bloc, satellite, and protectorate attest to the fact that large states still encroach indirectly upon the independence of their smaller neighbors, sovereign status in the postwar period is rarely challenged directly. Moreover, the international community has bestowed sovereign status on a steadily increasing number of political entities. From those important perspectives, at least, the concept appears to be more respected today than ever before.

To promote orderly relations among states, the international community must somehow separate what states rightfully view as their own business from that of their neighbors and the international community. Supplying this delineation is sovereignty's most useful and prominent function. A cardinal virtue of the concept is that it allocates responsibility as well as authority. The concept of sovereignty helps to create stable expectations that distinguish the business of one state from that of another.

In sum, then, while we view sovereignty as a mixed blessing, we value the benefits it delivers to the international community more than we rue its imperfections. The defenders of sovereignty who cite its beneficial influences for international order seem more persuasive than the critics who focus upon its drawbacks for human rights endeavors, supranationalism, and international organization.

Conclusion:
Will Sovereignty Prosper
or Decline?

> [W]hen a society is ruled by means of the state the concept of
> sovereignty is unavoidable. Questions about the final author-
> ity, what that implies and where it lies, must sooner or later
> in such conditions acquire a fundamental and perhaps a
> permanent significance.
>
> —F. H. Hinsley[1]

Having determined that news of the demise of sovereignty has been
inaccurate, we turn, in closing, to speculation about what might lie
ahead for the concept. What does the future hold for the venerable
notion of sovereignty? Is sovereignty approaching the end of a long
and useful life in international affairs? Alternatively, is the concept
likely to survive even while shedding particular, outmoded uses,
much as a snake wriggles out of its spent skin but continues to
slither forward?

For the foreseeable future we will live in an international community in which the status of political entities is far from self-evident.
As Quincy Wright once noted: "[I]nstead of a world of equal,
territorially defined, sovereign states we have a world of political
entities displaying a tropical luxuriance of political and legal orga-

---

1. F. H. Hinsley, *Sovereignty* (New York: Basic Books, 1966), p. 17.

nization, competence, and status."[2] The lines between sovereign states, federations of sovereign states, once sovereign states, constituent parts of sovereign states, nonsovereign territories, territories shortly to become sovereign states, and territories merely aspiring to future sovereign statehood may be difficult to distinguish today and nearly impossible to decipher as one looks out over the curve of the horizon.

For example, while few could confidently categorize each of the political entities on the following list, fewer still would be comfortable predicting how the status of those entities might change in the next fifty years. Consider, for instance, Andorra, Antarctica, Chad, the Cook Islands, the European Union, the Falkland Islands, Gibraltar, Hong Kong, Lebanon, Liechtenstein, Micronesia, the Netherlands Antilles, the Organization of Eastern Caribbean States, Outer Mongolia, Palau, Palestine, the Punjab, Quebec, San Marino, Somalia, Timor, Tristan da Cunha, the United Arab Emirates, the Vatican, the Virgin Islands, and the Western Sahara.[3] Such a list suggests to us that the status of sovereignty is likely to continue to help organize the cluttered roster of modern political entities for decades to come.

This is especially so, given the continued prominence and the changing interpretations of the principle of self-determination. Advocates of self-determination, from Woodrow Wilson forward, have long spoken in terms of every nation being entitled to its own state. However, the international community actually interpreted self-determination more narrowly than all the rhetoric might suggest. A spectrum of states, both within the United Nations and on their own, vocally opposed the efforts of various peoples at achieving their own states. In reality, the international community plainly endorsed only the right of colonial self-determination: that is, the right of a people to break away from a subservient, colonial status and form their own state.

With the passing of the age of colonialism, advocates of self-determination have started to focus again on broader interpretations. Should people around the world clothe the notion of national

2. Quincy Wright, *Mandates Under the League of Nations* (New York: Greenwood Press, 1968), p. 276.
3. For a similar argument tailored to a different era, see ibid., pp. 276–77.

self-determination with the same legitimacy that was once reserved for colonial self-determination, such a philosophical shift might herald an era marked by unprecedented splintering of states. One would expect sovereignty to remain the rallying cry for such secessionist efforts.

Even apart from issues of secession and self-determination, future international affairs are likely to be marked by constant flux, as states are buffeted by powerful religious, ideological, and nationalist forces. Conceivably, within the next century large swaths of the maps of Africa, the Indian subcontinent, central Europe, or central Asia could be entirely redrawn, much as the map of the former Soviet Union has already been transformed.[4] Moreover, the critical components for explosive future disorder are readily apparent: clashing ideologies; the proliferation of conventional and high-technology weapons; the power of terrorists, narcotics traffickers, and insurgents; and the widespread vulnerabilities of states still emerging from colonial or Cold War pasts. All these factors point to the potential for a new Balkanization, an era characterized by much tension within and among states and, perhaps, by widespread bloodshed.

We would venture to predict that international turmoil in decades ahead will more often be associated with the numerous weak, chaotic, anarchical, or internally tyrannical states than with the strong and stable, militaristic and adventuristic powers that have long been the subject of so much international relations scholarship.[5] The prospects of being drawn into involvement in situations like those in present-day Haiti or Somalia, Mozambique or Rwanda, may well haunt leaders more than the more remote possibility of being overrun by a latter-day Adolf Hitler or Saddam Hussein.

We have already started to see the response to such a state of affairs: the crumbling of the venerable principle of nonintervention under the weight of "humanitarian" interventions of many different

4. For an interesting theoretical discussion of state-building and state-contracting processes related to this point, see Ian S. Lustick, *Unsettled States, Disputed Lands: Britain and Ireland, France and Algeria, Israel and West Bank–Gaza* (Ithaca: Cornell University Press, 1993), especially pp. 442–45.

5. For extended discussions of this point, see Inis L. Claude, Jr., "The New International Security Order: Changing Concepts," *The Naval War College Review* 47 (1994): 9–17, and Inis L. Claude, Jr., *States and the Global System: Politics, Law, and Organization* (New York: St. Martin's Press, 1988), pp. 20–22.

stripes. In all likelihood a hallmark of the post–Cold War world will be a "New Interventionism,"[6] as large and small powers wrestle with the moral and practical implications of intervening, or not intervening, in what once would have been considered the internal affairs of other states.

We expect that under such daunting circumstances sovereignty will remain useful in providing answers to critical questions for the international system, such as:

—Who is in charge in which territory?

—Who is accountable for the uses made of a particular territory?

—Who is entitled, indeed who is obligated, to control the activities of a particular group?

As Inis Claude declared: "This new period of hijacking and piracy, kidnapping and assassination of diplomats and sacking of embassies, and private warfare conducted by guerrilla organizations and soldiers of fortune, may yet teach us to appreciate rather than merely to deplore the enormous historical significance of the sovereign state as a disciplined and disciplining agent in human affairs."[7]

In this regard one might usefully contrast nationalism with sovereigntyism. Nationalism, or aspirations to advance the national cause, ignores the current order and focuses on largely moral claims to legitimacy. Nationalism is thus inherently revolutionary. Sovereigntyism, or devotion to the sovereignty of a state, is stabiliz-

---

6. The phrase is drawn from Inis L. Claude, Jr., "Moral Dilemmas in International Relations," in *The Virginia Papers*, ed. Kenneth W. Thompson (Lanham, Md.: University Press of America, forthcoming), and "The United States and Changing Approaches to National Security and World Order," *The Naval War College Review* (forthcoming). The notion of a New Interventionism is that in the post–Cold War era old legal and moral strictures against intervention in the affairs of other sovereign states have come to be regarded as outmoded. In the *Virginia Papers* article Claude argued: "The New Interventionism reflects the growing notion that intervention is not merely a right, derived from interdependence, but also a moral obligation, rooted in the world's need for human rights, democracy, and peace." And, he added: "The New Interventionism stirs concern about the possible arrogance and abusiveness of its agents."

7. Inis L. Claude, Jr., "The Peace-Keeping Role of the United Nations," in *The United Nations in Perspective*, ed. E. Berkeley Tompkins (Stanford, Calif.: Hoover Institution Press, 1972), p. 58.

ing. Sovereignty arguments stress the just and legal sanctity of the state. To counter man's natural belligerence, the principle of sovereignty provides a framework upon which political groups can build their hopes for security and independence. Thus, sovereignty-ism might be equated with satisfied nationalism.

Because of its positive features, although certain outdated implications of sovereignty may well be cast aside, people are likely to continue to use the concept with great frequency, elasticity, and at times ambiguity. The term's very flexibility will help to ensure that sovereignty will remain alive and well. Indeed, one might say, the multiple uses of sovereignty over the ages attest to the concept's procreative abilities. During the upcoming decades sovereignty will enter into discussions regarding a spectrum of vital international issues. Whether and how such issues are resolved will be determined to some degree by the manner in which leaders choose to approach this time-honored, yet steadily evolving, concept.

In some areas of international life views of sovereign rights may well threaten cooperative resolutions to problems that extend beyond national borders. For instance, efforts to control the proliferation of nuclear weapons will likely clash with the notion that states enjoy a sovereign right to determine what measures ought to be taken to provide for national defense. The recent experiences of Iran and North Korea, whose leaders have faced international condemnation and pressure for attempting to develop their nuclear capabilities, suggest that the international community would like to remove the right to develop such weapons from the baskets of aggressive states. While the success of that ongoing campaign remains open to speculation, a substantial portion of the debate is likely to center on the meaning of sovereignty.

A similar tension between cooperation and sovereignty is likely to continue to arise in law enforcement as well.[8] Until World War II American authorities and their colleagues in many other countries considered crime to be largely a local matter. However, in the twentieth century several critical developments moved law enforcement onto the national and, ultimately, the international stage.

---

8. For a more detailed analysis of the following points, see Ethan A. Nadelmann, *Cops Across Borders: The Internationalization of U.S. Criminal Law Enforcement* (University Park: The Pennsylvania State University Press, 1993).

First, governments around the world criminalized actions that once would have been considered perfectly legal in fields as diverse as narcotics, securities, and finance. Second, criminals took advantage of the transportation and communication revolutions, and their enterprises multiplied in sophistication and scope.

Police forces responded by vastly increasing cooperative efforts across national borders. Consequently, detectives, prosecutors, and diplomats scoff at the popular academic hypothesis that the concept of sovereignty has long been lapsing in relevance. To the contrary, notions of sovereignty amount to the chief difficulty in mounting law-enforcement efforts across boundaries. Police officials acting in foreign countries soon find themselves mired in difficulties quite unlike those encountered in the course of asserting their authority within the boundaries of their own states. Police officers abroad are often strictly constrained by foreign colleagues, guardians of their state's sovereign prerogative to monopolize the official use of force within its borders.

Thus, an official who wishes to gain custody of a suspect who has fled abroad will soon contend with the sovereignty of that foreign country. The police officer who wishes to investigate criminal activity that extends abroad, or who would like to hire informants or carry out undercover operations abroad, must confront the implications of sovereignty. So, too, is sovereignty uppermost in the mind of the prosecutor who needs evidence to be collected abroad for use in a domestic court.

To assuage the tension between cooperation and sovereignty in the law-enforcement realm, states have increasingly signed extradition and mutual legal assistance treaties to formalize just when and how cooperation will be forthcoming. At the same time it should be recognized that those upholding law and order in one country are often sympathetic to the efforts of foreign colleagues intent on the same task. This helps to explain the many efforts to evade sovereignty issues by cooperating informally or extralegally. Nonetheless, the specter of sovereignty hangs over all the interactions aimed at fostering cooperative law enforcement.

A like tension between cooperation and sovereignty exists when states attempt to settle environmental affairs. For example, to what extent are sovereign states obligated to restrict or cease polluting activities within their boundaries that adversely affect the inhabitants or territory of other states?[9] International and domestic courts, international organizations, and individual governments have already examined this issue for half a century and are likely to continue to do so through the foreseeable future.[10]

The difficulties inherent in forging agreements among sovereign states suffering from pollution drifting across international frontiers is illustrated by the acid rain disputes among European states and between Canada and the United States.[11] The pressing need to confront other international environmental problems involving oil spills, nuclear energy and explosions,[12] rain forests and climate change, toxic chemicals and hazardous wastes,[13] and even biodiversity and the transfer of plant genes[14] with lasting and effective environmental agreements ensures continuing tension between traditional notions of sovereign independence and popular, cooperative environmental movements aimed at curtailing pollution at its source.

Yet while some may rue the pernicious influence of the sovereign prerogative of domestic jurisdiction in many environmental matters, it may be more reasonable to appreciate that positive environmental behavior may be reached most readily by self-confident, secure sovereign states, not by states of doubtful sovereignty or by troubled states with tenuous control over their people and over

9. For a provocative, early discussion of such environmental problems see George F. Kennan, "To Prevent a World Wasteland," *Foreign Affairs* 48 (1970): 401–13.

10. See *Trail Smelter* [US/Can.] 17 *Reports of International Arbitral Awards* 1 (1949). See also Richard Bilder, "Settlement of Disputes in the Field of the International Law of the Environment," *Recueil des cours: Collected Courses of the Hague Academy of International Law* 144 (1975): 139–239.

11. See generally Cees Flinterman, Barbara Kwiatkowska, and Johan G. Lammers, eds. *Transboundary Air Pollution: International Legal Aspects of the Co-Operation of States* (The Hague: Martinus Nijhoff, 1986).

12. See, for instance, *Nuclear Tests* [*Australia v Fr.*], 1974 *International Court of Justice Reports of Judgments, Advisory Opinions, and Orders* 253 (Judgment).

13. See F. James Handley, "Hazardous Waste Exports: A Leak in the System of International Legal Controls," *Environmental Law Reporter* 19: 10,171–82. See also Philip Alston, "International Regulation of Toxic Chemicals," *Ecology Law Quarterly* 7 (1979): 397–456.

14. See Jack R. Kloppenburg, Jr., *Seeds and Sovereignty: The Use and Control of Plant Genetic Resources* (Durham, N.C.: Duke University Press, 1988). See also S. H. Bragdon, "National Sovereignty and Global Environmental Responsibility: Can the Tension be Reconciled for the Conservation of Biological Diversity?" *Harvard International Law Journal* 33 (1992): 381–92.

corporations operating within their boundaries. A state whose government is fighting for its survival, such as that of Saddam Hussein during the Gulf War, is more likely to unleash environmental terrorism than to sign sensible accords and otherwise take on the responsibilities of acting as a good environmental citizen.

While the international community has also traditionally relied upon the concept of sovereign rights to determine who owns and may exploit natural resources, some fresh thinking on this score seems to be emerging. In the past the territorial sovereign owned all the natural resources on land within the sovereign's borders, defined as its territory and its territorial waters. Alternatively, on the high seas resources were the property of all states. In recent years this simple division has started to break down as states have claimed exclusive economic zones far beyond their coastal waters. In addition, the Law of the Sea Conference raised the prospect of the international community granting to particular states either exclusive or competitive rights over certain marine resources within designated areas of the high seas.[15]

One might expect to see the notion of sovereign rights grow ever more complicated, if only because equitably dividing natural resources is often a complicated task in a world marked by increasing population pressures and extraordinary technological advances. Consider, for instance, a river that flows through the territories of several states; schools of fish that migrate through the coastal waters and, perhaps, journey up the rivers of different states; or an aquifer or large oil deposit that lies under the territory of more than one state. That such circumstances could lead to a competition between two or more states to exploit the resources as rapidly as possible has long been recognized.[16] To avoid wasteful or hasty exploitation,

15. Friedrich V. Kratochwil, Paul Rohrlich, and Harpreet Mahjan, *Peace and Disputed Sovereignty: Reflections on Conflict over Territory* (Lanham, Md.: University Press of America, 1985), p. 19. The authors continued: "Functional regimes and the unbundling of rights have often been advocated as solutions to the 'all or nothing' concept of national sovereignty. Even if such arrangements have considerably contributed to the de-escalation of conflict, they do not resolve all such issues." And, they concluded: "The advantage of the 'all-or-nothing' view of territorial sovereignty is not only its simplicity but its implicit *presumption* that in the face of newly emerging problems *the territorial unit (and the territorial 'sovereign') has the right to regulate matters*" (italics in original).

16. For an early chapter on this subject see F. A. Váli, *Servitudes of International Law: A Study of Rights in Foreign Territory*, 2d ed. rev. (New York: Frederick A. Praeger, 1958), pp. 153–66.

states may increasingly choose to rethink traditional notions of sovereign rights.

Another source of continuing conflict that will be centered on the idea of sovereignty may be seen in the field of human rights. As noted in the prior chapter, governments no longer comfortably declare: "Within our borders we, as sovereigns, do as we please and brook no foreign interference. We exercise our legislative, executive, and judicial functions as we like since it is our sovereign prerogative to do so."[17] Nevertheless, even in the field of human rights traditional views of state sovereignty are not inconsequential barriers to those pressing for change.

In the immediate future totalitarian and authoritarian governments are likely to continue to use supposed sovereign prerogatives to try to stem the flow of information about abuses and to forestall efforts to assist victims. To shield themselves from the scrutiny of human rights advocates, such leaders may be expected to call upon the chunk approach to sovereignty in a defensive manner. At the same time human rights groups will continue their efforts to underscore the key responsibilities of sovereign statehood. To promote humanitarian intervention and to circumscribe the principle of nonintervention is a task more comfortably associated with basket theory. In any event the different principal approaches to the concept of sovereignty are very likely to frame future controversies regarding human rights.

Along with security, law-enforcement, environmental, and human rights issues, sovereignty is likely to be a focal point of discussion as international and regional organizations attempt to gain strength and stature. To the chunk theorists such organizations naturally clash with expressions of sovereignty.[18] From this per-

17. See Michael Ross Fowler, *Thinking about Human Rights: Contending Approaches to Human Rights in U.S. Foreign Policy* (Lanham, Md.: University Press of America, 1987), p. 218.

18. Elmer Plischke wrote: "Whenever states create an international agency to perform certain responsibilities on their behalf and empower it to direct, manage, or regulate, they are . . . restricting their own governmental authority and freedom of action. Absolute sovereignty and international organization therefore appear to be contradictory and mutually exclusive." Plischke continued: "While it may be argued that fundamental sovereignty remains unaffected and only governmental authority is relinquished in the formation of an international agency, the practical effect is the same. In essence what formerly were matters that transcended national frontiers but nevertheless were treated as domestic issues and were dealt with purely on the basis of national policy have

spective the campaigns that are gaining momentum to rest authority in supranational organizations still face critical battles in contending with the tradition of sovereign rights.[19] For the basket thinker, perhaps, delegating certain traditionally sovereign rights and duties to an international body is viewed as a much more natural phenomenon. The effect of the process of international organization on a state's sovereign rights and duties simply reflects the manner in which the contents of sovereignty baskets continually and naturally change over time.[20]

The basket theorists might add that international organizations also reap important benefits from the notion of sovereignty. International organizations need members who can exercise the responsibilities now associated with sovereign rule. They need members who can control their territories and commit their peoples. Above all, perhaps, international organizations need members who are able to cooperate when they promise to do so. Strong sovereign states can thus be a boon for international organizations, not a burden.[21] One might well conclude that whether sovereignty is

---

become circumscribed by international commitments enforceable by international machinery." Elmer Plischke, *Conduct of American Diplomacy* (Princeton: D. Van Nostrand Co., 1961), pp. 527–28.

19. See Neil MacCormick, "Beyond the Sovereign State," *The Modern Law Review* 56 (1993): 1–18. See also Joseph Frankel, *The Making of Foreign Policy: An Analysis of Decisionmaking* (London: Oxford University Press, 1963), pp. 66–67. The Basic Law of the Federal Republic of Germany provided: "[T]he parliament will consent to such limitations upon its sovereign powers as will bring about and secure a peaceful and lasting order in Europe and among the nations of the world" (p. 66). The Draft Constitution of Ghana of 1960 stated: ". . . in the confident expectation of an early surrender of sovereignty to a union of African states and territories, the people now confer on the Parliament the power to provide for the surrender of the whole or of any part of the sovereignty of Ghana" (p. 67).

20. See Inis L. Claude, Jr., *Swords into Plowshares: The Problems and Progress of International Organization*, 4th ed. rev. (New York: Random House, 1971), p. 4.

21. Inis Claude wrote: "[International] agencies . . . are organizations not only of states but also by states and for states. They are not imposed upon states by some outside force, nor are they conceived as working to diminish the significance of states and ultimately to dismantle and replace the multistate system. On the contrary, they are created by states in response to needs, dangers, and opportunities, with a view to using them for their own purposes. States may, on occasion, lose control of some of them; . . . organizational tendencies to develop autonomy sometimes prevail. Nevertheless, . . . it is a mistake to regard the international organization movement as an antistate design, or to conceive the relationship between states and international organizations as a zero-sum game, in which the flourishing of the latter implies the weakening of the former."

viewed as a positive or a negative factor in international organization depends in large measure on whether the chunk or the basket
approach is being asserted. In either case scholars and politicians
alike are quite likely to continue to refer to the concept of sovereignty in discussions regarding the future of the process of organizing international society.

Conclusion

Those who would think clearly about modern international relations should study the value, meanings, complexities, and incon-
sistencies inherent in the concept of sovereignty. Operating on the
assumption that those writing on international relations should
analyze the actual conduct of states as well as the writings of
scholars, we have approached sovereignty trying to discover what
states say about the concept through their behavior as well as what
academics say about sovereignty in their works. After all, in our
view states remain the most prominent political groups that set the
rules for and play the game of international politics that scholars
study. And as has recently been observed: "Concepts are rarely
products of pure cogitation; they generally derive from practice,
from the trial and error of effort. We reflect upon our experiences
and thus develop concepts to explain and justify, to make sense of,
what we have done."[22]

This approach has underscored for us the fact that sovereignty is
a practical concept as well as an abstract one. It is a concept that in
the first instance is derived from the practice of states. As practices
change, so too have the uses of the term. The "skin of the living
thought" of sovereignty is likely to continue to adapt to future
circumstances within the international society.

Reports of its demise notwithstanding, sovereignty appears to us
to be prospering, not declining, as the twentieth century draws to a
close. It still serves as an indispensable component of international

Inis L. Claude, Jr., *The Record of International Organizations in the Twentieth Century*
(Taipei, Taiwan: Tamkang University Press, 1986), p. 4.
  22. Claude, "The New International Security Order," p. 9.

politics. So long as many in the society of states view sovereignty as contributing to world stability, security, and peace, the concept will remain a sturdy foundation for the superstructure of international politics for years to come. We would conclude that, although sovereignty is perhaps not an inevitable concept in international relations, its future in the current international community continues to be most promising.

Table of Cases

Bibliography

Books and Articles

Alcock, Antony E. *The History of the South Tyrol Question.* London: Michael Joseph, 1970.

Alexis, Francis. "British Intervention in St. Kitts." *New York University Journal of International Law and Politics* 16 (1983–84): 581–600.

Alston, Philip. "International Regulation of Toxic Chemicals." *Ecology Law Quarterly* 7 (1979): 394–456.

Andrews, J. A. "The Concept of Statehood and the Acquisition of Territory in the Nineteenth Century." *The Law Quarterly Review* 94 (1978): 408–27.

Arend, Anthony Clark. "The United Nations and the New World Order." *The Georgetown Law Journal* 81 (1993): 491–533.

Armstrong, J. D. "The International Committee of the Red Cross and Political Prisoners." *International Organization* 39 (1985): 615–42.

Aron, Raymond. *Peace and War: A Theory of International Relations.* Translated by Richard A. Howard and Annette Baker-Fox. New York: Frederick A. Praeger, 1967.

Azar, Edward E. *The Management of Protracted Social Conflicts: Theory and Cases.* Hanover, N.H.: Dartmouth College Press, 1990.

———, and Pickering, Anthony F. "The Problem-Solving Forums: The Falklands/Malvinas Islands." In *The Management of Protracted Social Conflicts: Theory and Cases,* edited by Edward E. Azar, pp. 82–108. Hanover, N.H.: Dartmouth College Press, 1990.

Ball, George. *Diplomacy for a Crowded World.* Boston: Little, Brown & Co., 1976.

Baroch, Charles T. *The Soviet Doctrine of Sovereignty.* New York: American Bar Association, 1970.

Bateson, Mary Catherine. "Beyond Sovereignty: An Emerging Global Civilization." In *Contending Sovereignties: Redefining Political Community*, edited by R.B.J. Walker and Saul H. Mendlovitz, pp. 145–58. Boulder, Colo.: Lynne Reinner Publishers, 1990.

Benn, Stanley I. "The Uses of 'Sovereignty.'" In *In Defense of Sovereignty*, edited by W. J. Stankiewicz, pp. 67–85. New York: Oxford University Press, 1969.

Bennett, Michael. "The People's Republic of China and the Use of International Law in the Spratly Islands Dispute." *Stanford Journal of International Law* 28 (1992): 425–50.

Bilder, Richard. "Settlement of Disputes in the Field of International Law of the Environment." *Recueil des cours: Collected Courses of the Hague Academy of International Law* 144 (1975): 139–239.

Bingham, June. *U Thant: The Search for Peace*. New York: Alfred A. Knopf, 1970.

Black, Cyril E.; Falk, Richard A.; Knorr, Klaus; and Young, Oran R. *Neutralization and World Politics*. Princeton: Princeton University Press, 1968.

Blake, Leslie L. *Sovereignty: Power Beyond Politics*. London: Shepheard-Walwyn, 1988.

Blix, Hans. *Sovereignty, Aggression, and Neutrality*. Stockholm: Amquist & Wiksell, 1970.

Bodin, Jean. *On Sovereignty: Four Chapters from the Six Books on the Commonwealth*. Edited and translated by Julian H. Franklin. New York: Cambridge University Press, 1992.

Booth, Ken. *Law, Force, and Diplomacy at Sea*. London: Allen & Unwin, 1985.

Bosco, Andrea. "National Sovereignty and Peace: Lord Lothian's Federalist Thought." In *The Larger Idea: Lord Lothian and the Problem of National Sovereignty*, edited by John Turner, pp. 108–23. London: Historians' Press, 1988.

Boutros-Ghali, Boutros. "Empowering the United Nations." *Foreign Affairs* 71 (1992/93): 89–102.

Boyle, Francis; Chayes, Abram; Dore, Isaak; Falk, Richard; Feinrider, Martin; Ferguson, C. Clyde, Jr.; Fine, J. David; Nunes, Keith; and Weston, Burns. "International Lawlessness in Grenada." *American Journal of International Law* (1984): 172–75.

Bragdon, S. H. "National Sovereignty and Global Environmental Responsibility: Can the Tension Be Reconciled for the Conservation of Biological Diversity?" *Harvard International Law Journal* 33 (1992): 381–92.

Brewin, Christopher. "Sovereignty." In *The Community of States*, edited by James Mayall, pp. 34–48. London: Allen & Unwin, 1982.

Brownlie, Ian. *Principles of Public International Law*. Oxford: Clarendon Press, 1979.

———. "Thoughts on Kind-Hearted Gunmen." In *Humanitarian Intervention and the United Nations*, edited by Richard B. Lillich, pp. 139–48. Charlottesville: University Press of Virginia, 1973.

Brunal-Perry, Omaira. *A Question of Sovereignty: What Legitimate Right Did Spain Have to Its Territorial Expansion?* Translated by Marjorie G. Driver. Mangilao, Guam: Micronesian Area Research Center, University of Guam, 1993.

Brzezinski, Zbigniew. *Power and Principle: Memoirs of the National Security Adviser, 1977–1981*. New York: Farrar, Straus & Giroux, 1983.

Bull, Hedley. *The Anarchical Society*. London: Macmillan, 1977.
――――. *Intervention in World Politics*. New York: Oxford University Press, 1984.
――――. "The State's Positive Role in World Affairs." *Daedalus* 108 (1979): 111–23.
Bunck, Julie Marie. *Fidel Castro and the Quest for a Revolutionary Culture in Cuba*. University Park, Pa.: The Pennsylvania State University Press, 1994.
Burgess, John W. *Political Science and Comparative Constitutional Law*. 2 vols. Boston: Ginn and Co., 1893.
Burns, E.L.M. "The Withdrawal of UNEF and the Future of Peacekeeping." *International Journal* 23 (1967–68): 1–17.
Buzan, Barry. *People, States, and Fear: The National Security Problem in International Relations*. Chapel Hill: University of North Carolina Press, 1983.
Camilleri, Joseph A. "Rethinking Sovereignty in a Shrinking, Fragmented World." In *Contending Sovereignties: Redefining Political Community*, edited by R.B.J. Walker and Saul H. Mendlovitz, pp. 13–44. Boulder, Colo.: Lynne Reinner Publishers, 1990.
――――, and Falk, Jim. *The End of Sovereignty? The Politics of a Shrinking and Fragmented World*. Brookfield, Vt.: Elgar, 1992.
Campbell, David. *Politics without Principle: Sovereignty, Ethics, and the Narratives of the Gulf War*. Boulder, Colo.: Lynne Reinner Publishers, 1993.
Carlisle, Rodney. *Sovereignty for Sale: The Origins and Evolution of the Panamanian and Liberian Flags of Convenience*. Annapolis, Md.: Naval Institute Press, 1981.
Cassese, Antonio. *International Law in a Divided World*. Oxford: Clarendon Press, 1988.
Chan, Ming K., and Clark, David J., eds. *The Hong Kong Basic Law: Blueprint for "Stability and Prosperity" under Chinese Sovereignty?* Armonk, N.Y.: M.E. Sharpe, 1991.
Chang, Jaw-ling Joanne. "Settlement of the Macao Issue: Distinctive Features of Beijing's Negotiating Behavior." *Case Western Reserve Journal of International Law* 20 (1988): 253–78.
Chao, John K. T. "South China Sea: Boundary Problems Relating to the Nansha and Hsisha Islands." *Chinese Yearbook of International Law and Affairs* 9 (1989–90): 66–156.
Chopra, Jarat, and Weiss, Thomas G. "Sovereignty Is No Longer Sacrosanct: Codifying Humanitarian Intervention." *Ethics and International Affairs* 6 (1992): 95–117.
Clark, Grenville, and Sohn, Louis B. *World Peace through World Law: Two Alternative Plans*. Cambridge, Mass.: Harvard University Press, 1966.
Claude, Inis L., Jr. *American Approaches to World Affairs*. Lanham, Md.: University Press of America, 1986.
――――. "The Balance of Power Revisited." *Review of International Studies* 15 (1989): 77–85.
――――. *The Changing United Nations*. New York: Random House, 1967.
――――. "The Common Defense and Great-Power Responsibilities." *Political Science Quarterly* 101 (1986): 719–32.

———. "The Gulf War and Prospects for World Order by Collective Security." In *The Persian Gulf Crisis: Power in the Post–Cold War World*, edited by Robert F. Helms II and Robert H. Dorff, pp. 23–38. Westport, Conn.: Praeger Publishers, 1993.

———. "Introduction—The Place of Theory in the Conduct and Study of International Relations." *Journal of Conflict Resolution* 4 (1960): 263–65.

———. "Moral Dilemmas in International Relations." In *The Virginia Papers*, edited by Kenneth W. Thompson. Lanham, Md.: University Press of America, forthcoming.

———. *National Minorities: An International Problem.* Cambridge, Mass.: Harvard University Press, 1955. Reprint, New York: Greenwood Press, 1969.

———. "The New International Security Order: Changing Concepts." *The Naval War College Review* 47 (1994): 9–17.

———. "The Peace-Keeping Role of the United Nations." In *The United Nations in Perspective*, edited by E. Berkeley Tompkins, pp. 49–63. Stanford, Calif.: Hoover Institution Press, 1972.

———. *Power and International Relations.* New York: Random House, 1962.

———. *The Record of International Organizations in the Twentieth Century.* Taipei, Taiwan: Tamkang University Press, 1986.

———. "Reflections on the Role of the UN Secretary-General." In *The Challenging Role of the UN Secretary-General*, edited by Benjamin Rivlin and Leon Gordenker, pp. 249–60. Foreword by Sir Brian Urquhart. Westport, Conn.: Frederick A. Praeger, 1993.

———. *States and the Global System: Politics, Law, and Organization.* New York: St. Martin's Press, 1988.

———. *Swords into Plowshares: The Problems and Progress of International Organization.* 4th ed. rev. New York: Random House, 1971.

———. "The Tension between Principle and Pragmatism in International Relations." *Review of International Studies* 19 (1993): 215–26.

———. "Theoretical Approaches to National Security and World Order." In *National Security Law*, edited by John Norton Moore, Frederick S. Tipson, and Robert F. Turner, pp. 31–45. Durham, N.C.: Carolina Academic Press, 1990.

———. "The United States and Changing Approaches to National Security and World Order." *The Naval War College Review* (forthcoming).

———. *The United States in a Changing World.* Jerusalem: The Academon Press, The Hebrew University, 1993.

Clinebell, John H., and Thompsen, Jim. "Sovereignty and Self-Determination: The Rights of Native Americans under International Law." *Buffalo Law Review* 27 (1978): 669–714.

Cohen Hymen Ezra. *Recent Theories of Sovereignty.* Chicago: University of Chicago Press, 1937.

Cohen, Maxwell. "Demise of UNEF." *International Journal* 23 (1967–68): 18–51.

Cole, Kenneth C. "The Theory of the State as a Sovereign Juristic Person." In *In Defense of Sovereignty*, edited by W. J. Stankiewicz, pp. 86–106. New York: Oxford University Press, 1969.

Commager, Henry Steele, ed. *Documents of American History.* Englewood Cliffs, N.J.: Prentice-Hall, 1973.

Cordier, Andrew W., and Harrelson, Max. *Public Papers of the Secretaries-General of the United Nations.* Vol. 7. New York: Cambridge University Press, 1976.

Crawford, James. *The Creation of States in International Law.* Oxford: Clarendon Press, 1979.

————. "Islands as Sovereign Nations." *International and Comparative Law Quarterly* 38 (1989): 277–98.

Curzon, George Nathaniel (Lord). *Frontiers.* Oxford: Clarendon Press, 1907; Greenwood Press, 1976.

Damis, John. *Conflict in North West Africa: The Western Sahara Dispute.* Stanford, Calif.: Hoover Institution Press, 1983.

————. "The Western Sahara Conflict: Myths and Realities." *The Middle East Journal* 37 (1983): 169–79.

DuLupis, Ingrid. *International Law and the Independent State.* New York: Crane, Russak and Co., 1974.

Deutsch, Karl. "Between Sovereignty and Integration: Conclusion." In *Between Sovereignty and Integration,* edited by Ghita Ionescu, pp. 181–87. New York: John Wiley and Sons, 1974.

————. "On the Concepts of Politics and Power." *Journal of International Affairs* 21 (1967): 232–41.

————. "Sovereignty and Vulnerability in Political Systems." In *In Defense of Sovereignty,* edited by W. J. Stankiewicz, pp. 107–14. New York: Oxford University Press, 1969.

de Vattel, Emerich. *The Law of Nations.* Edited by Joseph Chitty. Philadelphia: T. and J. W. Johnson & Co., 1983.

Dingley, Mark. "Eruptions in International Law: Emerging Volcanic Islands and the Law of Territorial Acquisition." *Cornell International Law Journal* 11 (1978): 121–35.

Dodwell, H. H. "The Development of Sovereignty in British India." In *The Cambridge History of India,* edited by H. H. Dodwell, pp. 589–608. 6 vols. New York: Macmillan, 1929.

Donnelly, Jack. "Human Rights and International Organizations: States, Sovereignty, and the International Community." In *International Organization: A Reader,* edited by Friedrich V. Kratochwil and Edward D. Mansfield, pp. 202–18. New York: HarperCollins College Publishers, 1994.

Dosman, Edgar J. *Sovereignty and Security in the Arctic.* Toronto: York University Centre for International and Strategic Studies, 1989.

Dreyss, Charles. *Etude sur les Mémoires de Louis XIV pour l'instruction du Dauphin.* Paris: Didier, 1860.

Duchacek, Ivo D. *Nations and Men: International Politics Today.* New York: Holt, Rinehart and Winston, 1966.

————. *The Territorial Dimension of Politics: Within, Among, and Across Nations.* Boulder, Colo.: Westview Press, 1986.

————; Latouche, Daniel; and Stevenson, Garth, eds. *Perforated Sovereignties and International Relations: Trans-Sovereign Contacts of Subnational Governments.* New York: Greenwood Press, 1988.

Dugard, John. *Recognition and the United Nations.* Cambridge: Grotius Publications, 1987.

Eban, Abba. *The New Diplomacy: International Affairs in the Modern Age.* New York: Random House, 1983.

Emerson, Rupert P. *From Empire to Nation: The Rise to Self-Assertion of Asian and African Peoples*. Cambridge, Mass.: Harvard University Press, 1960.
——. *State and Sovereignty in Modern Germany*. Westport, Conn.: Hyperion Press, 1977.
Encarnation, Dennis J., and Well, Louis T., Jr. "Sovereignty En Garde: Negotiating with Foreign Investors." *International Organization* 39 (1985): 47–78.
Falk, Richard A. "Evasions of Sovereignty." In *Contending Sovereignties: Redefining Political Community*, edited by R.B.J. Walker and Saul H. Mendlovitz, pp. 61–78. Boulder, Colo.: Lynne Reinner Publishers, 1990.
——. *Human Rights and State Sovereignty*. New York: Holmes & Meier, 1981.
——; Kratochwil, Friedrich V.; and Mendlovitz, Saul H., eds. *International Law: A Contemporary Perspective*. Boulder, Colo.: Westview Press, 1985.
Farer, Tom J. "Humanitarian Intervention: The View from Charlottesville." In *Humanitarian Intervention and the United Nations*, edited by Richard B. Lillich, Charlottesville: University Press of Virginia, 1973.
Fishel, Wesley R. *The End of Extraterritoriality in China*. New York: Octagon Books, 1974.
Fisher, David I. *Prior Consent to International Direct Satellite Broadcasting*. Boston: Kluwer Academic Publishers, 1990.
Fisher, Roger. "Fractionating Conflict." In *International Conflict and Behavioral Science*, ed. Roger Fisher, pp. 91–109. New York: Basic Books, 1964.
——. "Intervention: Three Problems of Policy and Law." In *Essays on Intervention*, edited by Roland J. Stanger, pp. 3–30. Columbus: Ohio State University Press, 1964.
——. *Points of Choice: International Crises and the Role of Law*. Oxford: Oxford University Press, 1978.
Flinterman, Cees; Kwiatkowska, Barbara; and Lammers, Johan G., eds. *Transboundary Air Pollution: International Legal Aspects of the Co-Operation of States*. The Hague: Martinus Nijhoff Publishers, 1986.
Forsythe, David, and Pease, Kelly Kate. "Human Rights, Humanitarian Intervention, and World Politics." *Human Rights Quarterly* 15 (1993): 290–314.
Foucault, Michel. "Power, Sovereignty and Discipline." In *States and Societies*, edited by David Held, pp. 306–13. New York: New York University Press, 1983.
Fourlanos, Gerassimos. *Sovereignty and the Ingress of Aliens: With Special Focus on Family Unit and Refugee Law*. Stockholm: Almquist & Wiksell, 1986.
Fowler, Michael Ross. *Thinking about Human Rights: Contending Approaches to Human Rights in U.S. Foreign Policy*. Lanham, Md.: University Press of America, 1987.
Fowler, Michael Ross, and Bunck, Julie Marie. "The Chunk and Basket Theories of Sovereignty." In *Community, Diversity, and a New World Order: Essays in Honor of Inis L. Claude, Jr.*, edited by Kenneth W. Thompson, pp. 137–44. Lanham, Md.: University Press of America, 1994.
——. "Legal Imperialism of Disinterested Assistance: American Legal Aid in the Caribbean Basin." *Albany Law Review* 55 (1992): 815–97.

Franck, Thomas M. *Control of Sea Resources by Semi-Autonomous States: Prevailing Legal Relationships between Metropolitan Governments and Their Overseas Commonwealths, Associated States, and Self-Governing Dependencies.* Washington, D.C.: Carnegie Endowment for International Peace, 1978.

———. "The Stealing of the Sahara." *American Journal of International Law* 70 (1976): 694–721.

———, and Weisband, Edward. *Word Politics: Verbal Strategy among the Superpowers.* New York: Oxford University Press, 1971.

Frankel, Joseph. *International Politics: Conflict and Harmony.* Baltimore: Penguin Books, 1973.

———. *The Making of Foreign Policy: An Analysis of Decisionmaking.* London: Oxford University Press, 1963.

Franklin, Julian H. *John Locke and the Theory of Sovereignty: Mixed Monarchy and the Right of Resistance in the Political Thought of the English Revolution.* Cambridge: Cambridge University Press, 1978.

Freedman, Lawrence. *Britain and the Falklands War.* Cambridge: Basil Blackwell, 1988.

Fulton, Thomas Wemyss. *The Sovereignty of the Sea: An Historical Account of the Claims of England to the Dominion of the British Seas, and of the Evolution of the Territorial Waters: With Special Reference to the Rights of Fishing and the Naval Salute.* London: William Blackwood and Sons, 1911.

Furlong, William L., and Scranton, Margaret E. *The Dynamics of Foreign Policymaking: The President, the Congress, and the Panama Canal Treaties.* Boulder, Colo.: Westview Press, 1984.

Galbraith, John Kenneth. *The Anatomy of Power.* Boston: Houghton Mifflin, 1985.

Gibson, Charles. *The Inca Concept of Sovereignty and the Spanish Administration in Peru.* Austin: University of Texas Press, 1948.

Gilson, Bernard. *The Conceptual System of Sovereign Equality.* Leuven: Peeters, 1984.

Goldstein, Walter. "Europe after Maastricht." *Foreign Affairs* 71 (1992): 117–32.

Goodwin, Geoffrey L. "The Erosion of External Sovereignty?" In *Between Sovereignty and Integration,* edited by Ghita Ionescu, pp. 100–117. New York: John Wiley and Sons, 1974.

Goria, Wade R. *Sovereignty and Leadership in Lebanon, 1943–1976.* London: Ithaca Press, 1985.

Gowlland-Debas, Vera. "Collective Responses to the Unilateral Declarations of Independence of Southern Rhodesia and Palestine: An Application of the Legitimizing Function of the United Nations." *The British Year Book of International Law* 61 (1990): 135–53.

Grady, Patrick. *The Economic Consequences of Quebec Sovereignty.* Vancouver: Fraser Institute, 1991.

Grant, Shelagh D. *Sovereignty or Security?: Government Policy in the Canadian North, 1936–1950.* Vancouver: University of British Columbia Press, 1988.

Greig, Donald W. "Sovereignty, Territory, and the International Lawyer's Dilemma." *Osgoode Hall Law Journal* 26 (1988): 163–69.

Gustafson, Lowell S. *The Sovereignty Dispute over the Falkland (Malvinas) Islands.* Oxford: Oxford University Press, 1988.

Haas, Ernst B., and Whiting, Alan S. *Dynamics of International Relations.* New York: McGraw-Hill, 1956.

Hackworth, Green Haywood, ed. *Digest of International Law.* 8 vols. Washington, D.C.: U.S. Government Printing Office, 1940.

Hamilton, Alexander; Jay, John; and Madison, James. "The Federalist No. 81." In *The Federalist: A Commentary on the Constitution of the United States.* New York: Random House, 1937.

Handley, F. James. "Hazardous Waste Exports: A Leak in the System of International Legal Controls." *Environmental Law Reporter* 19: 10,171–82.

Hannum, Hurst. *Autonomy, Sovereignty, and Self-Determination: The Accommodation of Conflicting Rights.* Philadelphia: University of Pennsylvania Press, 1990.

———. "The Foreign Affairs Powers of Autonomous Regions." *Nordic Journal of International Law* 57 (1988): 273–88.

Hartmann, Frederick H. *The Relations of Nations.* New York: Macmillan, 1966.

Hassan, Sir Joshua. "Gibraltar's Political and Constitutional Future: The Spanish Sovereignty Claim versus Gibraltar's Continuing Relationship with Britain and the Commonwealth." *Parliamentarian* 68 (1987): 58–61.

Hawtrey, R[alph] G[eorge]. *Economic Aspects of Sovereignty.* 2d ed. rev. New York: Longmans, Green, 1952.

Hehir, J. Bryan. "World of Faultlines: Sovereignty, Self-Determination, Intervention." *Commonweal* 119 (25 September 1992): 8–9.

Henkin, Louis. *How Nations Behave: Law and Foreign Policy.* 2d ed. rev. New York: Columbia University Press, 1979.

Herr, Richard A. "Microstate Sovereignty in the South Pacific: Is Small Practical?" *Contemporary Southeast Asia* 10 (1988): 182–96.

Hinsley, F[rancis] H[arry]. "The Concept of Sovereignty and the Relations between States." In *In Defense of Sovereignty,* edited by W. J. Stankiewicz, pp. 275–90. New York: Oxford University Press, 1969.

———. "The Concept of Sovereignty and the Relations between States." In *Theory and Reality in International Relations,* edited by John C. Farrell and Asa P. Smith, pp. 58–68. New York: Columbia University Press, 1967.

———. *Sovereignty.* New York: Basic Books, 1966.

———. *Sovereignty.* 2d ed. rev. New York: Basic Books, 1986.

Hodges, Tony. *Western Sahara: The Roots of a Desert War.* Westport, Conn.: Lawrence Hill, 1984.

Hoffmann, Fritz L., and Hoffmann, Olga Mingo. *Sovereignty in Dispute: The Falklands/Malvinas, 1493–1982.* Boulder, Colo.: Westview Press, 1984.

Hoffmann, Stanley. "In Search of a Thread: The UN in the Congo Labyrinth." In *United Nations Political Systems,* edited by David A. Kay, pp. 230–60. New York: John Wiley and Sons, 1967.

———. *Primacy or World Order: American Foreign Policy since the Cold War.* New York: McGraw-Hill, 1978.

Holsti, K. J. "The Concept of Power in the Study of International Relations." *Background* 7 (1964): 179–94.

"Hong Kong: Transfer of Sovereignty." *Case Western Reserve Journal of International Law* 20 (1988): 1–278; 301–68.

Hossain, Kamal, and Chowdhury, Subrata Roy. *Permanent Sovereignty over Natural Resources in International Law: Principle and Practice.* New York: St. Martin's Press, 1984.

Hudson, Manley O., ed. *Cases and Other Materials on International Law.* St. Paul, Minn.: West Publishing Co., 1929.

———. *World Court Reports.* Washington, D.C.: Carnegie Endowment for International Peace, 1934.

Ionescu, Ghita, ed. *Between Sovereignty and Integration.* New York: John Wiley and Sons, 1974.

al-Iryan, Abdallah Ali. *Condominium and Related Situations in International Law with Special Reference to the Dual Administration of the Sudan and the Legal Problems Arising Out of It.* Cairo: Fouad University Press, 1952.

Ishida, Takeshi, and Krauss, Ellis S. "Democracy in Japan: Issues and Questions." In *Democracy in Japan,* edited by Takeshi Ishida and Ellis S. Krauss, pp. 3–16. Pittsburgh: University of Pittsburgh Press, 1989.

Jackson, Robert H. *Quasi-States: Sovereignty, International Relations, and the Third World.* New York: Cambridge University Press, 1990.

———, and Rosberg, Carl G. "Why Africa's Weak States Persist: The Empirical and the Juridical in Statehood." *World Politics* 35 (1982): 1–24.

Jaffe, Louis L. *Judicial Aspects of Foreign Relations: In Particular of the Recognition of Foreign Powers.* Cambridge, Mass.: Harvard University Press, 1933.

James, Alan. "The Contemporary Relevance of National Sovereignty." In *Constraints and Adjustments in British Foreign Policy,* edited by Michael Leifer, pp. 16–34. London: Allen & Unwin, 1972.

———. *Sovereign Statehood: The Basis of International Society.* London: Allen & Unwin, 1986.

———. "The UN Force in Cyprus." *International Affairs* 65, no. 3 (Summer 1989): 481–500.

———. "Unit Veto Dominance in United Nations Peace-Keeping." In *Politics in the United Nations System,* edited by Lawrence S. Finkelstein, pp. 75–105. Durham, N.C.: Duke University Press, 1988.

———, ed. *The Bases of International Order: Essays in Honor of C.A.W. Manning.* New York: Oxford University Press, 1973.

Janis, Mark W. *An Introduction to International Law.* Boston: Little, Brown, 1988.

Jessup, Philip C. *The Price of International Justice.* New York: Columbia University Press, 1971.

Jiménez de Arechaga, Eduardo. "State Responsibility for the Nationalization of Foreign-Owned Property." In *International Law: A Contemporary Perspective,* edited by Richard A. Falk, Friedrich V. Kratochwil, and Saul H. Mendlovitz, pp. 546–57. Boulder, Colo.: Westview Press, 1985.

Johnson, W. Ross. *Sovereignty and Protection: A Study of British Jurisdictional Imperialism in the Late Nineteenth Century.* Durham: Duke University Press, 1973.

Jones, Robert A. *The Soviet Concept of "Limited Sovereignty" from Lenin to Gorbachev: The Brezhnev Doctrine.* New York: St. Martin's Press, 1990.

Jouvenal, Bertran de. *Sovereignty: An Inquiry into the Political Good.* Translated by J. F. Huntington. Chicago: University of Chicago Press, 1957.

Joyner, Christopher C. "Reflections on the Lawfulness of Invasion." *American Journal of International Law* 78 (1984): 131–44.

——. "Sanctions, Compliance, and International Law: Reflections on the United Nations' Experience against Iraq." *Virginia Journal of International Law* 32 (1991): 1–46.

Kageyama, Sei. "International Cooperation and National Sovereignty— Unchanged Role of National Sovereignty in the Provision of International Telecommunications Services." *Case Western Reserve Journal of International Law* 16 (1984): 265–85.

Kaikobad, Kaiyan Homi. *The Shatt-al-Arab Boundary Question: A Legal Reappraisal*. Oxford: Clarendon Press, 1988.

Keller, Arthur S.; Lissitzyn, Oliver J.; and Mann, Frederick J. *Creation of Rights of Sovereignty through Symbolic Acts, 1400–1800*. New York: Columbia University Press, 1938.

Kelsen, Hans. "Sovereignty and International Law." In *In Defense of Sovereignty*, edited by W. J. Stankiewicz, pp. 115–31. New York: Oxford University Press, 1969.

Kennan, George F. *Around the Cragged Hill: A Personal and Political Philosophy*. New York: Norton, 1993.

——. *The Cloud of Danger: Current Realities of American Foreign Policy*. Boston: Little, Brown & Co., 1977.

——. "To Prevent a World Wasteland." *Foreign Affairs* 48 (1970): 401–13.

Keohane, Robert O. *Hobbes's Dilemma and Institutional Change in World Politics: Sovereignty in International Society*. Working Paper no. 93-3. Cambridge, Mass.: Harvard University, Center for International Affairs, 1993.

——. *Sovereignty, Interdependence, and International Institutions*. Working Paper no. 1. Cambridge, Mass.: Harvard University, Center for International Affairs, 1991.

——, ed. *Neorealism and Its Critics*. New York: Columbia University Press, 1986.

——, and Hoffmann, Stanley, eds. *The New European Community: Decision-Making and Institutional Change*. Boulder, Colo.: Westview Press, 1991.

Khadduri, Majid. "Iraq's Claim to the Sovereignty of Kuwayt." *New York University Journal of International Law and Politics* 23 (1990): 5–34.

Khan, Ali. "The Extinction of Nation-States." *American University Journal of International Law and Policy* 7 (1992): 197–234.

Kis, Theofil I. *Nationhood, Statehood, and the International Status of the Ukrainian SSR/Ukraine*. Ottawa: University of Ottawa Press, 1989.

Klein, Robert A. *Sovereign Equality among States: The History of an Idea*. Foreword by Louis Halle. Toronto: University of Toronto Press, 1974.

Kloppenburg, Jack R., Jr. *Seeds and Sovereignty: The Use and Control of Plant Genetic Resources*. Durham: Duke University Press, 1988.

Knight, Franklin W. "The State of Sovereignty and the Sovereignty of States." In *Americas: New Interpretive Essays*, edited by Alfred Stepan, pp. 11–29. New York: Oxford University Press, 1992.

Krasner, Stephen D. "Sovereignty: An Institutional Perspective." In *The Elusive State: International and Comparative Perspectives*, edited by James A. Caporaso, pp. 69–96. Newbury Park, Calif.: Sage Publications, 1989.

Kratochwil, Friedrich V. "Of Systems, Boundaries, and Territoriality: An

Inquiry into the Formation of the State System." *World Politics* 39 (1986): 27–52.

———; Rohrlich, Paul; and Mahajan, Harpreet. *Peace and Disputed Sovereignty: Reflections on Conflict over Territory.* Lanham, Md.: University Press of America, 1985.

Lallier, Adalbert. *Sovereignty Association: Economic Realism or Utopia?* New York: Mosaic Press, 1991.

Lane, Kevin P. *Sovereignty and the Status Quo: The Historical Roots of China's Hong Kong Policy.* Boulder, Colo.: Westview Press, 1990.

Lansing, Robert. *Notes On Sovereignty: From the Standpoint of the State and of the World.* Washington, D.C.: Carnegie Endowment for International Peace, 1921.

Larson, Arthur, and Jenks, C. Wilfred, eds. *Sovereignty within the Law.* Dobbs Ferry, N.Y.: Oceana Publications, 1965.

Laski, Harold J. *The Foundations of Sovereignty and Other Essays.* New York: Harcourt Brace & Co., 1921.

———. *Studies in the Problem of Sovereignty.* New Haven: Yale University Press, 1917. Reprint, New York: Howard Fertig, 1968.

Lee, Rensselaer W. "Why the U.S. Cannot Stop South American Cocaine." *Orbis* 32 (1988): 513–19.

Lenarcic, David, and Reford, Robert. "Sovereignty versus Defense: The Arctic in Canadian-American Relations." In *Sovereignty and Security in the Arctic,* edited by Edgar J. Dosman, pp. 159–75. New York: Routledge, 1989.

Lerche, Charles O., Jr., and Said, Abdul A. *Concepts of International Politics.* Englewood Cliffs, N.J.: Prentice-Hall, 1970.

Levie, Howard S. *The Status of Gibraltar.* Boulder, Colo.: Westview Press, 1983.

Lillich, Richard B. "A United States Policy of Humanitarian Intervention and Intercession." In *Human Rights and American Foreign Policy,* edited by Donald P. Kommers and Gilburt D. Loescher, pp. 278–98. Notre Dame, Ind.: University of Notre Dame Press, 1979.

Lin, Mousheng. *Men and Ideas: An Informal History of Chinese Political Thought.* New York: John Day, 1942.

Lobingier, Charles Sumner. *Extraterritorial Cases.* 2 vols. Manila: Bureau of Printing, 1920.

Lochen, Einar, and Torgerson, Rolf N. *Norway's Views on Sovereignty: A Report Prepared for Unesco.* Bergen: A.S. John Griegs Boktrykkeri, 1955.

Luard, Evan. *The Blunted Sword: The Erosion of Military Power in World Politics.* New York: New Amsterdam Books, 1989.

———. *Types of International Society.* New York: The Free Press, 1976.

Lustick, Ian S. *Unsettled States, Disputed Lands: Britain and Ireland, France and Algeria, Israel and the West Bank–Gaza.* Ithaca: Cornell University Press, 1993.

Luxemburgensis. "The Emergence of a European Sovereignty." In *Between Sovereignty and Integration,* edited by Ghita Ionescu, pp. 118–34. New York: John Wiley and Sons, 1974.

Lyon, Peter. "New States and International Order." In *The Bases of International Order: Essays in Honor of C.A.W. Manning,* edited by Alan James, pp. 24–59. New York: Oxford University Press, 1973.

Lyons, Gene, and Mastanduno, Michael, eds. *Beyond Westphalia: National*

Sovereignty and International Intervention. Baltimore: Johns Hopkins University Press, 1995.

McClanahan, Grant. *Diplomatic Immunity: Principles, Practices, Problems.* Foreword by Sir Nicholas Henderson. New York: St. Martin's Press, 1989.

MacCormick, Neil. "Beyond the Sovereign State." *The Modern Law Review* 56 (1993): 1–18.

McDougal, Myres, and Chen, Lung-Chu. "Introduction: Human Rights and Jurisprudence." *Hofstra Law Review* 9 (1981): 337–46.

MacMurray, John V. A. *Treaties and Agreements with and Concerning China, 1894–1919.* New York: Oxford University Press, 1921.

Maine, Sir Henry. *International Law.* London: J. Murray, 1890.

Malcolm, Noel. *Sense on Sovereignty.* London: Centre for Policy Studies, 1991.

Mansbach, Richard W.; Ferguson, Yale H.; and Lampert, Donald E. *The Web of World Politics: Nonstate Actors in the Global System.* Englewood Cliffs, N.J.: Prentice-Hall, 1976.

———, and Vasquez, John A. *In Search of Theory: A Paradigm for Global Politics.* New York: Columbia University Press, 1981.

Maritain, Jacques. "The Concept of Sovereignty." In *In Defense of Sovereignty,* edited by W. J. Stankiewicz, pp. 41–66. New York: Oxford University Press, 1969.

Mark, Max. *Beyond Sovereignty.* Washington, D.C.: Public Affairs Press, 1985.

Marshall, Charles Burton. *The Exercise of Sovereignty: Papers on Foreign Policy.* Baltimore: Johns Hopkins University Press, 1965.

Marshall, James. *Swords and Symbols: The Technique of Sovereignty.* New York: Funk and Wagnalls, 1969.

Marston, Geoffrey. "Abandonment of Territorial Claims: The Cases of Bouvet and Spratly Islands." *The British Year Book of International Law* 57 (1986): 337–56.

Martin, Thomas R. *Sovereignty and Coinage in Classical Greece.* Princeton: Princeton University Press, 1985.

Meissner, Boris. *The Brezhnev Doctrine.* Kansas City, Mo.: Park College, Governmental Research Bureau, 1970.

Meron, Ya'akov. "Waste Land (*Mewat*) in Judea and Samaria." *Boston College International and Comparative Law Review* 4 (1981): 1–37.

Merriam, Charles E., Jr., *History of the Theory of Sovereignty Since Rousseau.* Columbia University Studies in the Social Sciences, vol. 38. New York: AMS Press, 1968.

———. *Systematic Politics.* Chicago: University of Chicago Press, 1945.

Middleton, K.W.B. "Sovereignty in Theory and Practice." In *In Defense of Sovereignty,* edited by W. J. Stankiewicz, pp. 132–59. New York: Oxford University Press, 1969.

Mitrany, David. "The Progress of International Government. New Haven: Yale University Press, 1933.

———. *A Working Peace System.* Chicago: Quadrangle Books, 1966.

Moore, John Bassett, ed. *A Digest of International Law.* 8 vols. Washington, D.C.: U.S. Government Printing Office, 1906.

Moore, John Norton. "Grenada and the International Double Standard." *American Journal of International Law* 78 (1984): 145–68.

———. *Law and the Grenada Mission.* Charlottesville: University of Virginia, Center for Law and National Security, 1984.

Morgan, Edmund S. *Inventing the People: The Rise of Popular Sovereignty in England and America*. New York: Norton, 1988.

Morgenthau, Hans J. "The Intellectual and Political Functions of a Theory of International Relations." In *The Role of Theory in International Relations*, edited by H. V. Harrison, pp. 99–118. Princeton, N.J.: D. Van Nostrand, 1964.

———. *Politics Among Nations: The Struggle for Power and Peace*. New York: Alfred A. Knopf, 1948.

———. "The Problem of Sovereignty Reconsidered." In *Essays on International Law from the Columbia Law Review*, edited by Columbia Law Review, pp. 338–63. New York: Columbia Law Review, 1965.

Morse, Hosea B[allou], and MacNair, Harley F[arnsworth]. *Far Eastern International Relations*. Boston: Houghton Mifflin, 1931.

Mosse, George L. *The Struggle for Sovereignty in England: From the Reign of Queen Elizabeth to the Petition of Right*. New York: Octagon Books, 1968.

Munkman, A.L.W. "Adjudication and Adjustment—International Judicial Decision and the Settlement of Territorial and Boundary Disputes." *The British Year Book of International Law* 46 (1972–73): 1–116.

Murphy, John F. *The United Nations and the Control of International Violence: A Legal and Political Analysis*. Totowa, N.J.: Allanheld, Osmun Publishers, 1982.

Nadelmann, Ethan A. *Cops Across Borders: The Internationalization of U.S. Criminal Law Enforcement*. University Park, Pa.: The Pennsylvania State University Press, 1993.

Netanyahu, Benjamin. "Terrorism: How the West Can Win." In *Terrorism: How the West Can Win*, edited by Benjamin Netanyahu, pp. 199–226. New York: Farrar, Straus & Giroux, 1986.

Nettl, J. P. "The State as a Conceptual Variable." *World Politics* 20 (1968): 559–92.

Nincic, Djura. *The Problem of Sovereignty in the Charter and in the Practice of the United Nations*. The Hague: Martinus Nijhoff Publishers, 1970.

Nordenstreng, Kaarle, and Schiller, Herbert, eds. *Beyond National Sovereignty: International Communication in the 1990s*. Norwood, N.J.: Ablex Publishing Co., 1992.

———. *National Sovereignty and International Communication*. Norwood, N.J.: Ablex Publishing Co., 1979.

Nye, Joseph S. "Soft Power." *Foreign Policy* 80 (1990): 153–71.

O'Rourke, Vernon A. *The Juristic Status of Egypt and the Sudan*. Baltimore: Johns Hopkins University Press, 1935.

Overholt, William H. "Hong Kong and the Crisis of Sovereignty." *Asian Survey* 24 (1984): 471–84.

Oxman, Bernard H. "Summary of the Law of the Sea Convention." In *International Law: A Contemporary Perspective*, edited by Richard A. Falk, Friedrich V. Kratochwil, and Saul H. Mendlovitz, pp. 559–69. Boulder, Colo.: Westview Press, 1985.

Pahre, Jennifer Noe. "The Fine Line Between the Enforcement of Human Rights Agreements and the Violation of National Sovereignty: The Case of the Soviet Dissidents." *Loyola of Los Angeles International and Comparative Law Journal* 7 (1984): 323–50.

Parry, Clive, ed. *The Consolidated Treaty Series*. Dobbs Ferry, N.Y.: Oceana Publications, 1980.

Pastor, Robert A. *Whirlpool: U.S. Foreign Policy toward Latin America and the Caribbean*. Princeton: Princeton University Press, 1992.

Pearcy, G. Etzel. *World Sovereignty*. Fullerton, Calif.: Plycon Press, 1977.

Pentland, Charles. "International Organizations and Their Roles." In *Perspectives on World Politics*, edited by Richard Little and Michael Smith, pp. 242–49. 2d ed. rev. New York: Routledge, 1981.

Pharand, Donat. "Canada's Sovereignty over the North West Passage." *Michigan Journal of International Law* 10 (1989): 653–78.

———. "Sovereignty in the Arctic: The International Legal Context." In *Sovereignty and Security in the Arctic*, edited by Edgar J. Dosman, pp. 145–58. New York: Routledge, 1989.

Plischke, Elmer. *Conduct of American Diplomacy*. Princeton, N.J.: D. Van Nostrand, 1961.

Pollard, A. F. "The Balance of Power." *Journal of the British Institute of International Affairs* 2 (1923): 51–64.

Prescott, J.R.V. *Political Frontiers and Boundaries*. London: Allen & Unwin, 1987.

"Questions for Readjustment, Submitted by China to the Peace Conference." *The Chinese Social and Political Science Review* 5A (1920): 115–61.

Raiffa, Howard. *The Art and Science of Negotiation*. Cambridge, Mass.: The Belknap Press of Harvard University Press, 1985.

Rajan, Mannaraswamighala Sreeranga. *Sovereignty over Natural Resources*. Atlantic Highlands, N.J.: Humanities Press, 1978.

Rees, W. J. "The Theory of Sovereignty Restated." In *In Defense of Sovereignty*, edited by W. J. Stankiewicz, pp. 209–40. New York: Oxford University Press, 1969.

———. "The Theory of Sovereignty Restated." In *Philosophy, Politics, and Society*, edited by Peter Laslett, pp. 56–82. New York: Macmillan, 1956.

Reid, Helen Dwight. *International Servitudes in Law and Practice*. Foreword by James Brown Scott. Chicago: University of Chicago Press, 1932.

Reisman, W. Michael. "Sovereignty and Human Rights in Contemporary International Law." *American Journal of International Law* 84 (1990): 866–76.

———, and Willard, Andrew R., eds. *International Incidents: The Law That Counts in World Politics*. Princeton: Princeton University Press, 1988.

Ricciardi, Matthew M. "Title to the Aouzou Strip: A Legal and Historical Analysis." *The Yale Journal of International Law* 17 (1992): 301–488.

Richardson, Elliot. "Climate Change: Problems of Law-Making." In *The International Politics of the Environment*, edited by Andrew Hurrell and Benedict Kingsbury, pp. 166–79. Oxford: Clarendon Press, 1992.

———. "Legal Regimes of the Arctic." *American Society of International Law Proceedings* 82 (1988): 315–34.

Rosenau, James N. "Pre-Theories and Theories of Foreign Policy." In *Approaches to Comparative and International Politics*, edited by R. Barry Farrell, pp. 53–92. Evanston, Ill.: Northwestern University Press, 1966.

———. "The State in an Era of Cascading Politics: Wavering Concept, Widening Competence, Withering Colossus, or Weathering Change?" In *The Elusive State: International and Comparative Perspectives*, edited by

James A. Caporaso, pp. 17–48. Newbury Park, Calif.: Sage Publications, 1989.

Rostow, Eugene. "Overcoming Denial." In Terrorism: How the West Can Win, edited by Benjamin Netanyahu, pp. 146–48. New York: Farrar, Straus & Giroux, 1986.

Ruggie, John Gerard. "Continuity and Transformation in the World Polity: Toward a Neorealist Synthesis." In Neorealism and Its Critics, edited by Robert O. Keohane, pp. 131–57. New York: Columbia University Press, 1986.

Ruiz, Lester Edwin J. "Sovereignty as Transformative Practice." In Contending Sovereignties: Redefining Political Community, edited by R.B.J. Walker and Saul H. Mendlovitz, pp. 79–96. Boulder, Colo.: Lynne Reinner Publishers, 1990.

Ryan, K. W., and White, M.W.D. "The Torres Strait Treaty." The Australian Year Book of International Law 7 (1981): 87–113.

Saseen, Sandra M. "The Taif Accord and Lebanon's Struggle to Regain Its Sovereignty." American University Journal of International Law and Policy 6 (1990): 57–75.

Scaperlanda, Michael. "Polishing the Tarnished Golden Door." Wisconsin Law Review (1993): 965–1032.

Schatz, Gerald S., ed. Science, Technology, and Sovereignty in the Polar Regions. Lexington, Mass.: D.C. Heath, 1974.

Scheffer, David J. "Use of Force after the Cold War: Panama, Iraq, and the New World Order." In Right v. Might: International Law and the Use of Force, edited by Louis Henkin and John Temple Swing, pp. 109–72. 2d ed. rev. New York: Council on Foreign Relations, 1991.

Schmitt, Carl. Political Theology: Four Chapters on the Concept of Sovereignty. Translated by George Schwab. Cambridge, Mass.: MIT Press, 1985.

Schott, Stephen. "United States Relief to Civilian Victims of the Biafra-Nigeria Civil War." In The United Nations: A Reassessment; Sanctions, Peace-keeping, and Humanitarian Assistance, edited by John M. Paxman and George T. Boggs, pp. 105–13. Charlottesville: University Press of Virginia, 1973.

Schwartz, Stuart B. Sovereignty and Society in Colonial Brazil: The High Court of Bahia and Its Judges, 1609–1751. Berkeley and Los Angeles: University of California Press, 1973.

Schwarzenberger, Georg. "The Forms of Sovereignty." In In Defense of Sovereignty, edited by W. J. Stankiewicz, pp. 160–95. New York: Oxford University Press, 1969.

Scott, James Brown. Sovereign States and Suits before Arbitral Tribunals and Courts of Justice. New York: New York University Press, 1925.

Shahabuddeen, M. The Conquest of Grenada: Sovereignty in the Periphery. Foreword by Hugh Desmond Hoyte. Georgetown, Guyana: University of Guyana, 1986.

Shaw, Malcolm N. International Law. 3d ed. rev. New York: Cambridge University Press, 1991.

Sherman, Mark Andrew. "An Inquiry Regarding the International and Domestic Legal Problems Presented in United States v. Noriega." University of Miami Inter-American Law Review 20 (1989): 393–428.

Shevtsov, Viktor Sergeevich. National Sovereignty and the Soviet State. Translated by Nick Bobrov. Moscow: Progress Publishers, 1974.

Sicherman, Harvey. *Palestinian Autonomy, Self-Government, & Peace.* Boulder, Colo.: Westview Press, 1993.

Sikkink, Kathryn. "Human Rights, Principled Issue-Networks, and Sovereignty in Latin America." *International Organization* 47 (1993): 411–41.

Simon, Yves R. "Sovereignty in Democracy." In *In Defense of Sovereignty,* edited by W. J. Stankiewicz, pp. 241–74. New York: Oxford University Press, 1969.

Smith, H. A. "Reviews of Books: Mandates." *The British Year Book of International Law* 12 (1931): 223–28.

Smith, Tony. *The Patterns of Imperialism: The United States, Great Britain, and the Late-Industrializing World since 1815.* Cambridge: Cambridge University Press, 1981.

Smith, Wayne S., ed. *Toward Resolution? The Falklands/Malvinas Dispute.* Boulder, Colo.: Lynne Reinner Publishers, 1991.

Snyder, Louis L. *Global Mini-Nationalisms: Autonomy or Independence.* Westport, Conn.: Greenwood Press, 1982.

Socarras, Michael P. "The Argentine Invasion of the Falklands: International Norms of Signaling." In *International Incidents: The Law That Counts in World Politics,* edited by W. Michael Reisman and Andrew R. Willard, pp. 115–43. Princeton: Princeton University Press, 1988.

Sohn, Louis B. "The International Court of Justice and the Scope of the Right of Self-Defense and the Duty of Non-Intervention." In *International Law at a Time of Perplexity,* edited by Yoram Dinstein and Mala Tabory, pp. 869–78. Boston: Martinus Nijhoff Publishers, 1989.

Sollie, Finn. "Nordic Perspectives on Arctic Sovereignty and Security." In *Sovereignty and Security in the Arctic,* edited by Edgar J. Dosman, pp. 194–210. New York: Routledge, 1989.

Soroos, Martin S. *Beyond Sovereignty: The Challenge of Global Policy.* Columbia: University of South Carolina Press, 1986.

Spiro, Herbert. "Interdependence: A Third Option between Sovereignty and Supranational Integration." In *Between Sovereignty and Integration,* edited by Ghita Ionescu, pp. 143–63. New York: John Wiley and Sons, 1974.

Spruyt, Hendrik. *The Sovereign State and Its Competitors: An Analysis of Systems Change.* Princeton: Princeton University Press, 1994.

Stankiewicz, W. J., ed. *In Defense of Sovereignty.* New York: Oxford University Press, 1969.

———. "In Defense of Sovereignty: A Critique and an Interpretation." In *In Defense of Sovereignty,* edited by W. J. Stankiewicz, pp. 3–40. New York: Oxford University Press, 1969.

———. "The Validity of the Concept of Sovereignty." In *In Defense of Sovereignty,* edited by W. J. Stankiewicz, pp. 291–98. New York: Oxford University Press, 1969.

Stevenson, Jonathan. "Hope Restored in Somalia?" *Foreign Policy* 91 (1993): 138–54.

Strayer, Joseph R. *On the Medieval Origins of the Modern State.* Princeton: Princeton University Press, 1970.

Swift, Richard N. *International Law: Current and Classic.* New York: John Wiley and Sons, 1969.

Takara, Tetsumi. "Peacekeeping without Force." *Japan Views* (August 1992), pp. 6–7.

Tanaka, Kotaro. "Japanese Law." In Sovereignty within the Law, edited by Arthur Larson and C. Wilfred Jenks, pp. 223–41. Dobbs Ferry, N.Y.: Oceana Publications, 1965.

Tapp, Nicholas. Sovereignty and Rebellion: The White Hmong of Northern Thailand. New York: Oxford University Press, 1989.

Tate, Jack B. "The Tate Letter: Letter from the Acting Legal Adviser of the Department of State to the Department of Justice, May 19, 1952." Department of State Bulletin 26 (1952): 984–85.

Theodoropoulos, Christos. Colonialism and General International Law: The Contemporary Theory of National Sovereignty and Self-Determination. Lagos, Nigeria: New Horizon Publishing House, 1988.

Thomas, Caroline. New States, Sovereignty, and Intervention. New York: St. Martin's Press, 1985.

Thompson, Kenneth W. Fathers of International Thought: The Legacy of Political Theory. Baton Rouge: Louisiana State University Press, 1994.

Thomson, Janice E. Mercenaries, Pirates, Sovereigns: State-Building and Extraterritorial Violence in Early Modern Europe. Princeton: Princeton University Press, 1994.

———. "Sovereignty in Historical Perspective: The Evolution of State Control over Extraterritorial Violence." In The Elusive State: International and Comparative Perspectives, edited by James A. Caporaso, pp. 227–54. Newbury Park, Calif.: Sage Publications, 1989.

Tomko, Jan. The Domestic Jurisdiction of States and the UNO. Bratislava: Publishing House of Slovak Academy of Sciences, 1967.

Trachtman, J. P. "L'état, c'est nous: Sovereignty, Economic Integration, and Subsidiarity." Harvard International Law Journal 33 (1992): 459–73.

Triggs, Gillian D. International Law and Australian Sovereignty in Antarctica. Sydney: Legal Books, 1986.

Vagts, Detlev. "International Law under Time Pressure." American Journal of International Law 78 (1984): 169–72.

Váli, F. A. Servitudes of International Law: A Study of Rights in Foreign Territory. 2d ed. rev. New York: Frederick A. Praeger, 1958.

Vance, Cyrus. Hard Choices: Critical Years in America's Foreign Policy. New York: Simon & Schuster, 1983.

Van der Vyver, Johan D. "The Concept of Political Sovereignty." In Essays in Honour of Ellison Kahn, edited by Coenraad Visser, pp. 289–360. Capetown: Juta & Co., 1989.

———. "Sovereignty and Human Rights in Constitutional and International Law." Emory International Law Review 5 (1991): 321–443.

———. "State Sovereignty and the Environment in International Law." South African Law Journal 109 (1992): 472–95.

Van Dyke, Jon M., and Brooks, Robert A. "Uninhabited Islands: Their Impact on the Ownership of the Oceans' Resources." Ocean Development and International Law Journal 12 (1983): 265–300.

Varley, H. Paul. Japanese Culture: A Short History. New York: Holt, Rinehart and Winston, 1977.

Vernon, Raymond. "Sovereignty at Bay: Ten Years After." International Organization 35 (1981): 517–29.

———. Sovereignty at Bay: The Multinational Spread of U.S. Enterprises. New York: Basic Books, 1971.

Vincent, R. J. *Human Rights and International Relations*. New York: Cambridge University Press, 1986.

———. *Nonintervention and International Order*. Princeton, N.J.: Princeton University Press, 1974.

Walker, R.B.J. "Sovereignty, Identity, Community: Reflections on the Horizons of Contemporary Political Practice." In *Contending Sovereignties: Redefining Political Community*, edited by R.B.J. Walker and Saul H. Mendlovitz, pp. 159–85. Boulder, Colo.: Lynne Reinner Publishers, 1990.

———. *State Sovereignty, Global Civilization, and the Rearticulation of Political Space*. World Order Studies Program Occasional Paper no. 18. Princeton, N.J.: Princeton University, Center of International Studies, 1988.

Walker, R.B.J., and Mendlovitz, Saul H. "Interrogating State Sovereignty." In *Contending Sovereignties: Redefining Political Community*, edited by R.B.J. Walker and Saul H. Mendlovitz, pp. 1–12. Boulder, Colo.: Lynne Reinner Publishers, 1990.

———, eds. *Contending Sovereignties: Redefining Political Community*. Boulder, Colo.: Lynne Reinner Publishers, 1990.

Wallace, William. "What Price Interdependence? Sovereignty and Interdependence in British Politics." *International Affairs* 62 (1986): 367–89.

Wallace-Bruce, Nii Lante. *Claims to Statehood in International Law*. New York: Carlton Press, 1994.

———. "Two Hundred Years On: A Reexamination of the Acquisition of Australia." *Georgia Journal of International Law and Comparative Law* 19 (1989): 87–116.

Waltz, Kenneth N. "Political Structures." In *Neorealism and Its Critics*, edited by Robert O. Keohane, pp. 70–97. New York: Columbia University Press, 1986.

Watanabe, Akio. *The Okinawa Problem: A Chapter in Japan-U.S. Relations*. Melbourne: Melbourne University Press, 1970.

Watson, Adam. *The Evolution of International Society*. London: Routledge, 1992.

Weber, Cynthia. *Simulating Sovereignty: Intervention, the State, and Symbolic Exchange*. New York: Cambridge University Press, 1994.

Werther, Guntram F. A. *Self-Determination in Western Democracies: Aboriginal Politics in a Comparative Perspective*. Westport, Conn.: Greenwood Press, 1992.

Wesley-Smith, Peter. *Unequal Treaty 1898–1997: China, Great Britain, and Hong Kong's New Territories*. Hong Kong: Oxford University Press, 1980.

Whitton, John B. "Hostile International Propaganda and International Law." In *National Sovereignty and International Communication*, edited by Kaarle Nordenstreng and Herbert I. Schiller, pp. 217–29. Norwood, N.J.: Ablex Publishing Co., 1979.

Wight, Martin. *Systems of States*. Edited and with an introduction by Hedley Bull. Leicester: Leicester University Press, 1977.

———. "Why There Is No International Theory?" In *Diplomatic Investigations*, edited by Herbert Butterfield and Martin Wight, pp. 17–34. Cambridge, Mass.: Harvard University Press, 1968.

Wilkinson, Herbert A. *The American Doctrine of State Succession*. Westport, Conn.: Greenwood Press, 1975.

Wilks, Ivor. "A Note on Sovereignty." In *In Defense of Sovereignty*, edited by W. J. Stankiewicz, pp. 197–208. New York: Oxford University Press, 1969.

Wilks, Michael. *The Problem of Sovereignty in the Later Middle Ages: The Papal Monarchy with Augustinus Triumphus and the Publicists*. Cambridge: Cambridge University Press, 1964.

Will, W. Marvin. "A Nation Divided: The Quest for Caribbean Integration." *Latin American Research Review* 26 (1991): 3–37.

Williams, Sharon Anne. *International Legal Effects of Secession by Quebec*. North York, Ontario: York University, Centre for Public Law and Public Policy, 1992.

Williams, Shirley. "Sovereignty and Accountability in the European Community." In *The New European Community: Decisionmaking and Institutional Change*, edited by Robert O. Keohane and Stanley Hoffmann, pp. 155–76. Boulder, Colo.: Westview Press, 1991.

Willoughby, Westel W[oodbury]. *Foreign Rights and Interests in China*. 2 vols. Baltimore: Johns Hopkins University Press, 1927.

———. *The Fundamental Concepts of Public Law*. New York: Macmillan, 1924.

Wolfers, Arnold. *Discord and Collaboration: Essays on International Politics*. Baltimore: Johns Hopkins University Press, 1962.

Wright, [Philip] Quincy. "Espionage and the Doctrine of Non-Intervention in Internal Affairs." In *Essays on Espionage and International Law*, edited by Roland J. Stanger, pp. 3–28. Columbus: Ohio State University Press, 1962.

———. *The Existing Legal Situation as it Relates to the Conflict in the Far East*. New York: Institute of Pacific Relations, 1939.

———. *Mandates under the League of Nations*. New York: Greenwood Press, 1968.

———. "Sovereignty of the Mandates." *American Journal of International Law* 17 (1923): 691–703.

Young, Crawford. "Comparative Claims to Political Sovereignty: Biafra, Katanga, Eritrea." In *State versus Ethnic Claims: African Policy Dilemmas*, edited by Donald Rothchild and Victor A. Olorunsolu, pp. 199–223. Boulder, Colo.: Westview Press, 1983.

Yu, Steven Kuan-Tsyh. "Who Owns the Paracels and Spratlys?—An Evaluation of the Nature and Legal Basis of the Conflicting Territorial Claims." *Chinese Yearbook of International Law and Affairs* 9 (1989–90): 1–28.

Ziegler, David W. *War, Peace, and International Politics*. Glenview, Ill.: Scott, Foresman, 1987.

Zulfaker, Sabry, Hussein. *Sovereignty for Sudan*. London: Ithaca Press, 1982.

Statutes, Treaties, and Diplomatic Correspondence

"Agreement between Egypt and Great Britain relative to the future Administration of the Sudan, signed at Cairo, 19 January 1899." *The Consolidated Treaty Series*. Edited and annotated by Clive Parry. Vol. 187, 1898–99. Dobbs Ferry, N.Y.: Oceana Publications, 1980. Pp. 155–57.

"Agreement for the Lease to the United States of Lands in Cuba for Coaling and Naval Stations, 23 February 1903." *Treaties, Conventions, International*

Acts, Protocols, and Agreements between the United States of America and Other Powers, 1776–1909. Edited by W. M. Malloy. Vol. 1 of 2. Washington, D.C.: U.S. Government Printing Office, 1910. Pp. 358–59.

"Boundary Treaty between the Netherlands and Prussia, signed at Aix-la-Chapelle, 26 June 1816." *The Consolidated Treaty Series.* Edited and annotated by Clive Parry. Vol. 66. 1816–17. Dobbs Ferry, N.Y.: Oceana Publications, 1980. Pp. 187–204.

"Convention between China and Great Britain respecting an Extension of Hong Kong Territory, signed at Peking, 9 June 1898." *The Consolidated Treaty Series.* Edited and annotated by Clive Parry. Vol. 186, 1897–98. Dobbs Ferry, N.Y.: Oceana Publications, 1980. Pp. 310–11.

"Convention of Friendship between China and Great Britain, signed at Peking, 24 October 1860." *The Consolidated Treaty Series,* Edited and annotated by Clive Parry. Vol. 123, 1860–61. Dobbs Ferry, N.Y.: Oceana Publications, 1980.

Cook Islands Constitution Act of 1964. *Statutes of New Zealand* 3, no. 69 (1966), pp. 2,029–63.

The Covenant of the League of Nations. New York: World Peace Foundation, 1936.

"Definitive Treaty of Peace between Great Britain and the United States, signed at Paris, 3 September 1789." *The Consolidated Treaty Series.* Edited and annotated by Clive Parry. Vol. 48, 1781–83. Dobbs Ferry, N.Y.: Oceana Publications, 1980. Pp. 487–502.

"Joint Declarations of the Government of the United Kingdom of Great Britain and Northern Ireland and the Government of the People's Republic of China on the Question of Hong Kong, initialed at Peking, 26 September 1984." *International Legal Materials* 23 (1984): 1,371–81.

League of Nations. Treaty Series. "Convention between Great Britain and Belgium with a View to Facilitating Belgian Traffic through the Territories of East Africa, signed at London." 15 March 1921. *Société des Nations* 5, no. 138 (1921), pp. 319–27.

———. "Convention on Certain Questions relating to the Conflict of Nationality Laws, signed at The Hague." 12 April 1930. *Société des Nations* 179, no. 4137 (1937), pp. 91–137.

"Lease to the United States by Cuba of Land and Water for Naval or Coaling Stations in Guantánamo and Bahia Honda, 2 July 1903." *Treaties, Conventions, International Acts, Protocols, and Agreements between the United States of America and Other Powers, 1776–1909.* Edited by W. M. Malloy. Vol. 1 of 2. Washington, D.C.: U.S. Government Printing Office, 1910. Pp. 360–61.

"Protocol between France and Great Britain concerning the New Hebrides, signed at London, 27 February 1906." *The Consolidated Treaty Series.* Edited and annotated by Clive Parry. Vol. 200, 1905–6. Dobbs Ferry, N.Y.: Oceana Publications, 1980. Pp. 328–51.

"Rights and Duties of States (Inter-American), signed at Montevideo, 26 December 1933." *Treaties and Other International Agreements of the United States of America 1776–1949.* Edited by W. M. Malloy. Vol. 3, 1931–45. Washington, D.C.: U.S. Government Printing Office, 1969, pp. 145–51.

"The Sino-Portuguese Joint Declaration on the Question of Macao, signed 13 April 1987." *Beijing Review* 30, no. 14 (6 April 1987), special insert.

"Treaty between China and Great Britain, signed at Nanking, 29 August 1842." *The Consolidated Treaty Series.* Edited and annotated by Clive Parry. Vol. 93, 1842. Dobbs Ferry, N.Y.: Oceana Publications, 1980. Pp. 465–74.

"Treaty between Germany and Spain confirming the Cession of the Carolines etc., signed at Madrid, 30 June 1899." *The Consolidated Treaty Series.* Edited and annotated by Clive Parry. Vol. 187, 1898–99. Dobbs Ferry, N.Y.: Oceana Publications, 1980. P. 375.

"Treaty of Commerce and Extradition between Great Britain and Portugal, signed at Lisbon, 26 December 1878." *The Consolidated Treaty Series.* Edited and annotated by Clive Parry. Vol. 154. 1878–79. Dobbs Ferry, N.Y.: Oceana Publications, 1980. Pp. 57–102.

"Treaty of Peace between Bulgaria, Greece, Montenegro, Servia, and Turkey, signed at London, 30 May 1913." *The Consolidated Treaty Series.* Edited and annotated by Clive Parry. Vol. 218, 1913. Dobbs Ferry, N.Y.: Oceana Publications, 1980. Pp. 159–61.

"Treaty with Cuba Embodying the Platt Amendment, signed at Havana, 22 May 1903." *Documents of American History.* Edited by Henry Steele Commager. Vol. 2. Englewood Cliffs, N.J.: Prentice-Hall, 1973. Pp. 28–29.

United Nations. General Assembly. "Question of American Samoa, Bahamas, Brunei, Cayman Islands, Cocos (Keeling) Islands, Gilbert and Ellice Islands, Guam, Montserrat, New Hebrides, Pitcairn, St. Helena, Seychelles, Solomon Islands, Turks and Caicos Islands, and the United States Virgin Islands." *United Nations Resolutions: Resolutions of the General Assembly,* ser. 1, vol. 13, 1970–71, pp. 180, 459–60.

United Nations. Security Council. "Cablegram dated 21 August 1948 from the Hyderabad Government to the President of the Security Council." *United Nations Security Council Official Records,* Suppl. (UN DOC S/986), September 1948, p. 5.

———. "Cablegram dated 12 September 1948 from the Hyderabad Government to the President of the Security Council." *United Nations Security Council Official Records,* Suppl. (UN DOC S/998), September 1948, p. 5.

———. "Cablegram dated 13 September 1948 from the Hyderabad Government to the President of the Security Council." *United Nations Security Council Official Records,* Suppl. (UN DOC S/1000), September 1948, p. 5.

———. "Cablegram dated 22 September 1948 from the Nizam of Hyderabad." *United Nations Security Council Official Records,* Suppl. (UN DOC S/1011), September 1948, p. 7.

———. "The Hyderabad Question." *United Nations Resolutions: Resolutions and Decisions of the Security Council,* ser. 2, vol. 2, 1948–50, p. 42.

United Nations. Treaty Series. "Agreement between the United Nations and the United States of America Regarding the Headquarters of the United Nations, signed at Lake Success." 26 June 1947. *Treaties and International Agreements Registered or Filed and Reported with the Secretariat of the United Nations,* vol. 11, no. 147 (1947), pp. 11–41.

———. "Convention on the Prohibition of the Development, Production, and Stockpiling of Bacteriological (Biological) and Toxin Weapons and on their Destruction." 10 April 1972. *Treaties and International Agreements Registered or Filed and Reported with the Secretariat of the United Nations,* vol. 1015, no. 14860 (1972), pp. 163–241.

————. "Exchange of Notes Constituting an Agreement between the United States of America and Canada Relating to the Construction and Maintenance of a Highway to Alaska, signed at Ottawa." 18 March 1942. *Treaties and International Agreements Registered or Filed and Reported with the Secretariat of the United Nations*, vol. 101, no. 294 (1951), pp. 205–13.

————. "Interim Arrangement on Privileges and Immunities of the United Nations concluded between the Secretary-General of the United Nations and the Swiss Federal Council." 11 June 1946 (Berne) and 1 July 1946 (New York). *Treaties and International Agreements Registered or Filed and Reported with the Secretariat of the United Nations*, vol. 1, no. 8 (1947), pp. 163–80.

————. "Joint Declaration by the Union of Soviet Socialist Republics and Japan, signed at Moscow." 19 October 1956. *Treaties and International Agreements Registered or Filed and Reported with the Secretariat of the United Nations*, vol. 263, no. 3768 (1957), pp. 112–16.

————. "State Treaty for the Re-establishment of an Independent and Democratic Austria, signed at Vienna." 15 May 1955. *Treaties and International Agreements Registered or Filed and Reported with the Secretariat of the United Nations*, vol. 217, no. 2949 (1955), pp. 225–93.

————. "Treaty Banning Nuclear Weapons Tests in the Atmosphere, in Outer Space, and under Water, signed at Moscow." 5 August 1963. *Treaties and International Agreements Registered or Filed and Reported with the Secretariat of the United Nations*, vol. 480, no. 6964 (1963), pp. 45–99.

————. "Treaty of Mutual Co-operation and Security between Japan and the United States of America, signed at Washington." 19 January 1960. *Treaties and International Agreements Registered or Filed and Reported with the Secretariat of the United Nations*, vol. 373, no. 5320 (1960), pp. 186–204.

————. "Treaty of Peace with Italy, signed at Paris." 10 February 1947. *Treaties and International Agreements Registered or Filed and Reported with the Secretariat of the United Nations*, vol. 49, no. 747 (1950), pp. 126–235.

————. "Treaty on the Non-Proliferation of Nuclear Weapons, signed at London, Moscow, and Washington." 1 July 1968. *Treaties and International Agreements Registered or Filed and Reported with the Secretariat of the United Nations*, vol. 729, no. 10485 (1968), pp. 161–75.

U.S. Congress. House. Committee on Foreign Affairs. *U.N. Security Council Resolutions on Iraq: Compliance and Implementation*. 101st Cong., 2d sess., 1992, pp. 27–36.

U.S. Department of State. "Demarcation of the New International Boundary (Chamizal), signed at Washington, D.C." 27 October 1967. TIAS no. 6372. *United States Treaties and Other International Agreements*, vol. 18, pt. 3, pp. 2,836–44.

————. "Extradition Treaty, United States–United Mexican States." 4 May 1978. TIAS no. 9656. *United States Treaties and Other International Agreements*, vol. 31, pt. 6, pp. 5,059–78.

West Indies Act of 1967. 4 *Halsbury's Statutes of England*, 3d ed. rev., p. 611.

Index

DATE DUE